MARVEL GRAPHIC NOVEL

SUPERIOR SPIDER-MAN ANNUAL #1

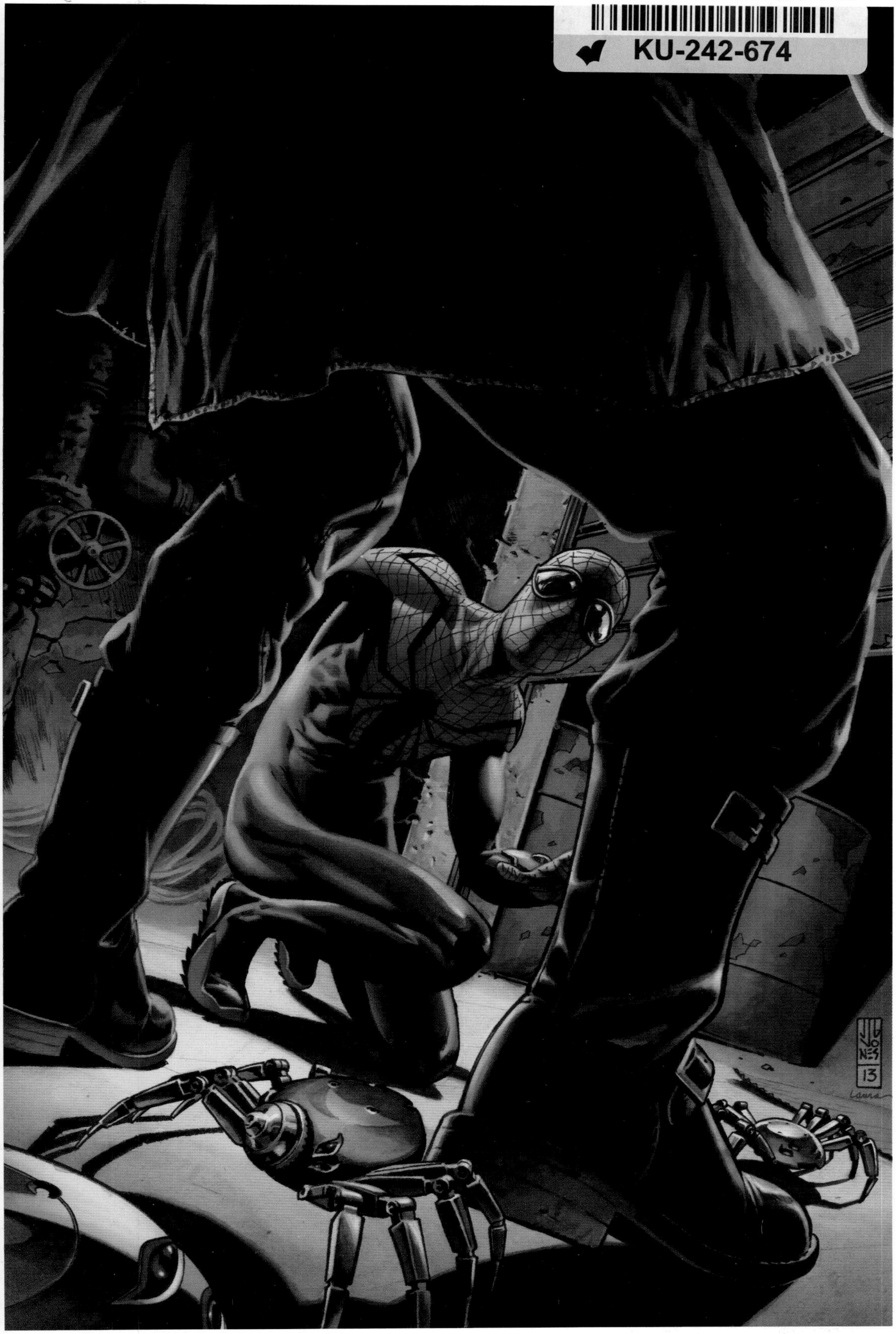

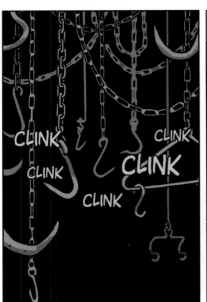

CLINK
CLINK
CLINK
CLINK
CLINK

SO YOU PROBABLY KNOW THE *KINGPIN* WAS WORKING WITH NINJAS LATELY. BUT HE KEPT SOME OF THE GUYS FROM THE OLD DAYS AROUND. LIKE ME.

YOU CAN'T SEND FREAKIN' *NINJAS* TO NEGOTIATE WITH THE *CHICAGO OUTFIT*, KNOW WHAT I'M SAYIN'?

DARK IN HERE.

ANYWAY, A WHILE BACK, MR. FISK GOT SOME DIRT ON *SPIDER-MAN.* Y'KNOW ALL THE TECH HE USES? WEB-SHOOTERS, GOGGLES, THOSE CREEPY ROBOT BUGS?

SOME TEST TUBE JOCKEY NAMED *PETER PARKER* MAKES IT ALL FOR 'IM. AND THAT'S *LEGIT,* 'CAUSE WHEN WE SNATCHED THE KID, SPIDEY CAME RUNNIN'.

NOW, I'M NO SNITCH, OKAY? I'M ONLY TELLIN' YOU 'CAUSE SINCE THE SPIDER WHACKED MR. FISK, I'M OUT OF A JOB.

AND I REMEMBER YOU FROM THE OLD DAYS. TOP-NOTCH BUTTON MAN. YOU DID NICE WORK FOR *THE HOOD.*

SO I KNOW YOU CAN USE THIS, AND YOU'RE GOOD FOR THE DOUGH, WHICH *I* CAN MOST DEFINITELY USE--

HUH?

NEWSPAPER?

REGRETTABLY, I FIND MYSELF UNEMPLOYED AS WELL.

HARD TIMES FOR US ALL.

NO! *WAIT!*

CLINK
CLINK
CLINK
CLIN
INK

SHRTCH

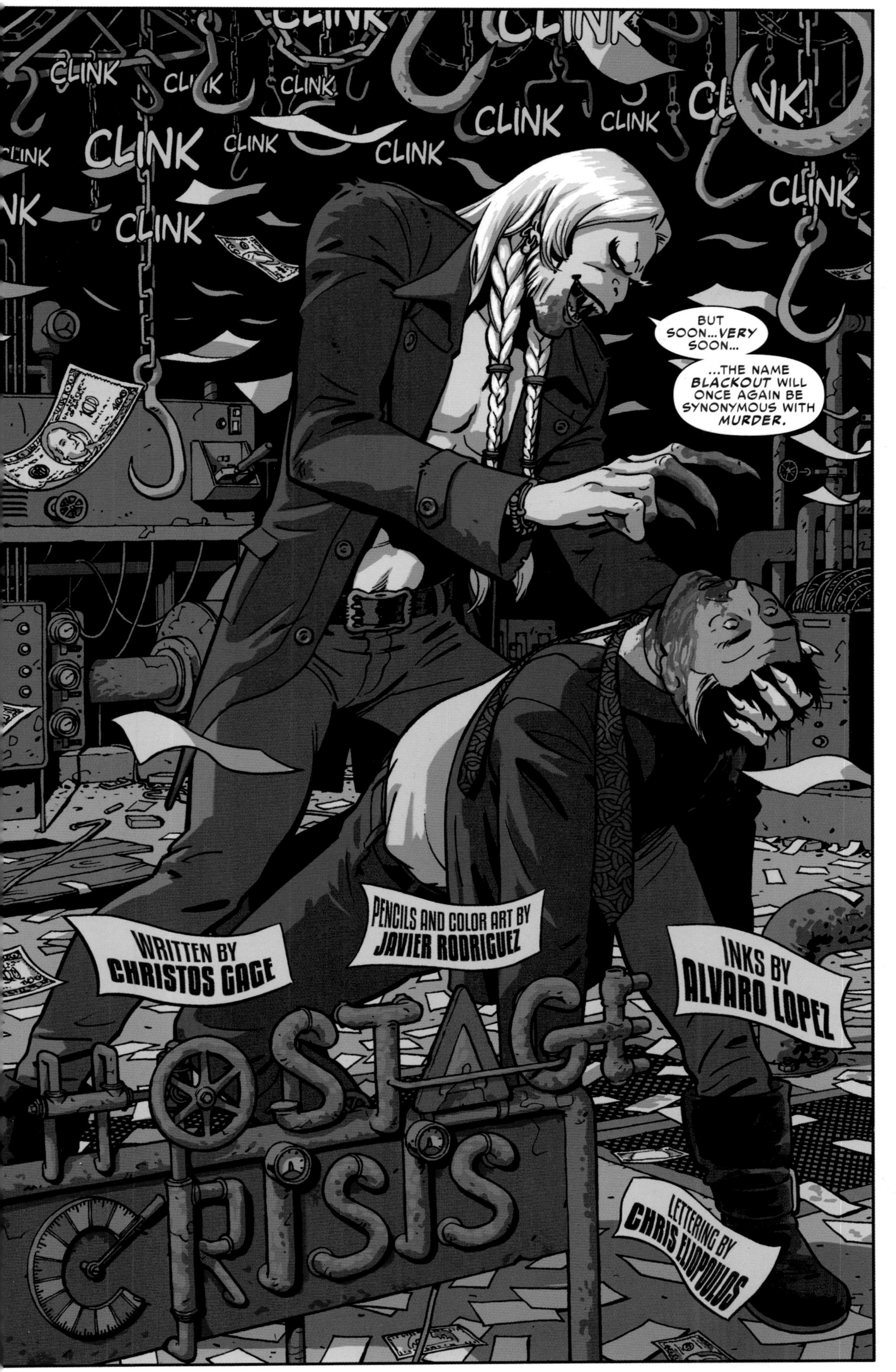
CLINK
CLINK
CLINK
CLINK
CLINK
CLINK
CLINK
CLINK
CLINK
CLINK
CLINK
CLINK
BUT SOON...VERY SOON...
...THE NAME BLACKOUT WILL ONCE AGAIN BE SYNONYMOUS WITH MURDER.
HOSTAGE CRISIS
WRITTEN BY CHRISTOS GAGE
PENCILS AND COLOR ART BY JAVIER RODRIGUEZ
INKS BY ALVARO LOPEZ
LETTERING BY CHRIS ELIOPOULOS

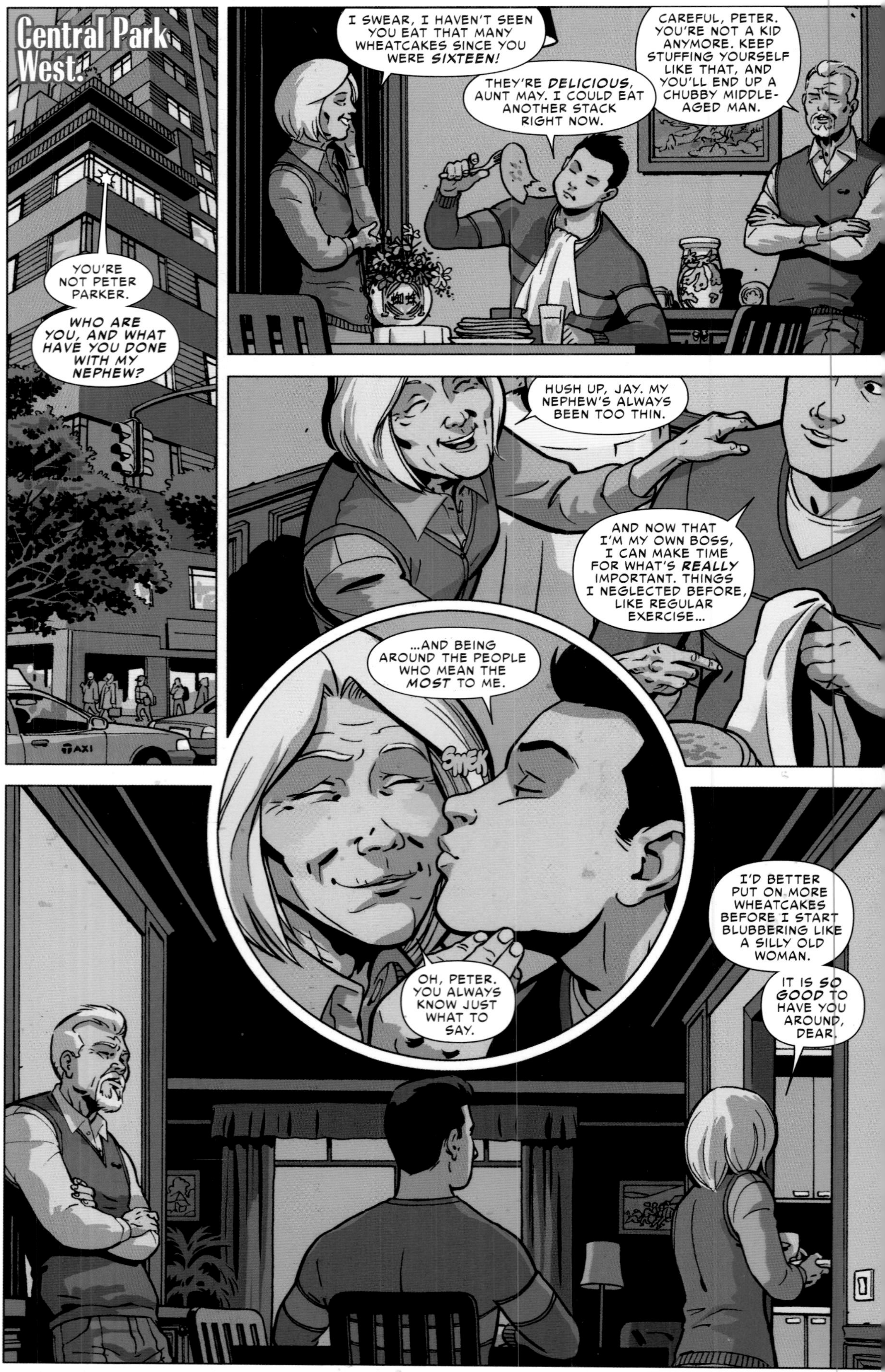
Central Park West.
YOU'RE NOT PETER PARKER.
WHO ARE YOU, AND WHAT HAVE YOU DONE WITH MY NEPHEW?
I SWEAR, I HAVEN'T SEEN YOU EAT THAT MANY WHEATCAKES SINCE YOU WERE SIXTEEN!
THEY'RE DELICIOUS, AUNT MAY. I COULD EAT ANOTHER STACK RIGHT NOW.
CAREFUL, PETER. YOU'RE NOT A KID ANYMORE. KEEP STUFFING YOURSELF LIKE THAT, AND YOU'LL END UP A CHUBBY MIDDLE-AGED MAN.
HUSH UP, JAY. MY NEPHEW'S ALWAYS BEEN TOO THIN.
AND NOW THAT I'M MY OWN BOSS, I CAN MAKE TIME FOR WHAT'S REALLY IMPORTANT. THINGS I NEGLECTED BEFORE, LIKE REGULAR EXERCISE...
...AND BEING AROUND THE PEOPLE WHO MEAN THE MOST TO ME.
SMEK
OH, PETER. YOU ALWAYS KNOW JUST WHAT TO SAY.
I'D BETTER PUT ON MORE WHEATCAKES BEFORE I START BLUBBERING LIKE A SILLY OLD WOMAN.
IT IS SO GOOD TO HAVE YOU AROUND, DEAR.

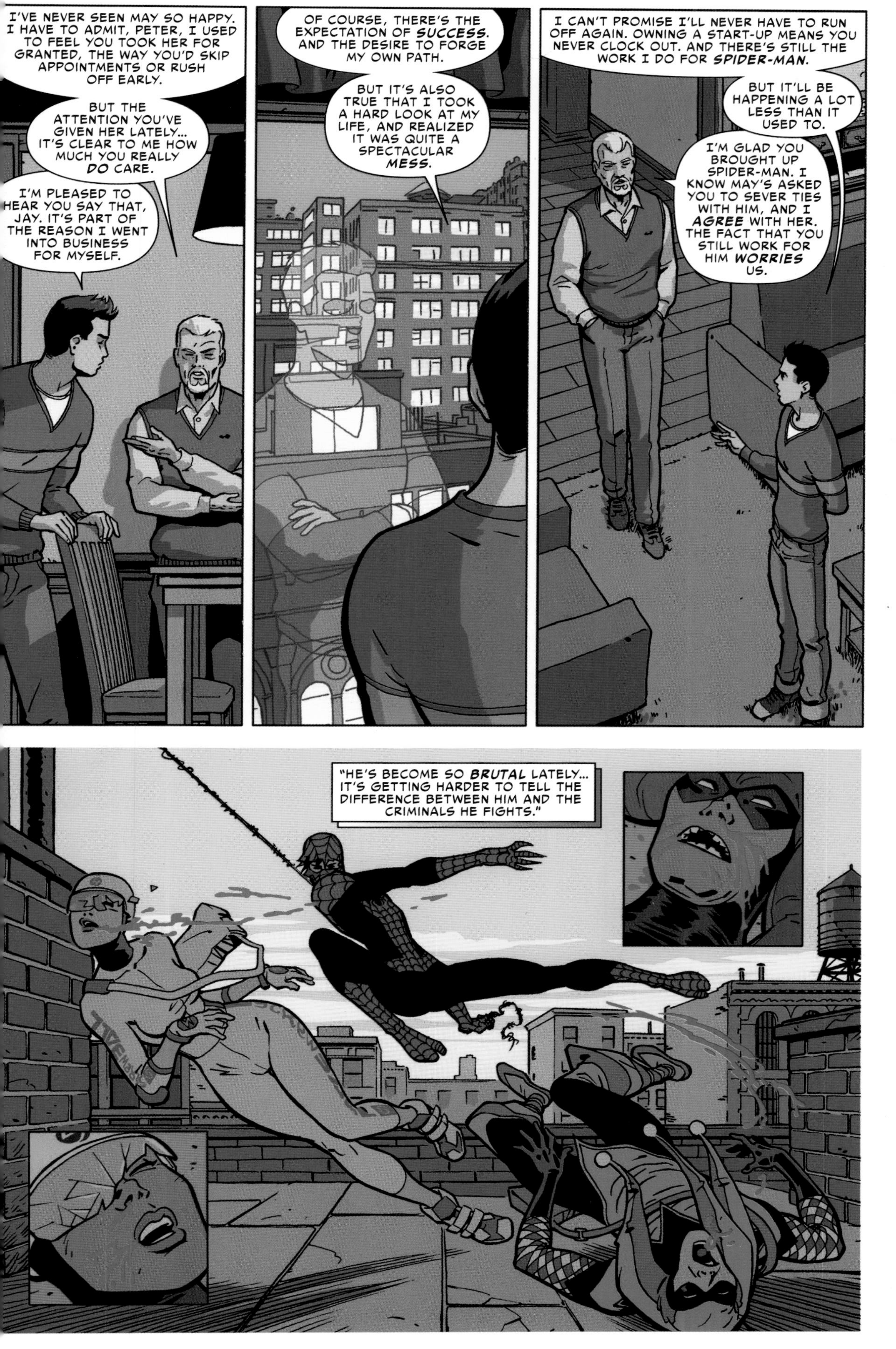

I'VE NEVER SEEN MAY SO HAPPY. I HAVE TO ADMIT, PETER, I USED TO FEEL YOU TOOK HER FOR GRANTED, THE WAY YOU'D SKIP APPOINTMENTS OR RUSH OFF EARLY.
BUT THE ATTENTION YOU'VE GIVEN HER LATELY... IT'S CLEAR TO ME HOW MUCH YOU REALLY DO CARE.
I'M PLEASED TO HEAR YOU SAY THAT, JAY. IT'S PART OF THE REASON I WENT INTO BUSINESS FOR MYSELF.
OF COURSE, THERE'S THE EXPECTATION OF SUCCESS. AND THE DESIRE TO FORGE MY OWN PATH.
BUT IT'S ALSO TRUE THAT I TOOK A HARD LOOK AT MY LIFE, AND REALIZED IT WAS QUITE A SPECTACULAR MESS.
I CAN'T PROMISE I'LL NEVER HAVE TO RUN OFF AGAIN. OWNING A START-UP MEANS YOU NEVER CLOCK OUT. AND THERE'S STILL THE WORK I DO FOR SPIDER-MAN.
BUT IT'LL BE HAPPENING A LOT LESS THAN IT USED TO.
I'M GLAD YOU BROUGHT UP SPIDER-MAN. I KNOW MAY'S ASKED YOU TO SEVER TIES WITH HIM, AND I AGREE WITH HER. THE FACT THAT YOU STILL WORK FOR HIM WORRIES US.
"HE'S BECOME SO BRUTAL LATELY... IT'S GETTING HARDER TO TELL THE DIFFERENCE BETWEEN HIM AND THE CRIMINALS HE FIGHTS."

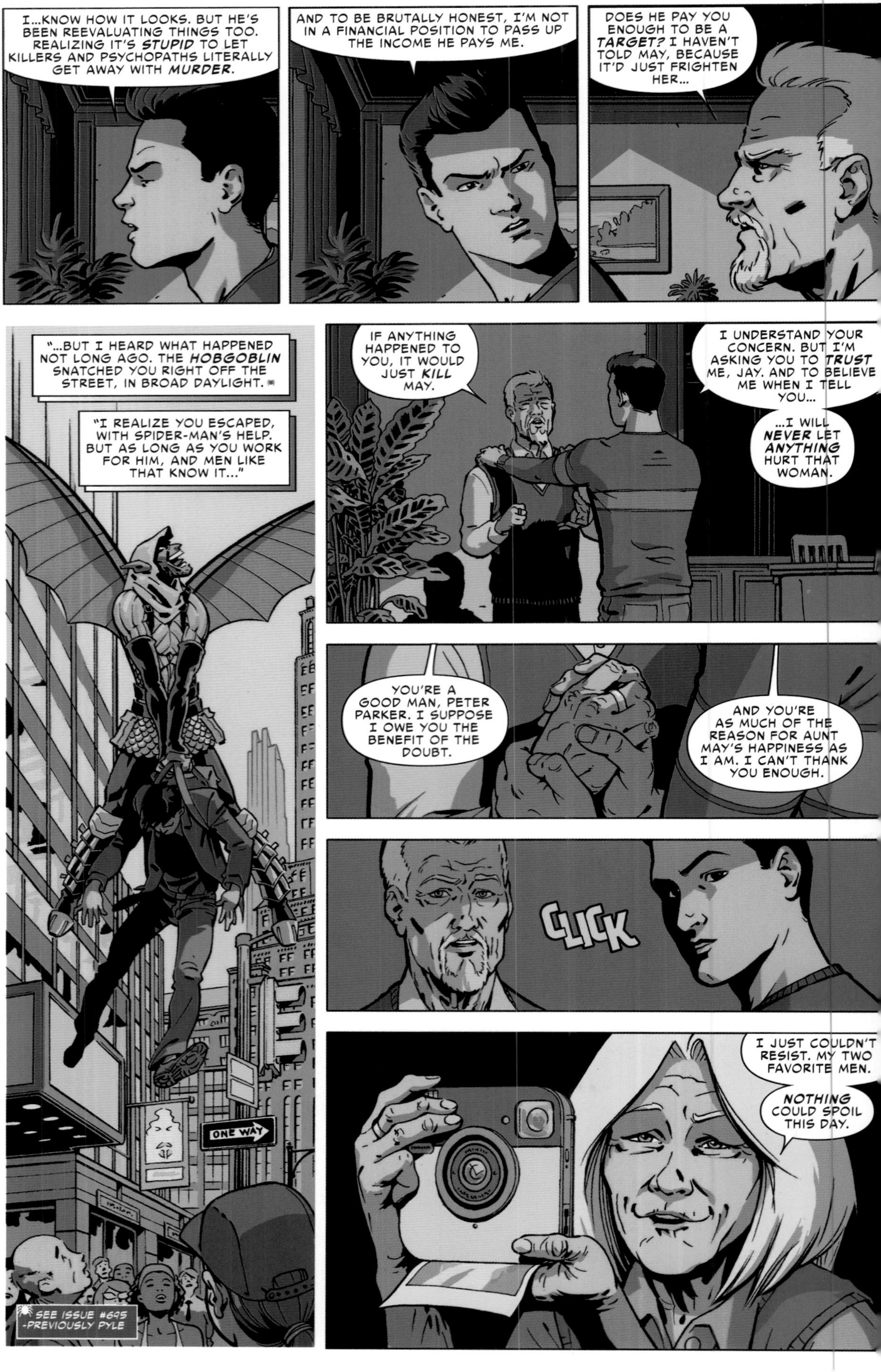

I...KNOW HOW IT LOOKS. BUT HE'S BEEN REEVALUATING THINGS TOO. REALIZING IT'S STUPID TO LET KILLERS AND PSYCHOPATHS LITERALLY GET AWAY WITH MURDER.
AND TO BE BRUTALLY HONEST, I'M NOT IN A FINANCIAL POSITION TO PASS UP THE INCOME HE PAYS ME.
DOES HE PAY YOU ENOUGH TO BE A TARGET? I HAVEN'T TOLD MAY, BECAUSE IT'D JUST FRIGHTEN HER...
"...BUT I HEARD WHAT HAPPENED NOT LONG AGO. THE HOBGOBLIN SNATCHED YOU RIGHT OFF THE STREET, IN BROAD DAYLIGHT.
"I REALIZE YOU ESCAPED, WITH SPIDER-MAN'S HELP. BUT AS LONG AS YOU WORK FOR HIM, AND MEN LIKE THAT KNOW IT..."
ONE WAY
SEE ISSUE #695 -PREVIOUSLY PYLE
IF ANYTHING HAPPENED TO YOU, IT WOULD JUST KILL MAY.
I UNDERSTAND YOUR CONCERN. BUT I'M ASKING YOU TO TRUST ME, JAY. AND TO BELIEVE ME WHEN I TELL YOU...
...I WILL NEVER LET ANYTHING HURT THAT WOMAN.
YOU'RE A GOOD MAN, PETER PARKER. I SUPPOSE I OWE YOU THE BENEFIT OF THE DOUBT.
AND YOU'RE AS MUCH OF THE REASON FOR AUNT MAY'S HAPPINESS AS I AM. I CAN'T THANK YOU ENOUGH.
CLICK
I JUST COULDN'T RESIST. MY TWO FAVORITE MEN.
NOTHING COULD SPOIL THIS DAY.

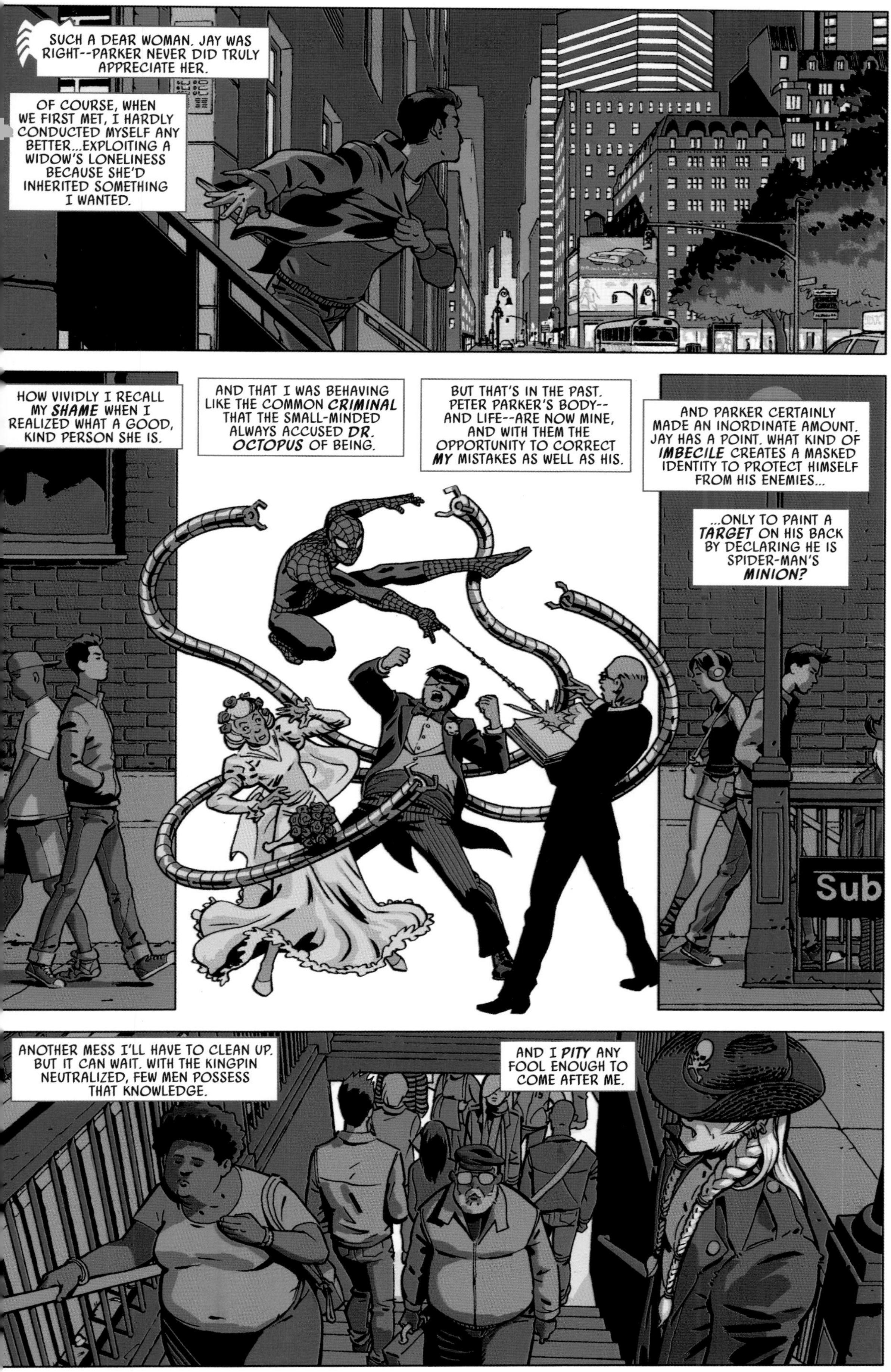

SUCH A DEAR WOMAN. JAY WAS RIGHT--PARKER NEVER DID TRULY APPRECIATE HER.
OF COURSE, WHEN WE FIRST MET, I HARDLY CONDUCTED MYSELF ANY BETTER...EXPLOITING A WIDOW'S LONELINESS BECAUSE SHE'D INHERITED SOMETHING I WANTED.
HOW VIVIDLY I RECALL MY SHAME WHEN I REALIZED WHAT A GOOD, KIND PERSON SHE IS.
AND THAT I WAS BEHAVING LIKE THE COMMON CRIMINAL THAT THE SMALL-MINDED ALWAYS ACCUSED DR. OCTOPUS OF BEING.
BUT THAT'S IN THE PAST. PETER PARKER'S BODY--AND LIFE--ARE NOW MINE, AND WITH THEM THE OPPORTUNITY TO CORRECT MY MISTAKES AS WELL AS HIS.
AND PARKER CERTAINLY MADE AN INORDINATE AMOUNT. JAY HAS A POINT. WHAT KIND OF IMBECILE CREATES A MASKED IDENTITY TO PROTECT HIMSELF FROM HIS ENEMIES...
...ONLY TO PAINT A TARGET ON HIS BACK BY DECLARING HE IS SPIDER-MAN'S MINION?
Sub
ANOTHER MESS I'LL HAVE TO CLEAN UP. BUT IT CAN WAIT. WITH THE KINGPIN NEUTRALIZED, FEW MEN POSSESS THAT KNOWLEDGE.
AND I PITY ANY FOOL ENOUGH TO COME AFTER ME.

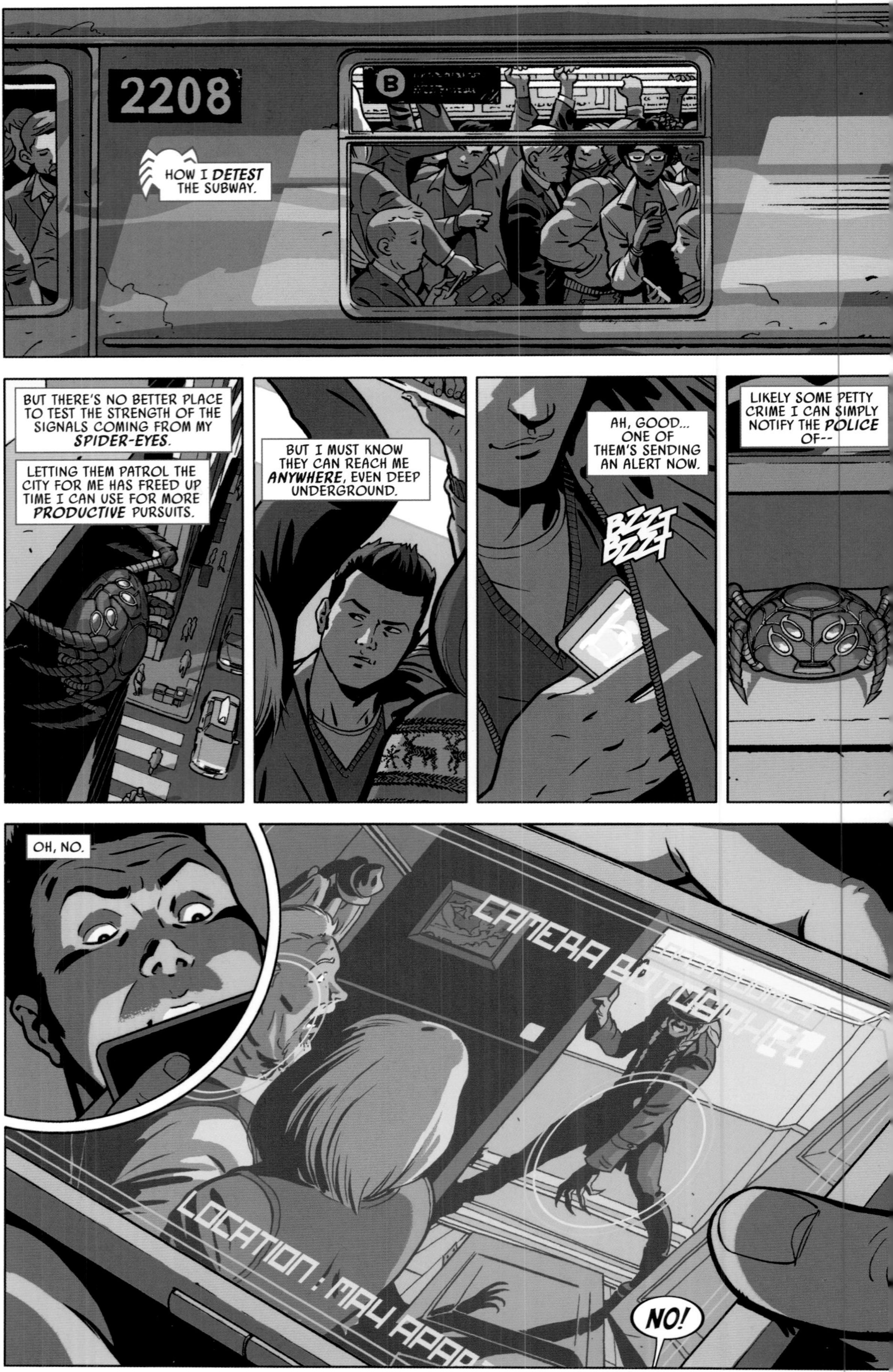

2208
B
HOW I DETEST THE SUBWAY.
BUT THERE'S NO BETTER PLACE TO TEST THE STRENGTH OF THE SIGNALS COMING FROM MY SPIDER-EYES.
LETTING THEM PATROL THE CITY FOR ME HAS FREED UP TIME I CAN USE FOR MORE PRODUCTIVE PURSUITS.
BUT I MUST KNOW THEY CAN REACH ME ANYWHERE, EVEN DEEP UNDERGROUND.
AH, GOOD... ONE OF THEM'S SENDING AN ALERT NOW.
BZZT BZZT
LIKELY SOME PETTY CRIME I CAN SIMPLY NOTIFY THE POLICE OF--
OH, NO.
CAMERA
LOCATION : MAY APAR
NO!

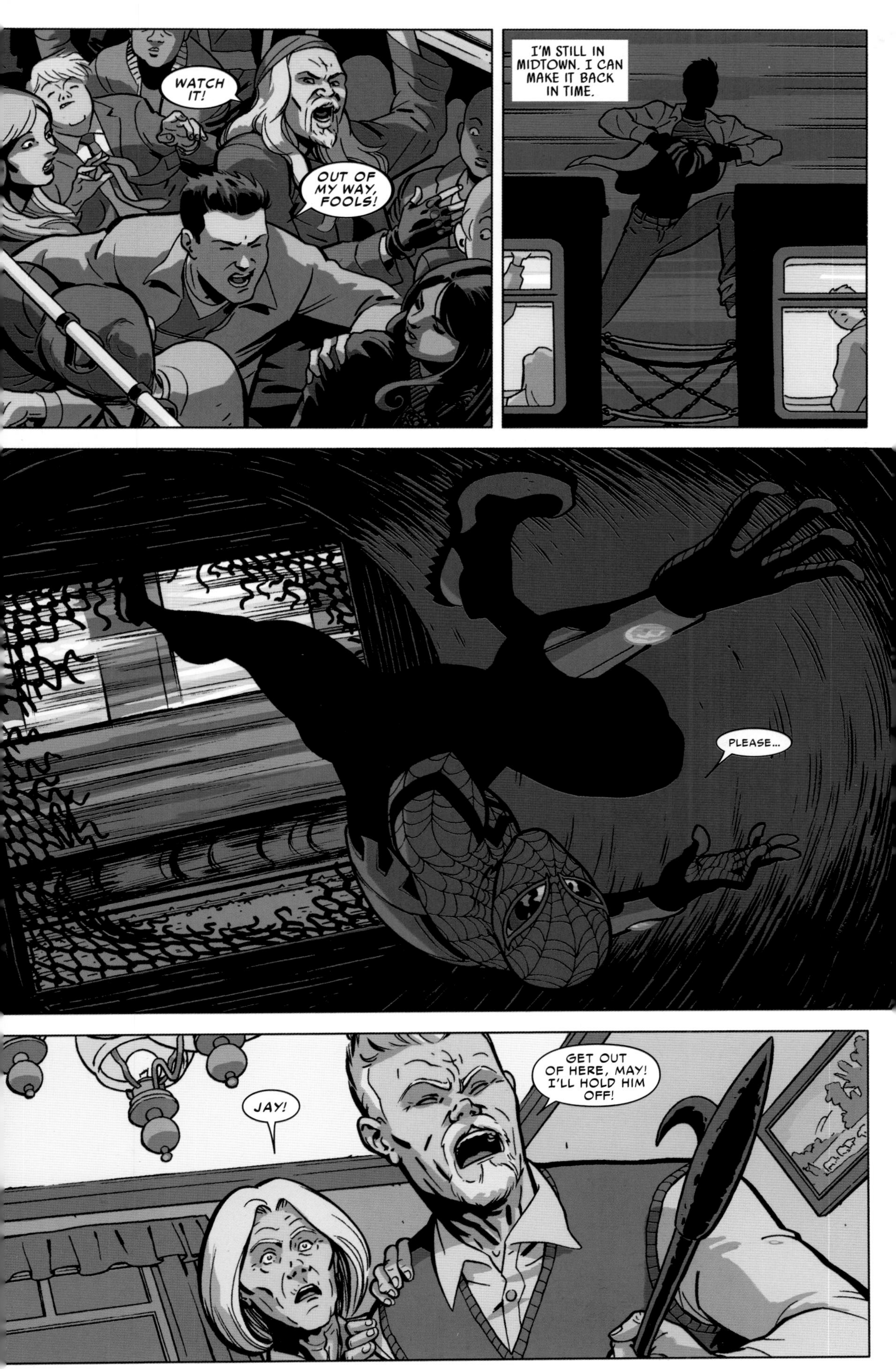
WATCH IT!
OUT OF MY WAY, FOOLS!
I'M STILL IN MIDTOWN. I CAN MAKE IT BACK IN TIME.
PLEASE...
JAY!
GET OUT OF HERE, MAY! I'LL HOLD HIM OFF!

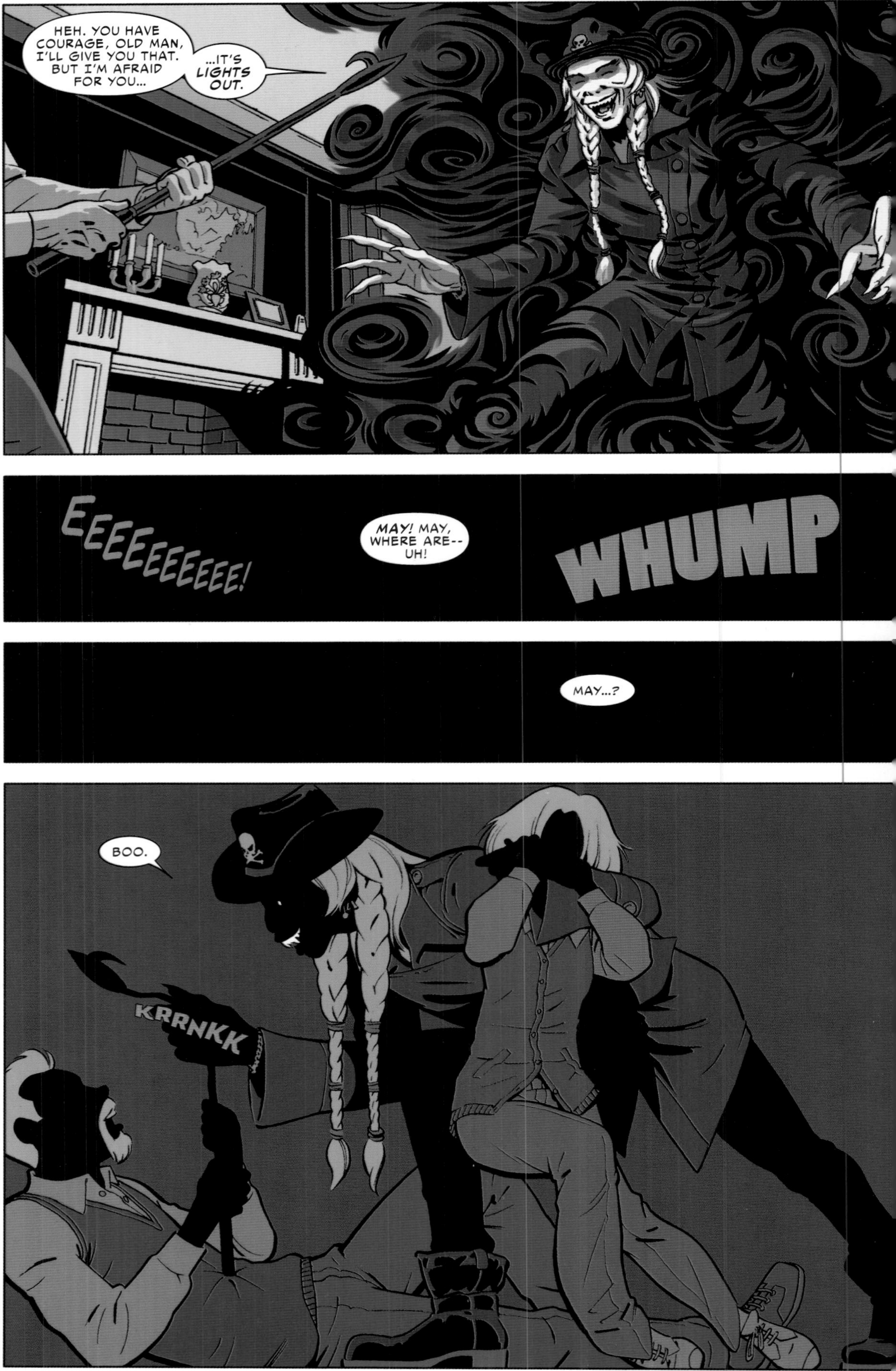
HEH. YOU HAVE COURAGE, OLD MAN, I'LL GIVE YOU THAT. BUT I'M AFRAID FOR YOU...
...IT'S LIGHTS OUT.
EEEEEEEEEE!
MAY! MAY, WHERE ARE-- UH!
WHUMP
MAY...?
BOO.
KRRNKK

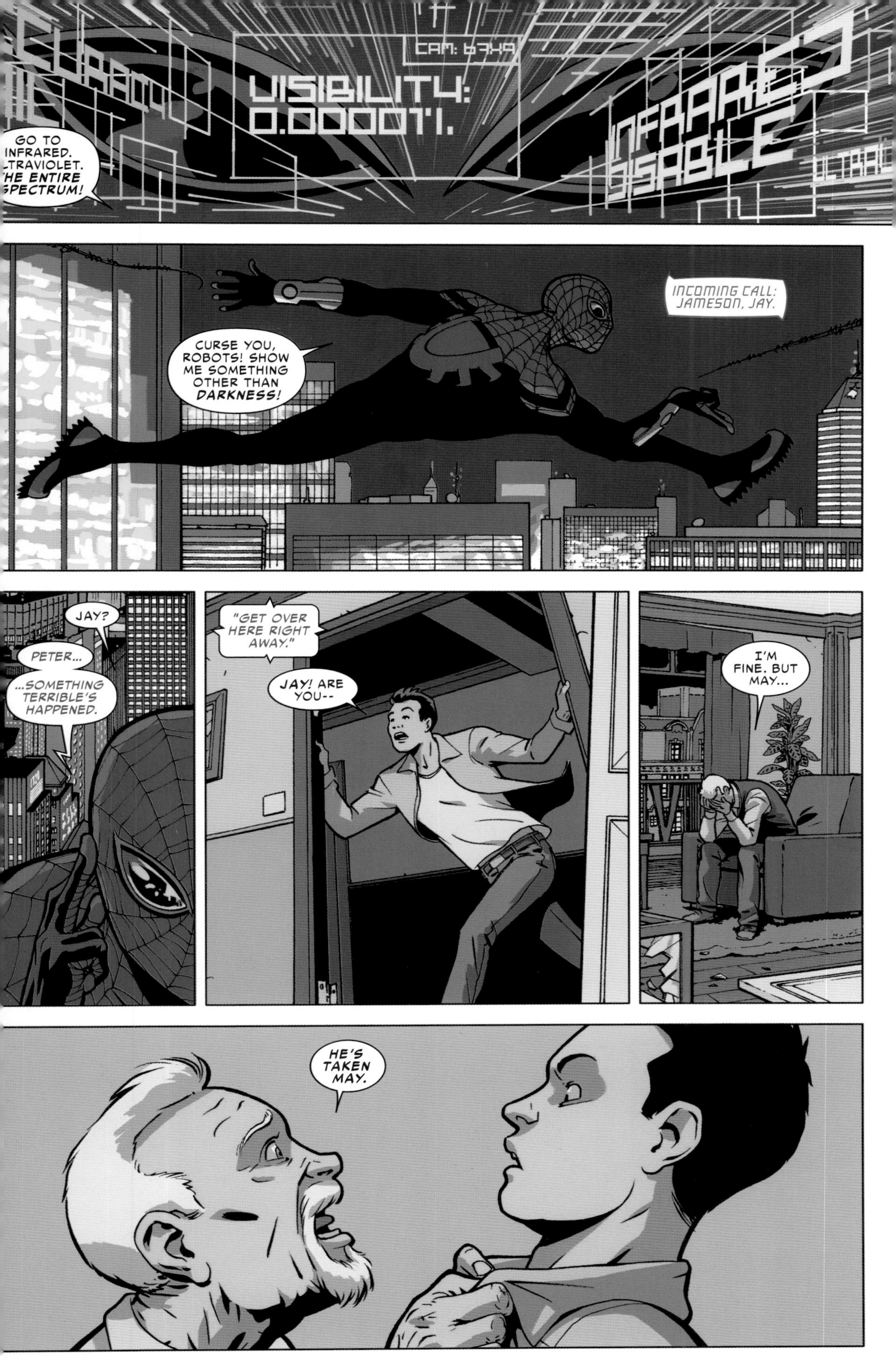
CAM: 63X9
VISIBILITY: 0.000071.
GO TO INFRARED. ULTRAVIOLET. THE ENTIRE SPECTRUM!
INFRARED
VISIBLE
CURSE YOU, ROBOTS! SHOW ME SOMETHING OTHER THAN DARKNESS!
INCOMING CALL: JAMESON, JAY.
JAY?
PETER...
...SOMETHING TERRIBLE'S HAPPENED.
"GET OVER HERE RIGHT AWAY."
JAY! ARE YOU--
I'M FINE. BUT MAY...
HE'S TAKEN MAY.

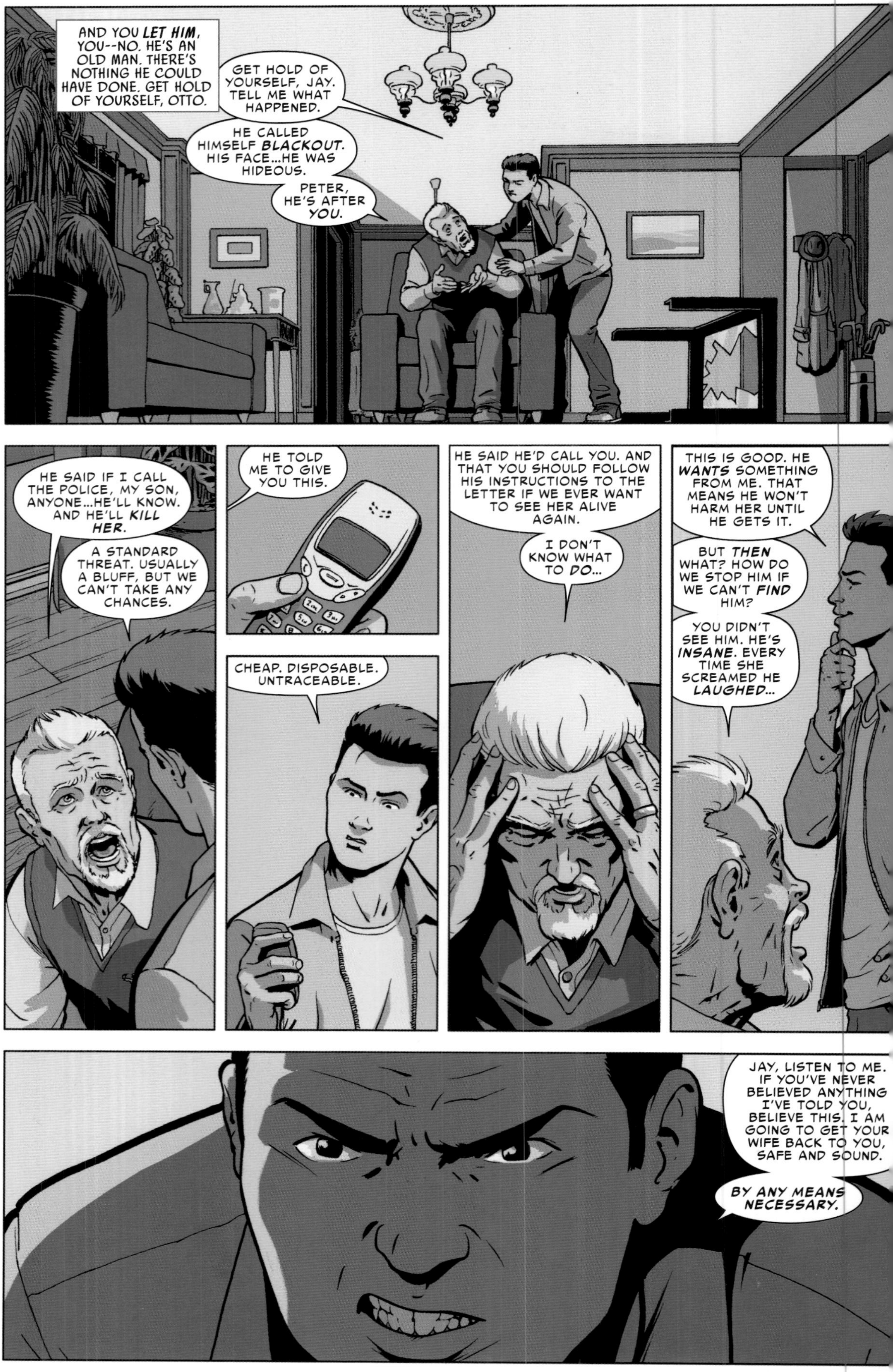
AND YOU LET HIM, YOU--NO. HE'S AN OLD MAN. THERE'S NOTHING HE COULD HAVE DONE. GET HOLD OF YOURSELF, OTTO.
GET HOLD OF YOURSELF, JAY. TELL ME WHAT HAPPENED.
HE CALLED HIMSELF BLACKOUT. HIS FACE...HE WAS HIDEOUS.
PETER, HE'S AFTER YOU.
HE SAID IF I CALL THE POLICE, MY SON, ANYONE...HE'LL KNOW. AND HE'LL KILL HER.
A STANDARD THREAT. USUALLY A BLUFF, BUT WE CAN'T TAKE ANY CHANCES.
HE TOLD ME TO GIVE YOU THIS.
CHEAP. DISPOSABLE. UNTRACEABLE.
HE SAID HE'D CALL YOU. AND THAT YOU SHOULD FOLLOW HIS INSTRUCTIONS TO THE LETTER IF WE EVER WANT TO SEE HER ALIVE AGAIN.
I DON'T KNOW WHAT TO DO...
THIS IS GOOD. HE WANTS SOMETHING FROM ME. THAT MEANS HE WON'T HARM HER UNTIL HE GETS IT.
BUT THEN WHAT? HOW DO WE STOP HIM IF WE CAN'T FIND HIM?
YOU DIDN'T SEE HIM. HE'S INSANE. EVERY TIME SHE SCREAMED HE LAUGHED...
JAY, LISTEN TO ME. IF YOU'VE NEVER BELIEVED ANYTHING I'VE TOLD YOU, BELIEVE THIS. I AM GOING TO GET YOUR WIFE BACK TO YOU, SAFE AND SOUND.
BY ANY MEANS NECESSARY.

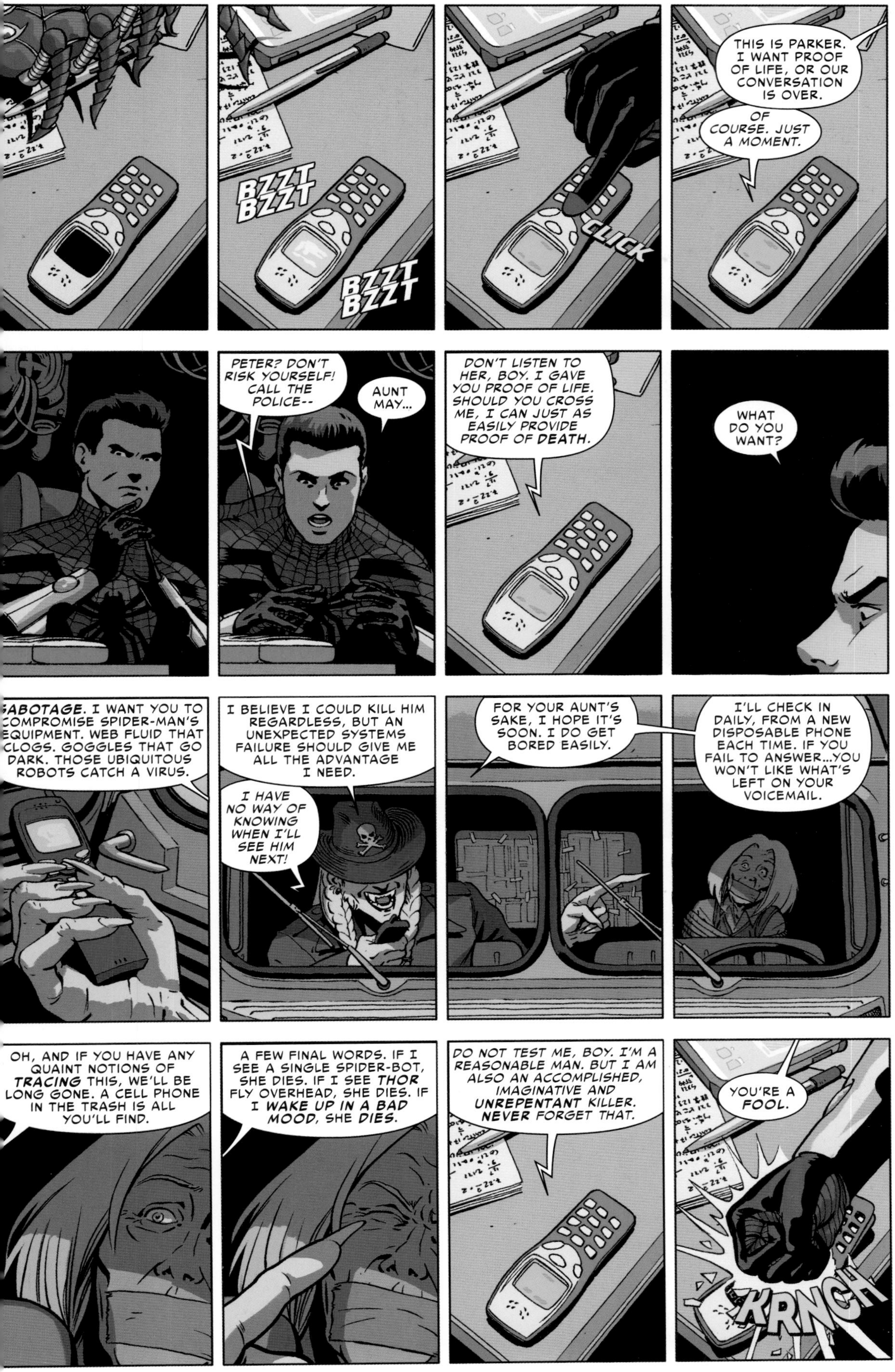
BZZT BZZT
BZZT BZZT
CLICK
THIS IS PARKER. I WANT PROOF OF LIFE, OR OUR CONVERSATION IS OVER.
OF COURSE. JUST A MOMENT.
PETER? DON'T RISK YOURSELF! CALL THE POLICE--
AUNT MAY...
DON'T LISTEN TO HER, BOY. I GAVE YOU PROOF OF LIFE. SHOULD YOU CROSS ME, I CAN JUST AS EASILY PROVIDE PROOF OF DEATH.
WHAT DO YOU WANT?
SABOTAGE. I WANT YOU TO COMPROMISE SPIDER-MAN'S EQUIPMENT. WEB FLUID THAT CLOGS. GOGGLES THAT GO DARK. THOSE UBIQUITOUS ROBOTS CATCH A VIRUS.
I HAVE NO WAY OF KNOWING WHEN I'LL SEE HIM NEXT!
I BELIEVE I COULD KILL HIM REGARDLESS, BUT AN UNEXPECTED SYSTEMS FAILURE SHOULD GIVE ME ALL THE ADVANTAGE I NEED.
FOR YOUR AUNT'S SAKE, I HOPE IT'S SOON. I DO GET BORED EASILY.
I'LL CHECK IN DAILY, FROM A NEW DISPOSABLE PHONE EACH TIME. IF YOU FAIL TO ANSWER...YOU WON'T LIKE WHAT'S LEFT ON YOUR VOICEMAIL.
OH, AND IF YOU HAVE ANY QUAINT NOTIONS OF TRACING THIS, WE'LL BE LONG GONE. A CELL PHONE IN THE TRASH IS ALL YOU'LL FIND.
A FEW FINAL WORDS. IF I SEE A SINGLE SPIDER-BOT, SHE DIES. IF I SEE THOR FLY OVERHEAD, SHE DIES. IF I WAKE UP IN A BAD MOOD, SHE DIES.
DO NOT TEST ME, BOY. I'M A REASONABLE MAN. BUT I AM ALSO AN ACCOMPLISHED, IMAGINATIVE AND UNREPENTANT KILLER. NEVER FORGET THAT.
YOU'RE A FOOL.
KRNCH

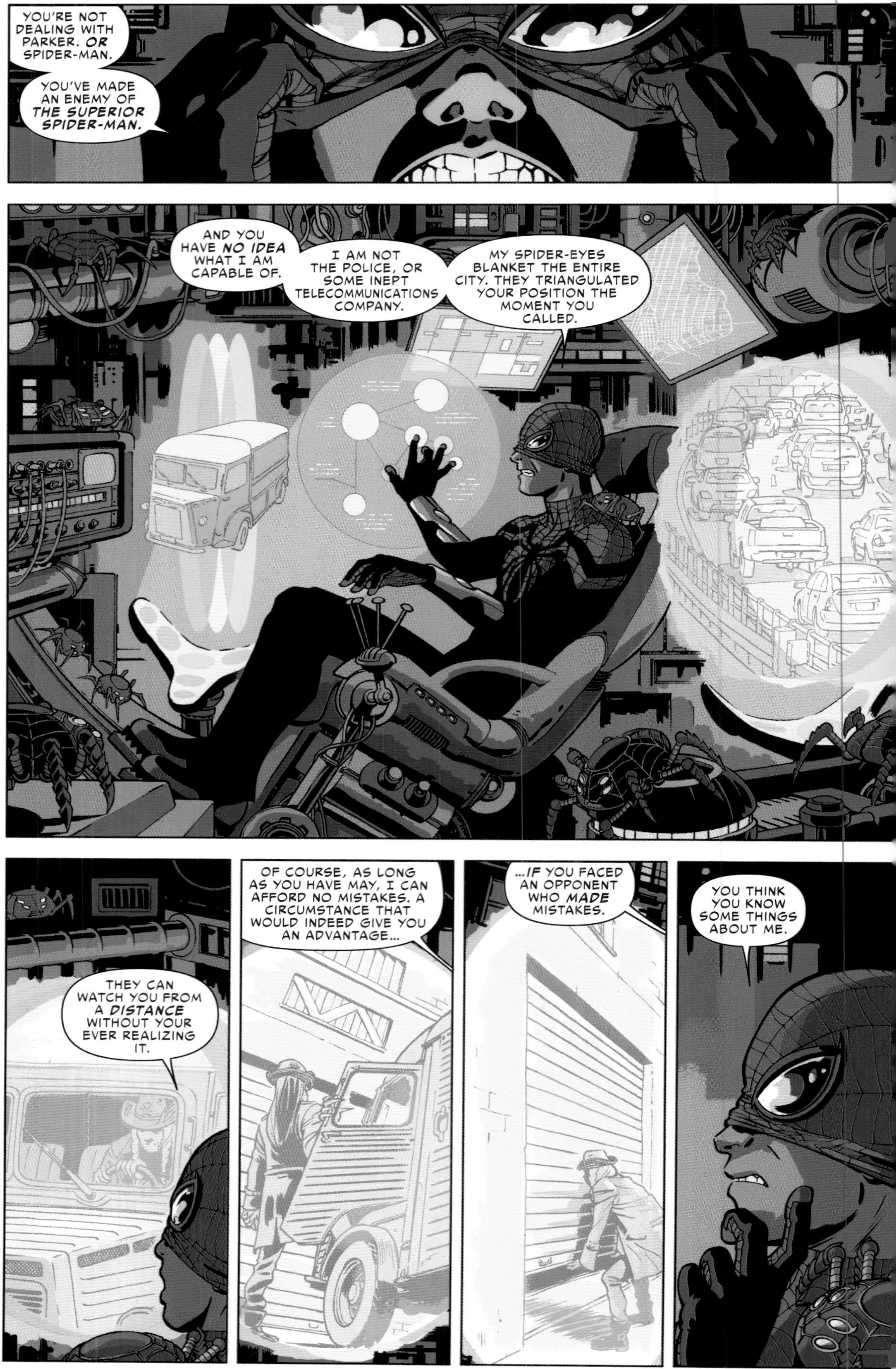
YOU'RE NOT DEALING WITH PARKER. OR SPIDER-MAN.
YOU'VE MADE AN ENEMY OF THE SUPERIOR SPIDER-MAN.
AND YOU HAVE NO IDEA WHAT I AM CAPABLE OF.
I AM NOT THE POLICE, OR SOME INEPT TELECOMMUNICATIONS COMPANY.
MY SPIDER-EYES BLANKET THE ENTIRE CITY. THEY TRIANGULATED YOUR POSITION THE MOMENT YOU CALLED.
THEY CAN WATCH YOU FROM A DISTANCE WITHOUT YOUR EVER REALIZING IT.
OF COURSE, AS LONG AS YOU HAVE MAY, I CAN AFFORD NO MISTAKES. A CIRCUMSTANCE THAT WOULD INDEED GIVE YOU AN ADVANTAGE...
...IF YOU FACED AN OPPONENT WHO MADE MISTAKES.
YOU THINK YOU KNOW SOME THINGS ABOUT ME.

"IT'S TIME I LEARNED MORE ABOUT *YOU*..."

Upstate.

BLACKOUT? YEAH, I KNOW HIM.

HE KILLED MY SISTER.

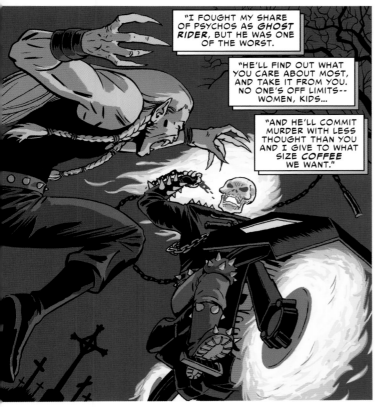

"I FOUGHT MY SHARE OF PSYCHOS AS *GHOST RIDER*, BUT HE WAS ONE OF THE WORST.

"HE'LL FIND OUT WHAT YOU CARE ABOUT MOST, AND TAKE IT FROM YOU. NO ONE'S OFF LIMITS-- WOMEN, KIDS...

"AND HE'LL COMMIT MURDER WITH LESS THOUGHT THAN YOU AND I GIVE TO WHAT SIZE *COFFEE* WE WANT."

I THOUGHT HE WAS DEAD, BUT I GUESS THAT ONLY MEANS SO MUCH WHEN A GUY'S *HALF DEMON.* NOT SURE HOW MUCH HELP I AM WITHOUT POWERS, BUT IF YOU WANT A HAND--

NO NEED, KETCH. I'M NOT CERTAIN IT'S HIM YET...JUST FOLLOWING A TIP. IT COULD BE THE *OTHER* BLACKOUT-- THE ONE WITH THAT RIDICULOUS LIGHTNING BOLT ON HIS HEAD.

BUT AS A PRECAUTION, I'M GATHERING INFORMATION ON YOUR OLD ENEMY-- STRENGTHS, WEAKNESSES, THAT SORT OF THING.

YOU CAN SEE WHO SPIDEY IS TALKING ABOUT IN *SUPERIOR TEAM-UP #6* -SELLIN' STEVE!

WELL, HE'S STRONG, FAST, DURABLE...RAZOR-SHARP CLAWS AND TEETH...LIKES TO RIP OUT THROATS...AND HE CAN LITERALLY SUCK THE LIGHT OUT OF A ROOM.

HE'S SENSITIVE TO SUNLIGHT. NOT BURSTING-INTO-FLAME SENSITIVE, BUT IT HURTS.

MY ADVICE? I KNOW THIS ISN'T YOUR STYLE. BUT IF YOU HAVE TO FIGHT HIM, KILL HIM.

OR YOU'RE PUTTING A NOOSE AROUND THE NECK OF EVERYONE YOU KNOW.

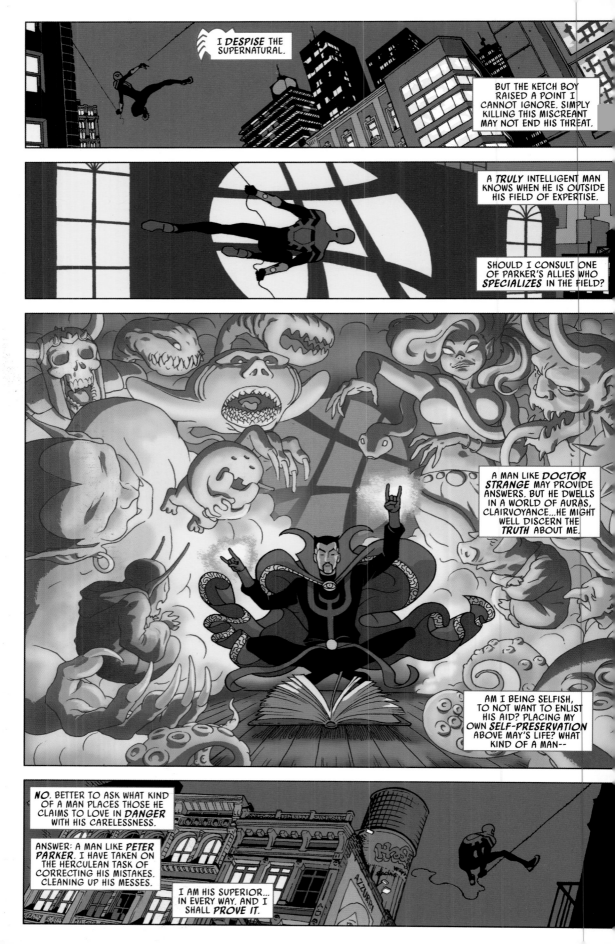

I *DESPISE* THE SUPERNATURAL.

BUT THE KETCH BOY RAISED A POINT I CANNOT IGNORE. SIMPLY KILLING THIS MISCREANT MAY NOT END HIS THREAT.

A *TRULY* INTELLIGENT MAN KNOWS WHEN HE IS OUTSIDE HIS FIELD OF EXPERTISE.

SHOULD I CONSULT ONE OF PARKER'S ALLIES WHO *SPECIALIZES* IN THE FIELD?

A MAN LIKE *DOCTOR STRANGE* MAY PROVIDE ANSWERS. BUT HE DWELLS IN A WORLD OF AURAS, CLAIRVOYANCE...HE MIGHT WELL DISCERN THE *TRUTH* ABOUT ME.

AM I BEING SELFISH, TO NOT WANT TO ENLIST HIS AID? PLACING MY OWN *SELF-PRESERVATION* ABOVE MAY'S LIFE? WHAT KIND OF A MAN--

NO. BETTER TO ASK WHAT KIND OF A MAN PLACES THOSE HE CLAIMS TO LOVE IN *DANGER* WITH HIS CARELESSNESS.

ANSWER: A MAN LIKE *PETER PARKER.* I HAVE TAKEN ON THE HERCULEAN TASK OF CORRECTING HIS MISTAKES. CLEANING UP HIS MESSES.

I AM HIS SUPERIOR... IN EVERY WAY. AND I SHALL *PROVE IT.*

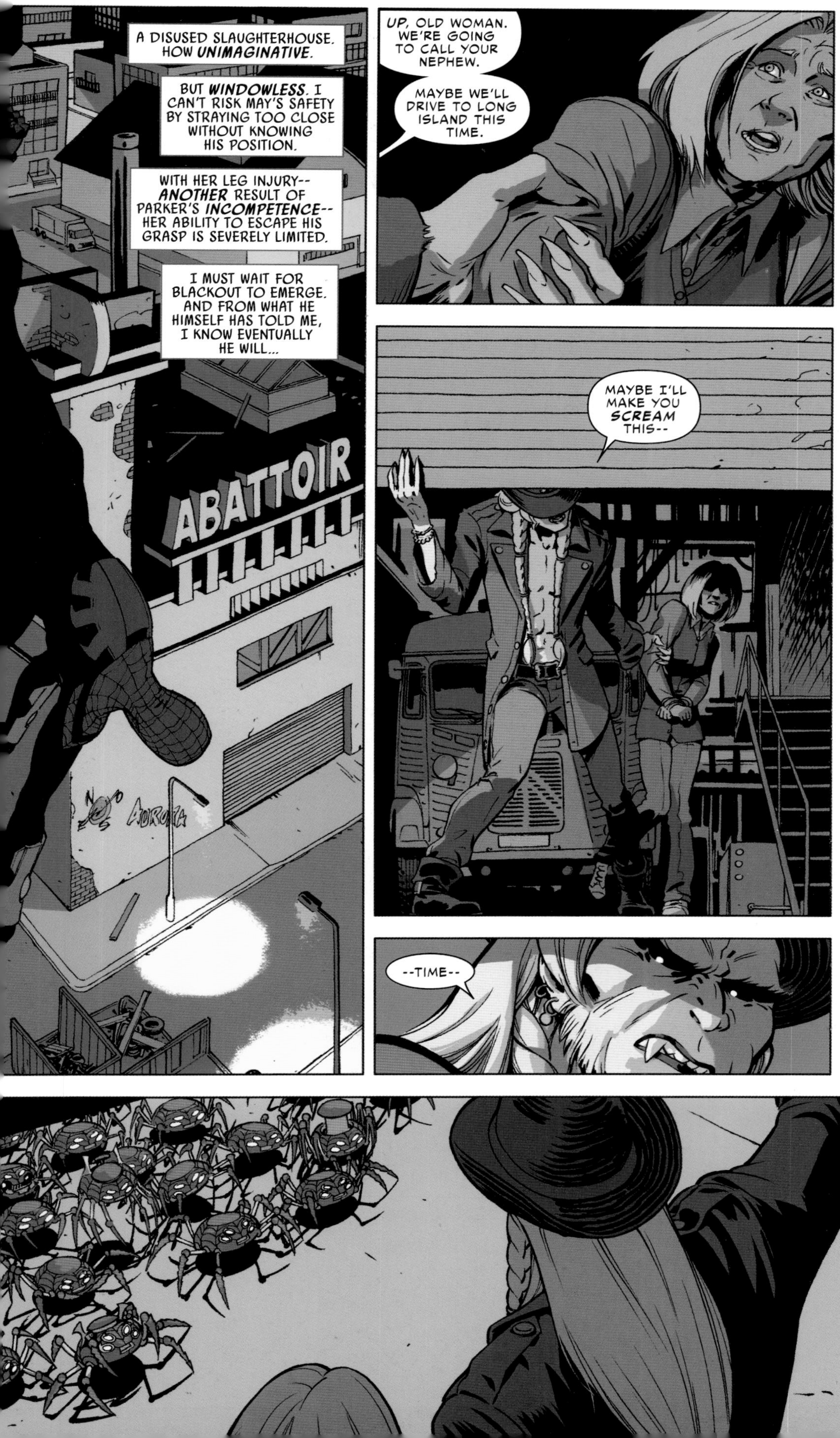
A DISUSED SLAUGHTERHOUSE. HOW UNIMAGINATIVE.
BUT WINDOWLESS. I CAN'T RISK MAY'S SAFETY BY STRAYING TOO CLOSE WITHOUT KNOWING HIS POSITION.
WITH HER LEG INJURY-- ANOTHER RESULT OF PARKER'S INCOMPETENCE-- HER ABILITY TO ESCAPE HIS GRASP IS SEVERELY LIMITED.
I MUST WAIT FOR BLACKOUT TO EMERGE. AND FROM WHAT HE HIMSELF HAS TOLD ME, I KNOW EVENTUALLY HE WILL...
ABATTOIR
UP, OLD WOMAN. WE'RE GOING TO CALL YOUR NEPHEW.
MAYBE WE'LL DRIVE TO LONG ISLAND THIS TIME.
MAYBE I'LL MAKE YOU SCREAM THIS--
--TIME--

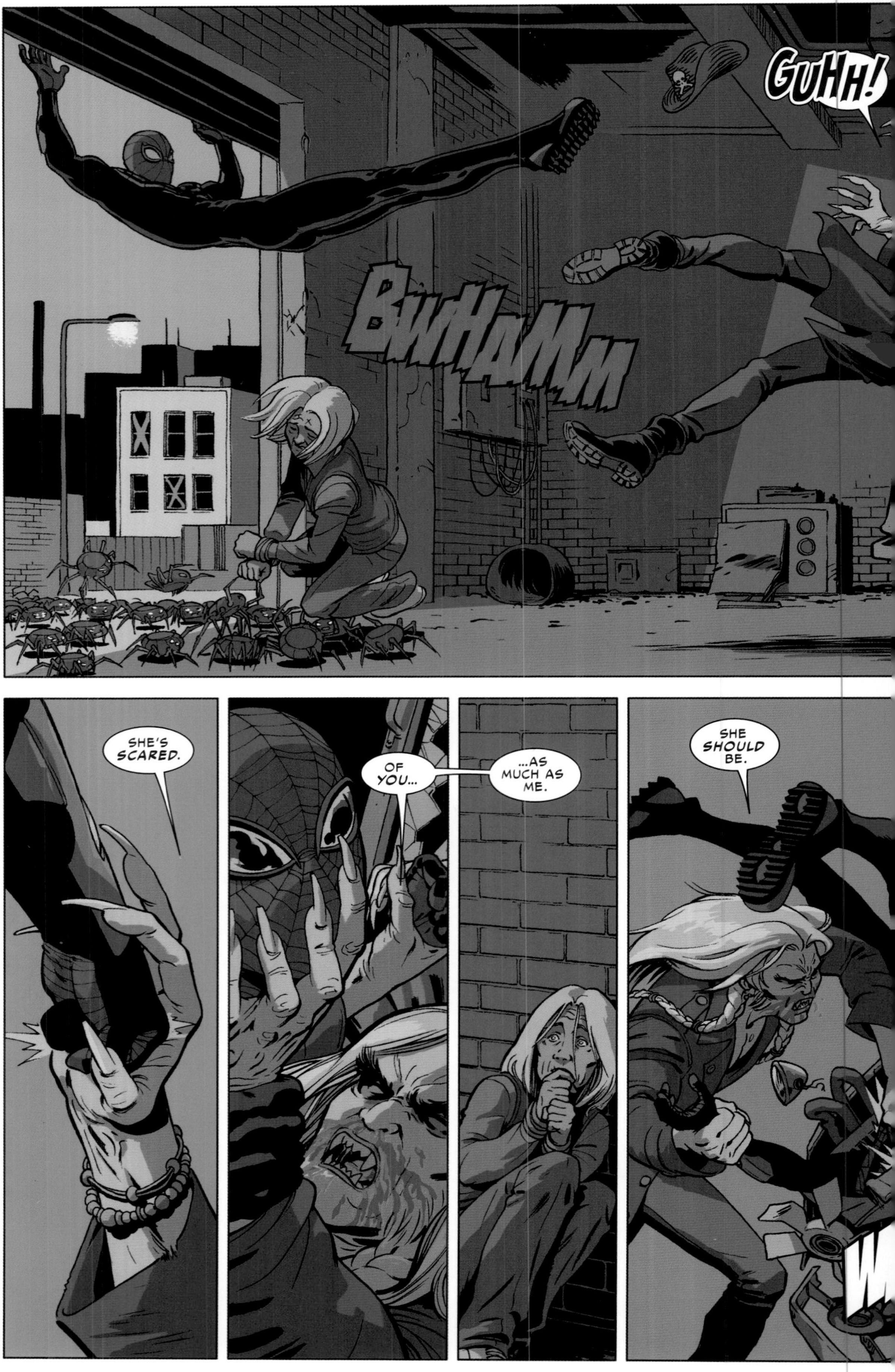
GUHH!
BWHAMMM
SHE'S SCARED.
OF YOU...
...AS MUCH AS ME.
SHE SHOULD BE.

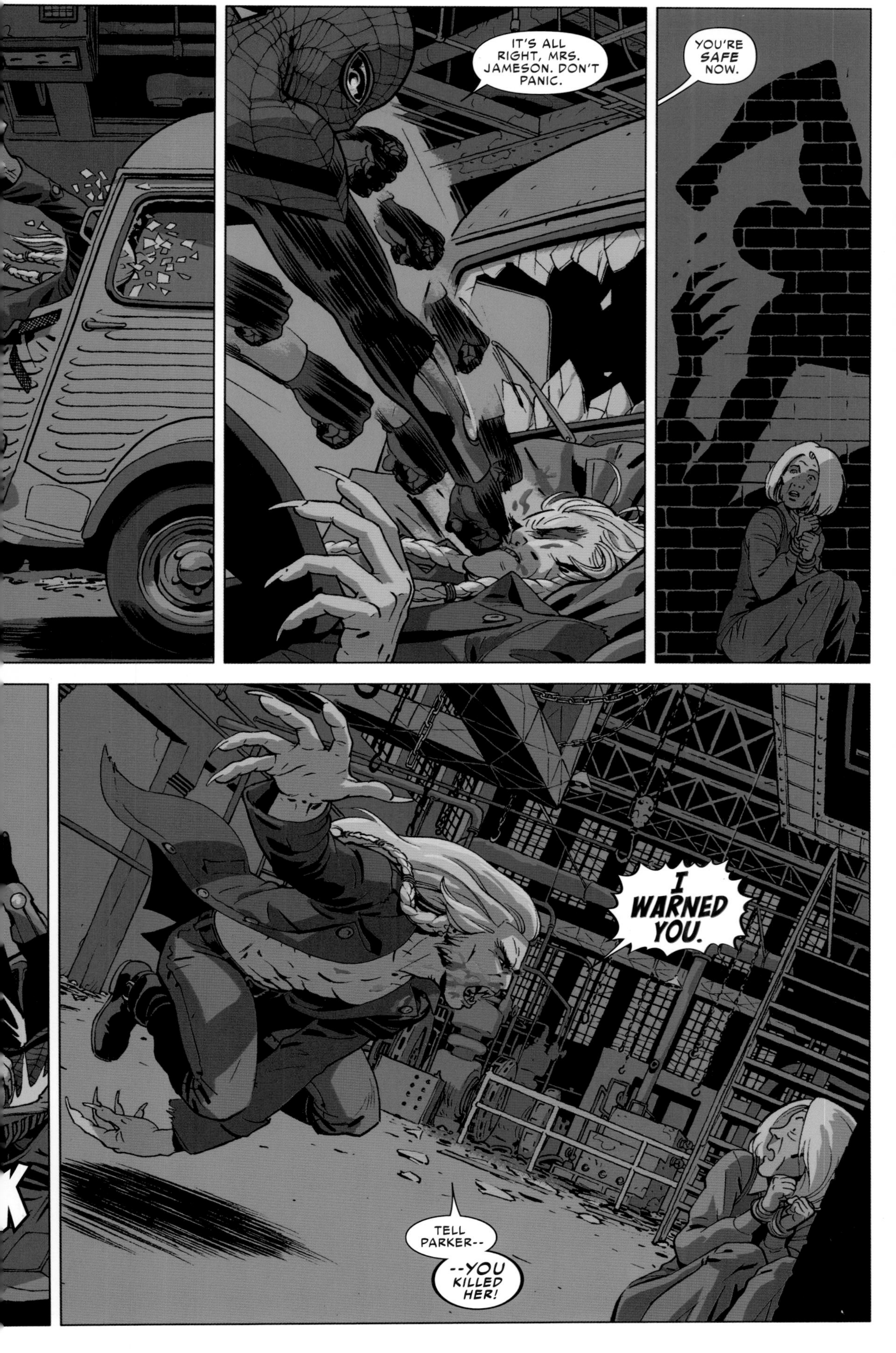

IT'S ALL RIGHT, MRS. JAMESON. DON'T PANIC.
YOU'RE SAFE NOW.
I WARNED YOU.
TELL PARKER--
--YOU KILLED HER!
K

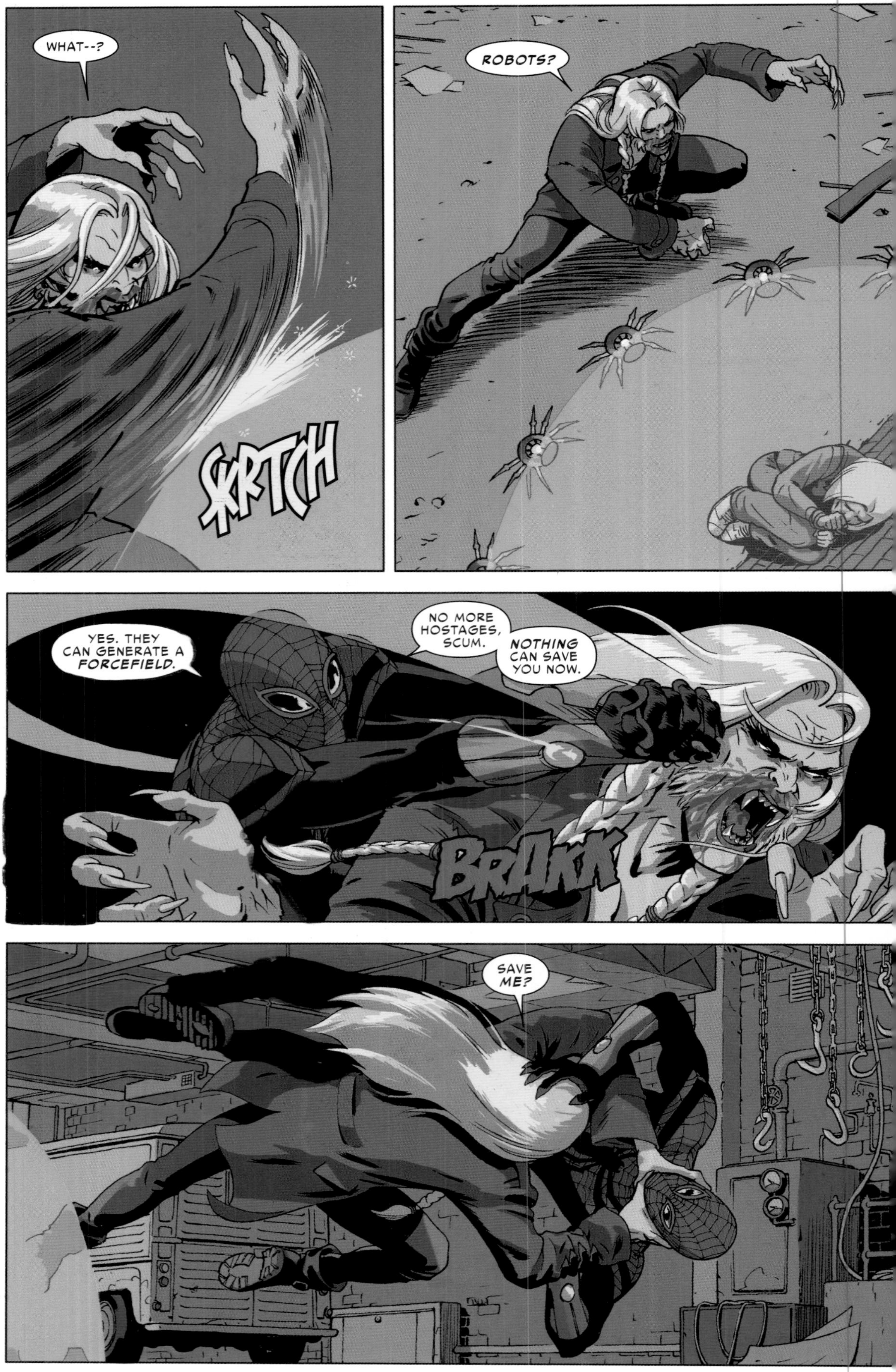
WHAT--?
SKRTCH
ROBOTS?
YES. THEY CAN GENERATE A FORCEFIELD.
NO MORE HOSTAGES, SCUM.
NOTHING CAN SAVE YOU NOW.
BRAKK
SAVE ME?

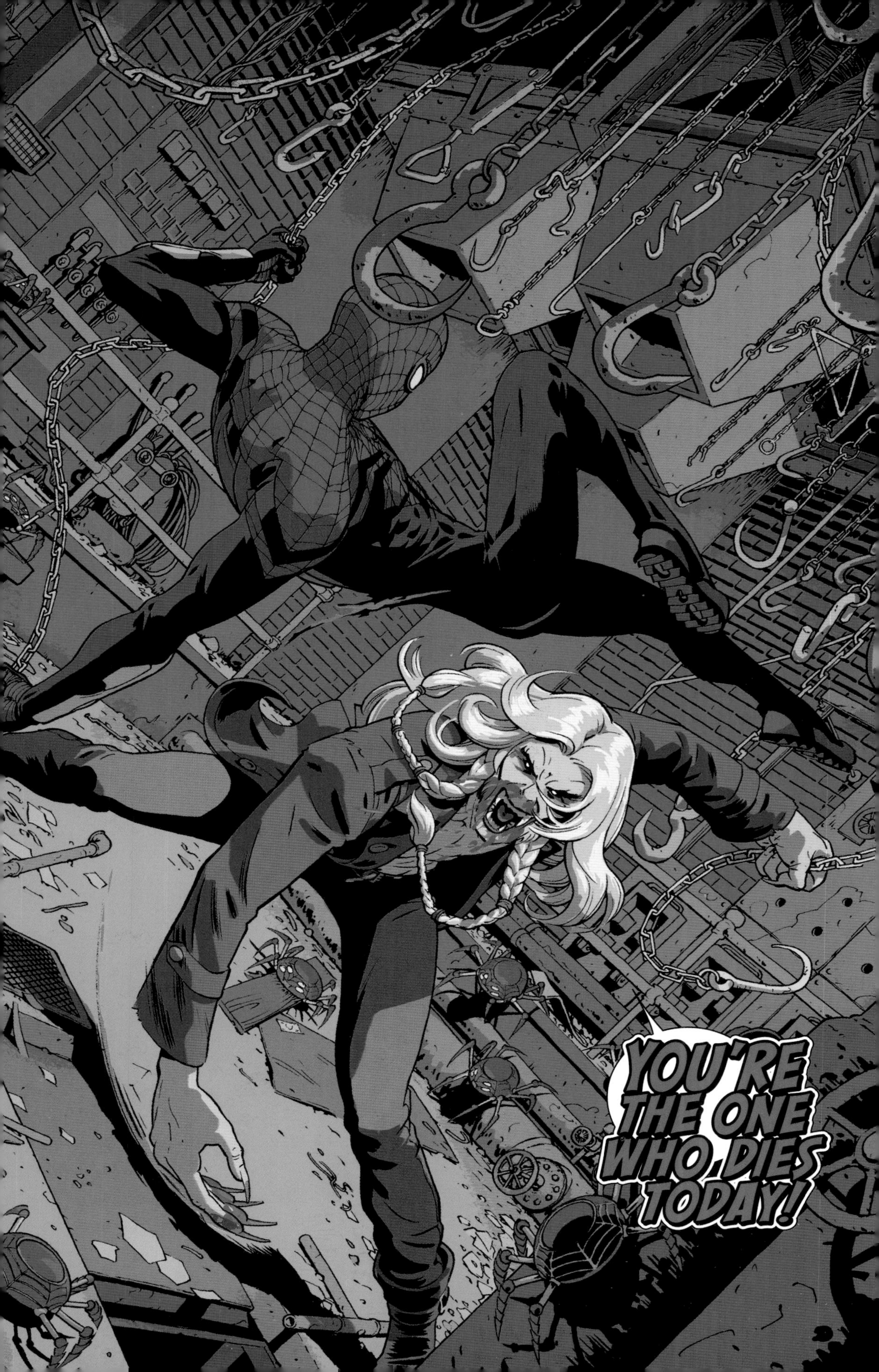
YOU'RE THE ONE WHO DIES TODAY!

KRTCH

GNH!

THERE. I'M NOT SURE THE TECH YOU'VE GOT IN THOSE EYEPIECES WOULD HAVE HELPED ANYWAY...

...BUT NOW THEY'RE *CLEARLY* USELESS.

AS ARE YOU.

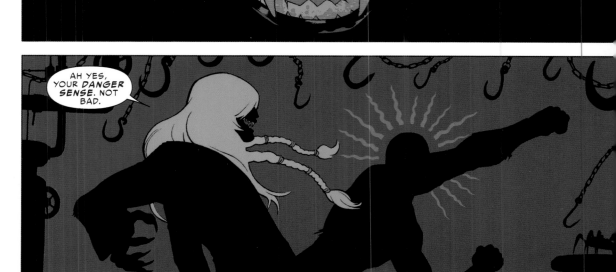

AH YES, YOUR *DANGER SENSE.* NOT BAD.

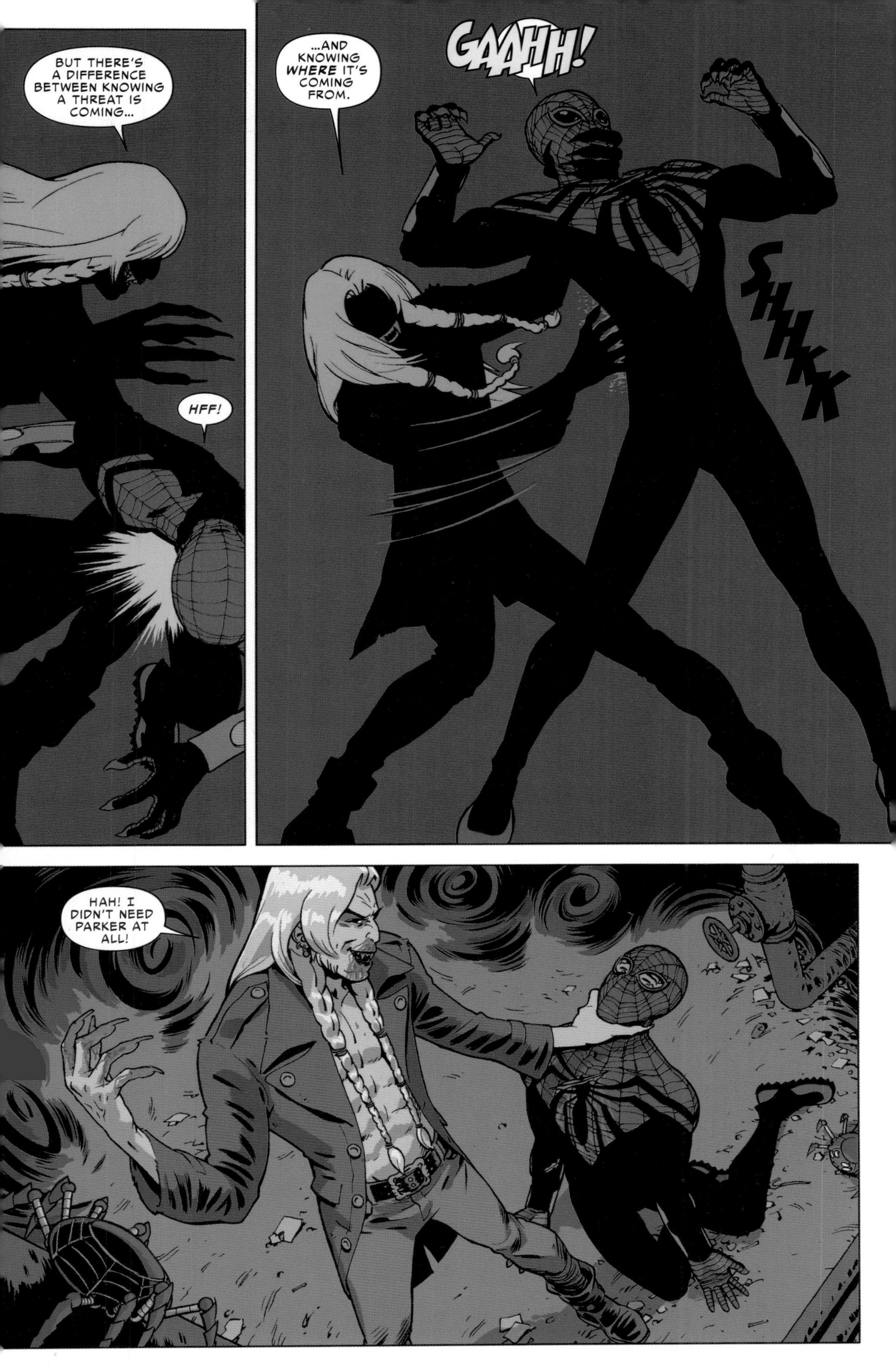

BUT THERE'S A DIFFERENCE BETWEEN KNOWING A THREAT IS COMING...
HFF!
...AND KNOWING *WHERE* IT'S COMING FROM.
GAAHH!
SHHKK
HAH! I DIDN'T NEED PARKER AT ALL!

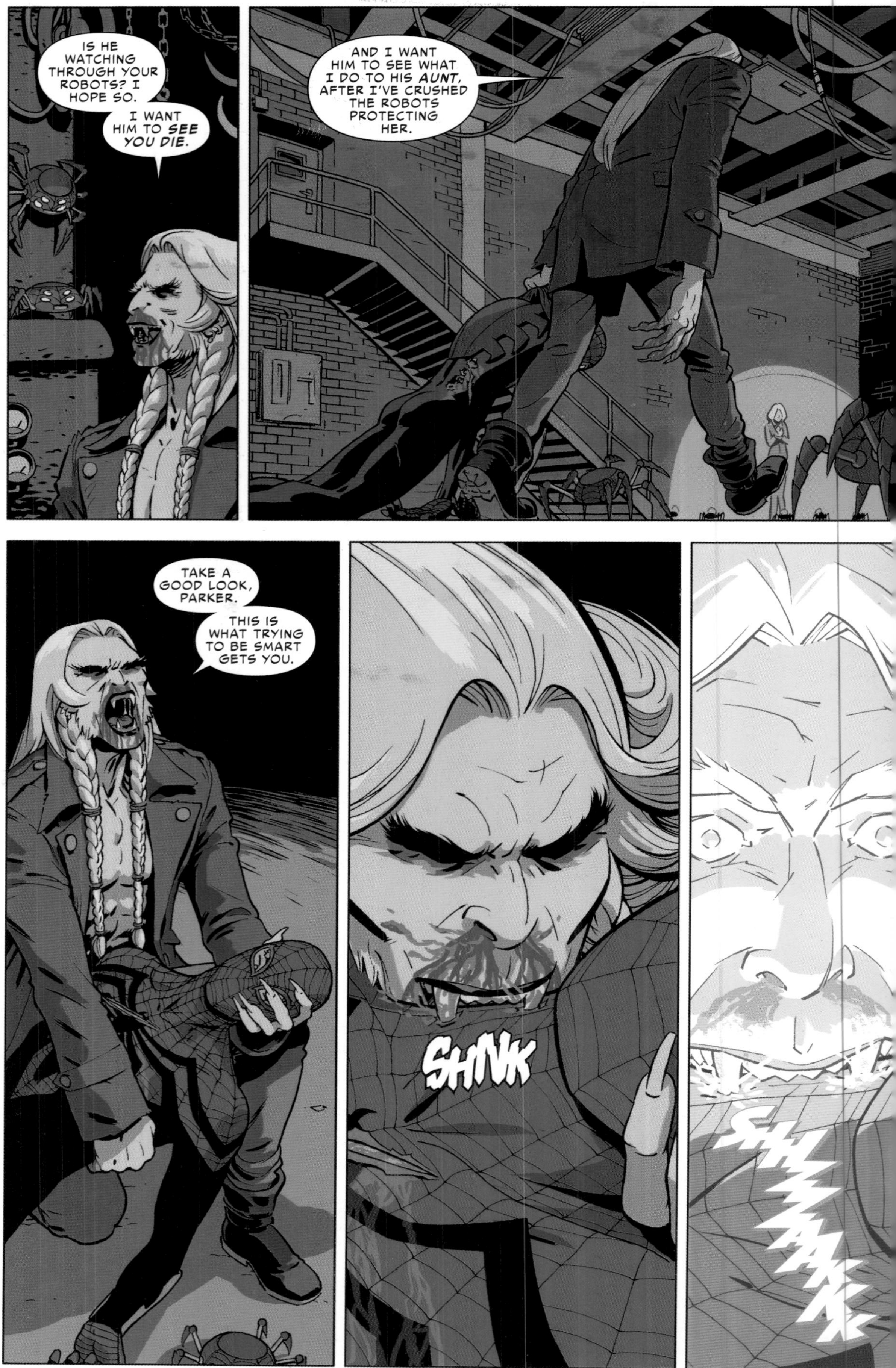
IS HE WATCHING THROUGH YOUR ROBOTS? I HOPE SO.
I WANT HIM TO SEE YOU DIE.
AND I WANT HIM TO SEE WHAT I DO TO HIS AUNT, AFTER I'VE CRUSHED THE ROBOTS PROTECTING HER.
TAKE A GOOD LOOK, PARKER.
THIS IS WHAT TRYING TO BE SMART GETS YOU.
SHINK
SHHAKK

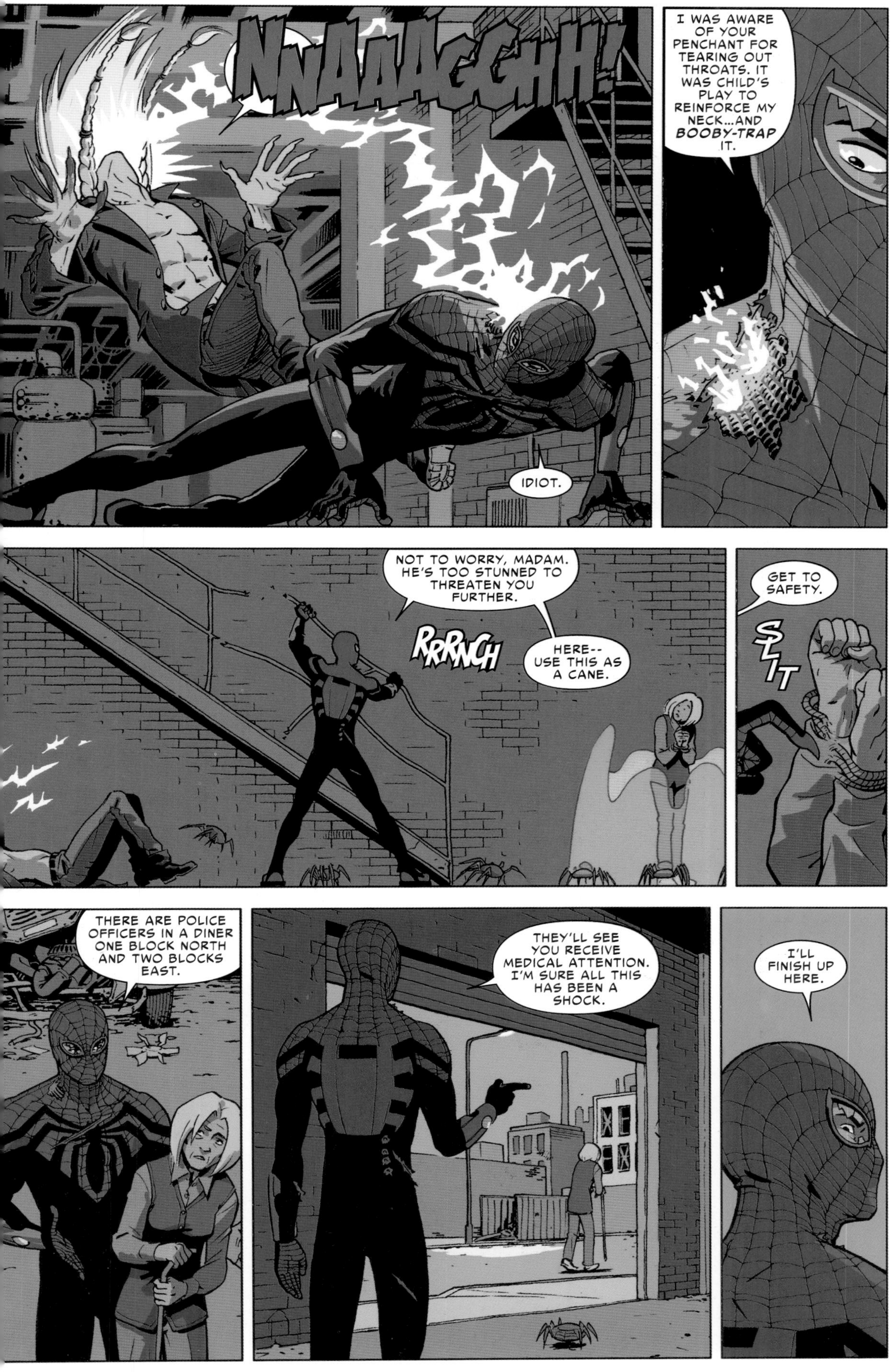
NNAAAAGGHH!
IDIOT.
I WAS AWARE OF YOUR PENCHANT FOR TEARING OUT THROATS. IT WAS CHILD'S PLAY TO REINFORCE MY NECK...AND BOOBY-TRAP IT.
NOT TO WORRY, MADAM. HE'S TOO STUNNED TO THREATEN YOU FURTHER.
RRRNCH
HERE-- USE THIS AS A CANE.
GET TO SAFETY.
SLIT
THERE ARE POLICE OFFICERS IN A DINER ONE BLOCK NORTH AND TWO BLOCKS EAST.
THEY'LL SEE YOU RECEIVE MEDICAL ATTENTION. I'M SURE ALL THIS HAS BEEN A SHOCK.
I'LL FINISH UP HERE.

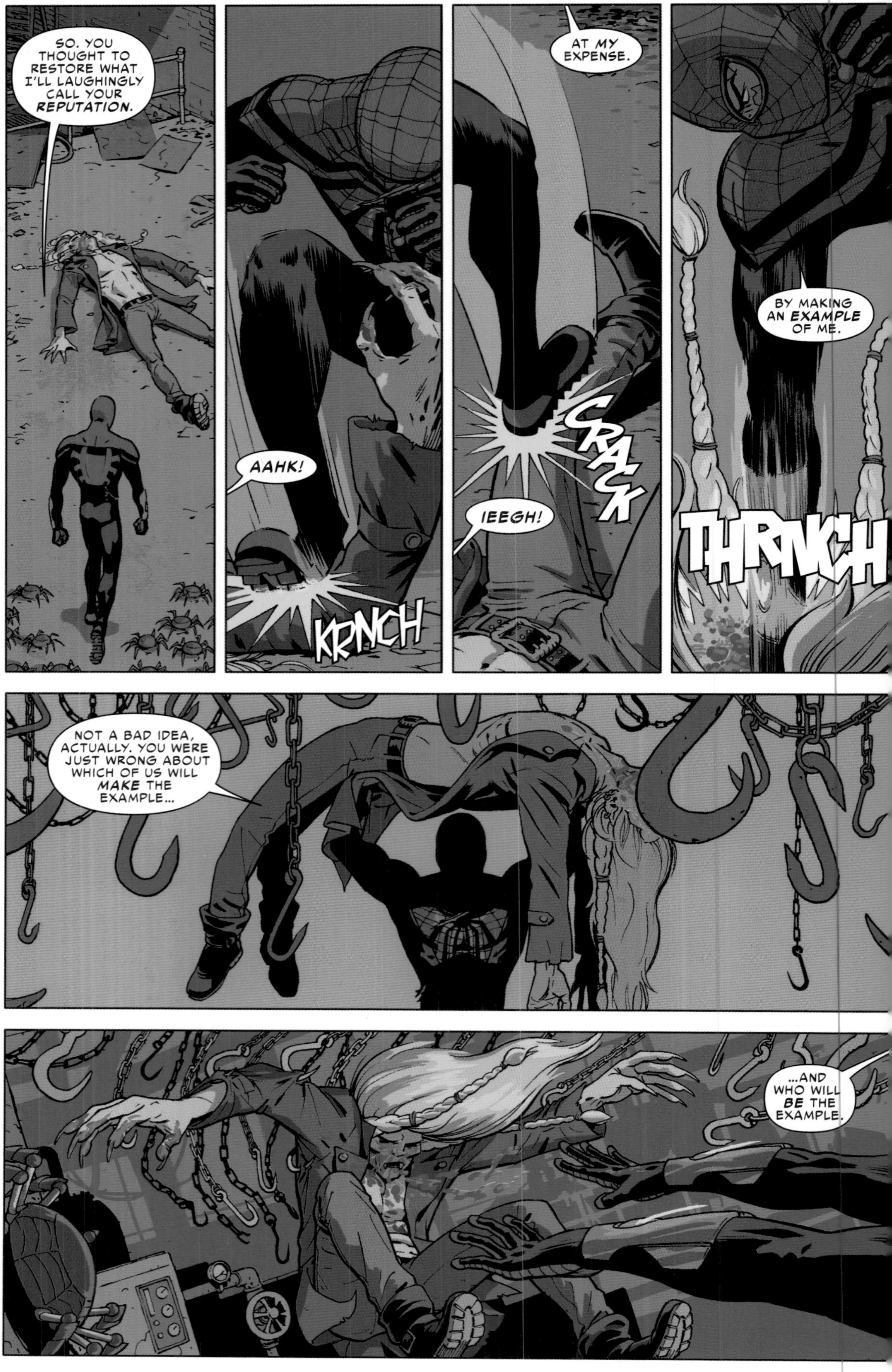
SO. YOU THOUGHT TO RESTORE WHAT I'LL LAUGHINGLY CALL YOUR *REPUTATION*.
AAHK!
KRNCH
AT MY EXPENSE.
CRACK
IEEGH!
BY MAKING AN *EXAMPLE* OF ME.
THRNCH
NOT A BAD IDEA, ACTUALLY. YOU WERE JUST WRONG ABOUT WHICH OF US WILL *MAKE* THE EXAMPLE...
...AND WHO WILL *BE* THE EXAMPLE.

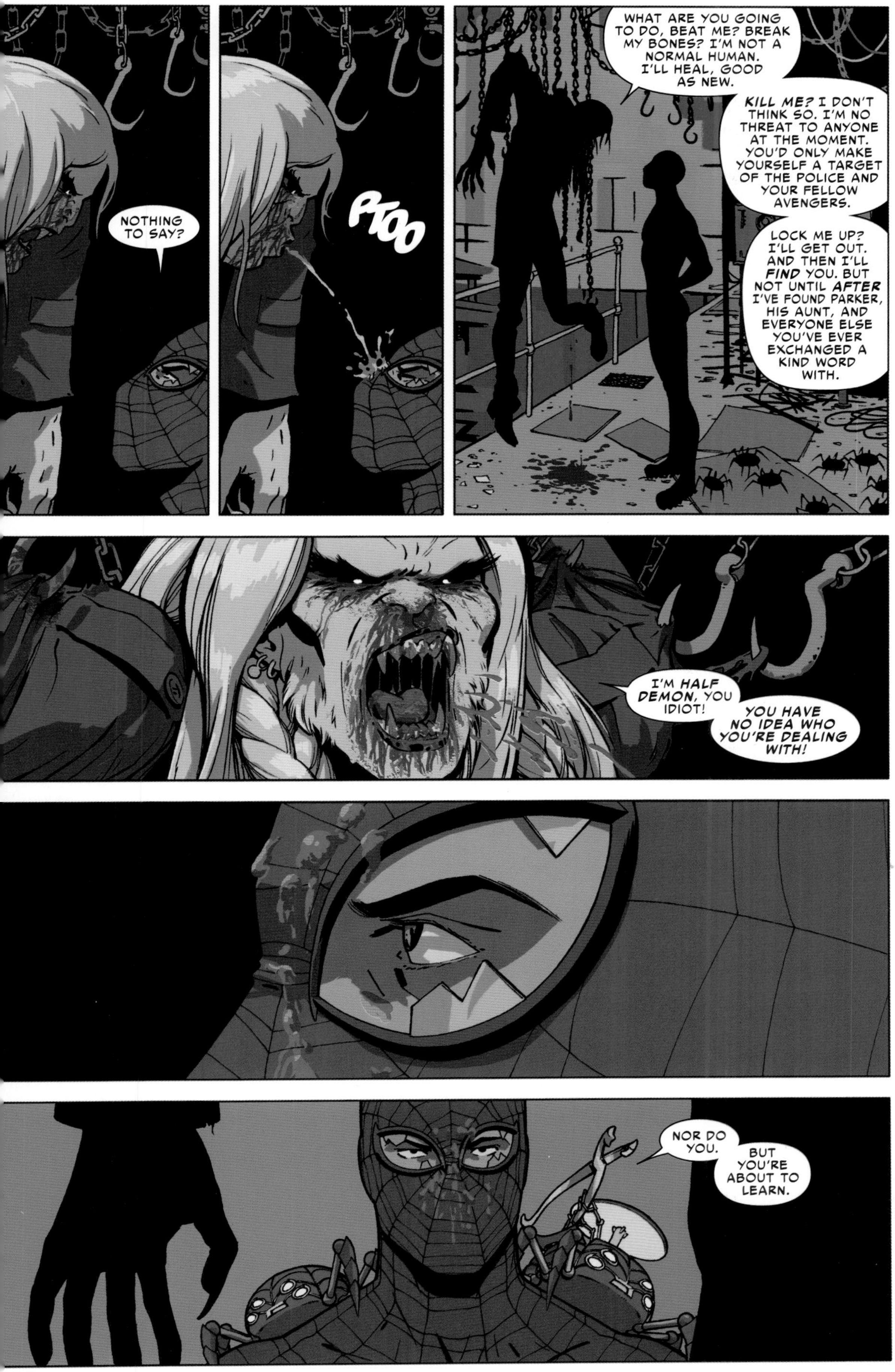

NOTHING TO SAY?
PTOO
WHAT ARE YOU GOING TO DO, BEAT ME? BREAK MY BONES? I'M NOT A NORMAL HUMAN. I'LL HEAL, GOOD AS NEW.
KILL ME? I DON'T THINK SO. I'M NO THREAT TO ANYONE AT THE MOMENT. YOU'D ONLY MAKE YOURSELF A TARGET OF THE POLICE AND YOUR FELLOW AVENGERS.
LOCK ME UP? I'LL GET OUT. AND THEN I'LL FIND YOU. BUT NOT UNTIL AFTER I'VE FOUND PARKER, HIS AUNT, AND EVERYONE ELSE YOU'VE EVER EXCHANGED A KIND WORD WITH.
I'M HALF DEMON, YOU IDIOT!
YOU HAVE NO IDEA WHO YOU'RE DEALING WITH!
NOR DO YOU.
BUT YOU'RE ABOUT TO LEARN.

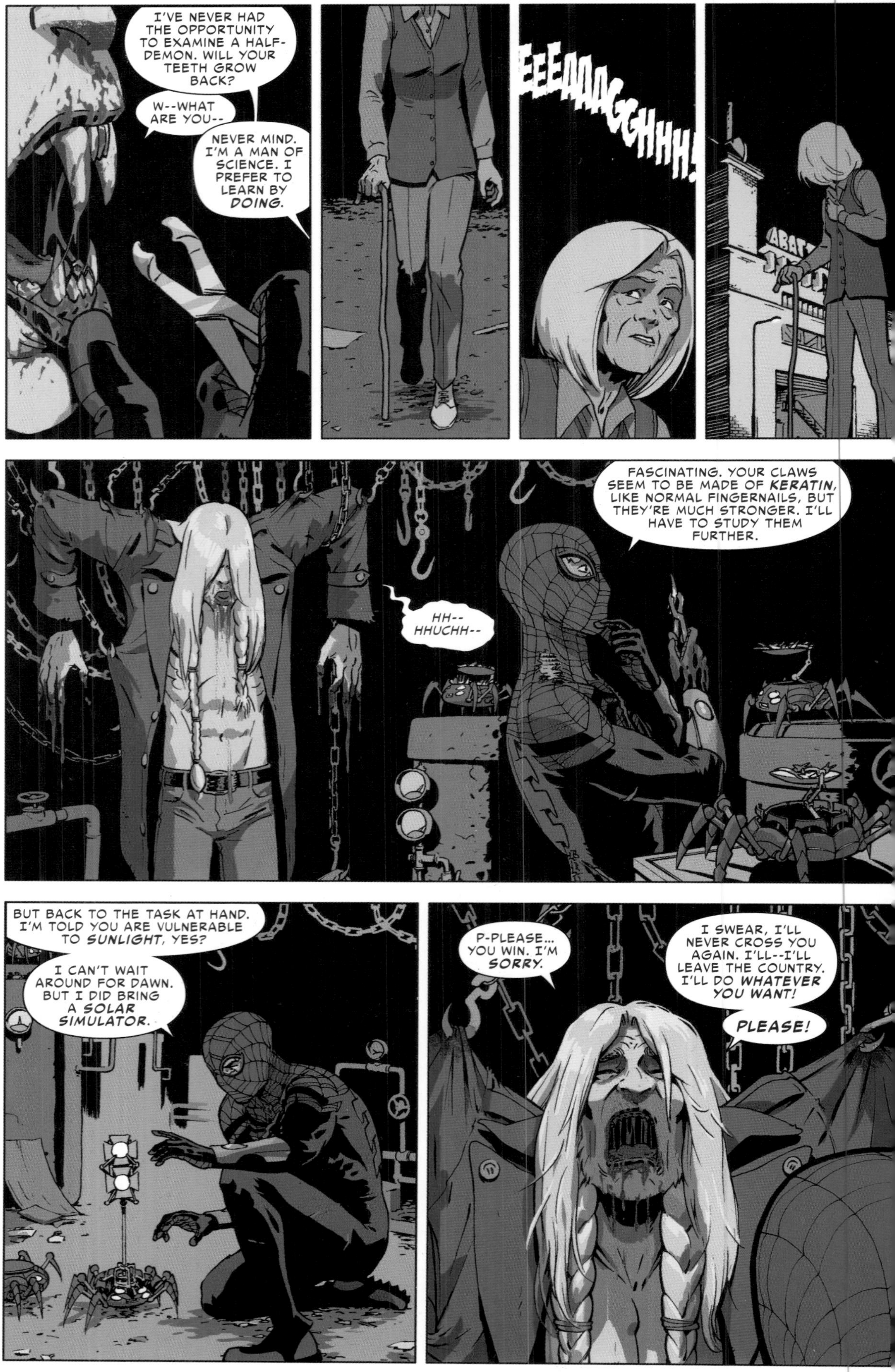
I'VE NEVER HAD THE OPPORTUNITY TO EXAMINE A HALF-DEMON. WILL YOUR TEETH GROW BACK?
W--WHAT ARE YOU--
NEVER MIND. I'M A MAN OF SCIENCE. I PREFER TO LEARN BY DOING.
EEEAAAGGHHHH!
FASCINATING. YOUR CLAWS SEEM TO BE MADE OF KERATIN, LIKE NORMAL FINGERNAILS, BUT THEY'RE MUCH STRONGER. I'LL HAVE TO STUDY THEM FURTHER.
HH-- HHUCHH--
BUT BACK TO THE TASK AT HAND. I'M TOLD YOU ARE VULNERABLE TO SUNLIGHT, YES?
I CAN'T WAIT AROUND FOR DAWN. BUT I DID BRING A SOLAR SIMULATOR.
P-PLEASE... YOU WIN. I'M SORRY.
I SWEAR, I'LL NEVER CROSS YOU AGAIN. I'LL--I'LL LEAVE THE COUNTRY. I'LL DO WHATEVER YOU WANT!
PLEASE!

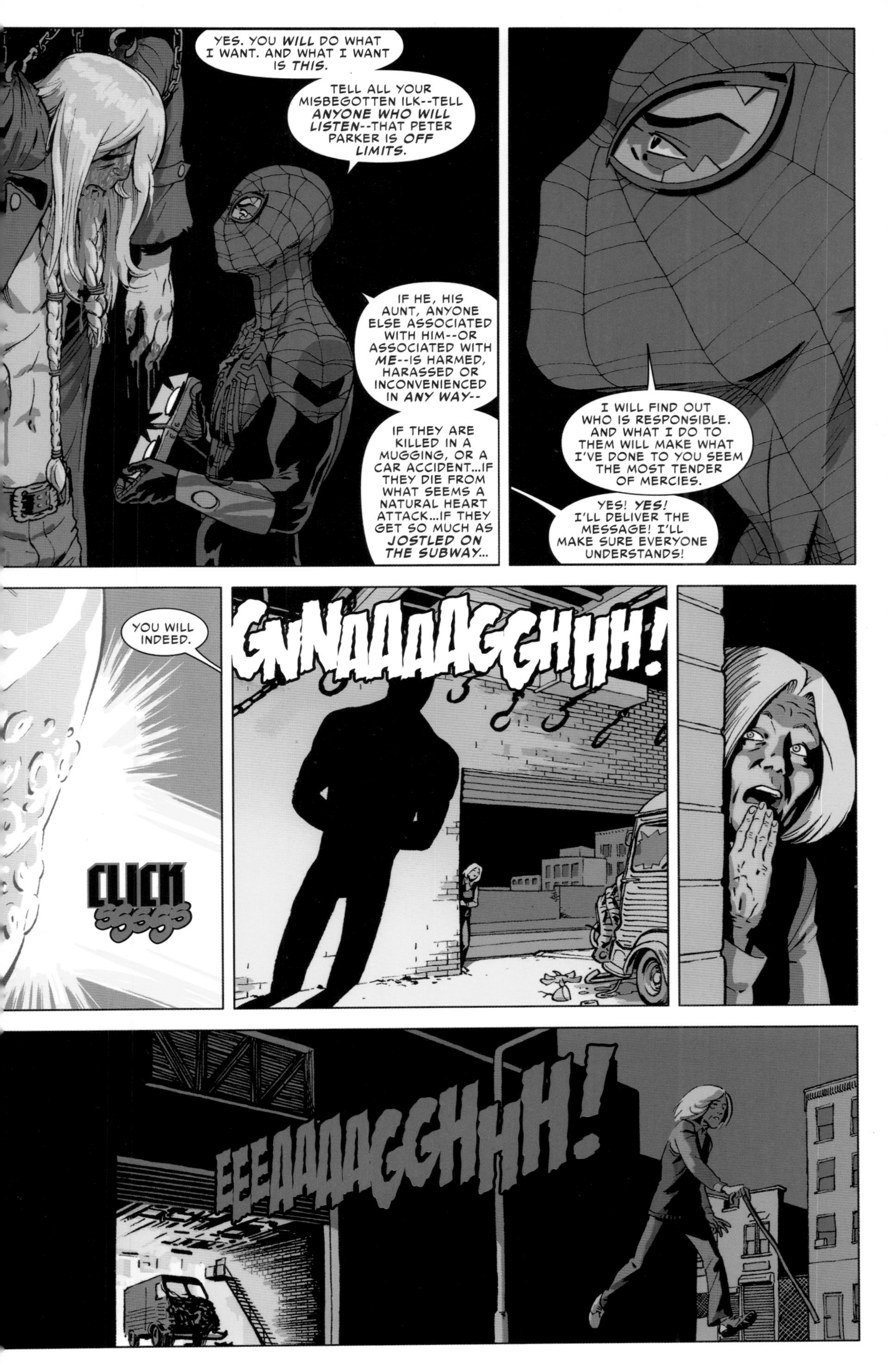
YES. YOU WILL DO WHAT I WANT. AND WHAT I WANT IS THIS.
TELL ALL YOUR MISBEGOTTEN ILK--TELL ANYONE WHO WILL LISTEN--THAT PETER PARKER IS OFF LIMITS.
IF HE, HIS AUNT, ANYONE ELSE ASSOCIATED WITH HIM--OR ASSOCIATED WITH ME--IS HARMED, HARASSED OR INCONVENIENCED IN ANY WAY--
IF THEY ARE KILLED IN A MUGGING, OR A CAR ACCIDENT...IF THEY DIE FROM WHAT SEEMS A NATURAL HEART ATTACK...IF THEY GET SO MUCH AS JOSTLED ON THE SUBWAY...
I WILL FIND OUT WHO IS RESPONSIBLE. AND WHAT I DO TO THEM WILL MAKE WHAT I'VE DONE TO YOU SEEM THE MOST TENDER OF MERCIES.
YES! YES! I'LL DELIVER THE MESSAGE! I'LL MAKE SURE EVERYONE UNDERSTANDS!
YOU WILL INDEED.
CLICK
GNAAAAAGGHHH!
EEEAAAAGGHHH!

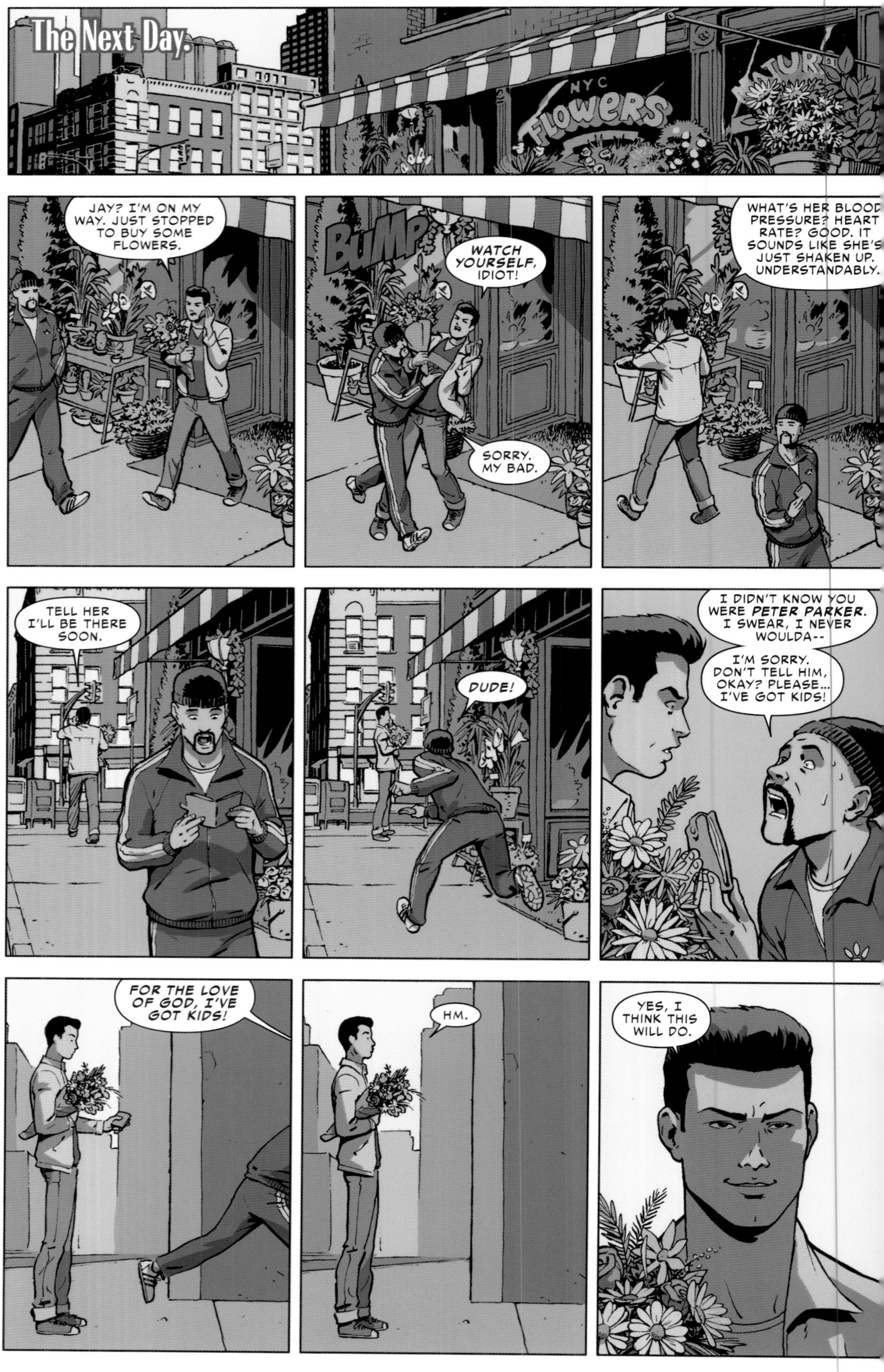
The Next Day.
NYC FLOWERS
JAY? I'M ON MY WAY. JUST STOPPED TO BUY SOME FLOWERS.
BUMP
WATCH YOURSELF, IDIOT!
SORRY. MY BAD.
WHAT'S HER BLOOD PRESSURE? HEART RATE? GOOD. IT SOUNDS LIKE SHE'S JUST SHAKEN UP. UNDERSTANDABLY.
TELL HER I'LL BE THERE SOON.
DUDE!
I DIDN'T KNOW YOU WERE PETER PARKER. I SWEAR, I NEVER WOULDA--
I'M SORRY. DON'T TELL HIM, OKAY? PLEASE... I'VE GOT KIDS!
FOR THE LOVE OF GOD, I'VE GOT KIDS!
HM.
YES, I THINK THIS WILL DO.

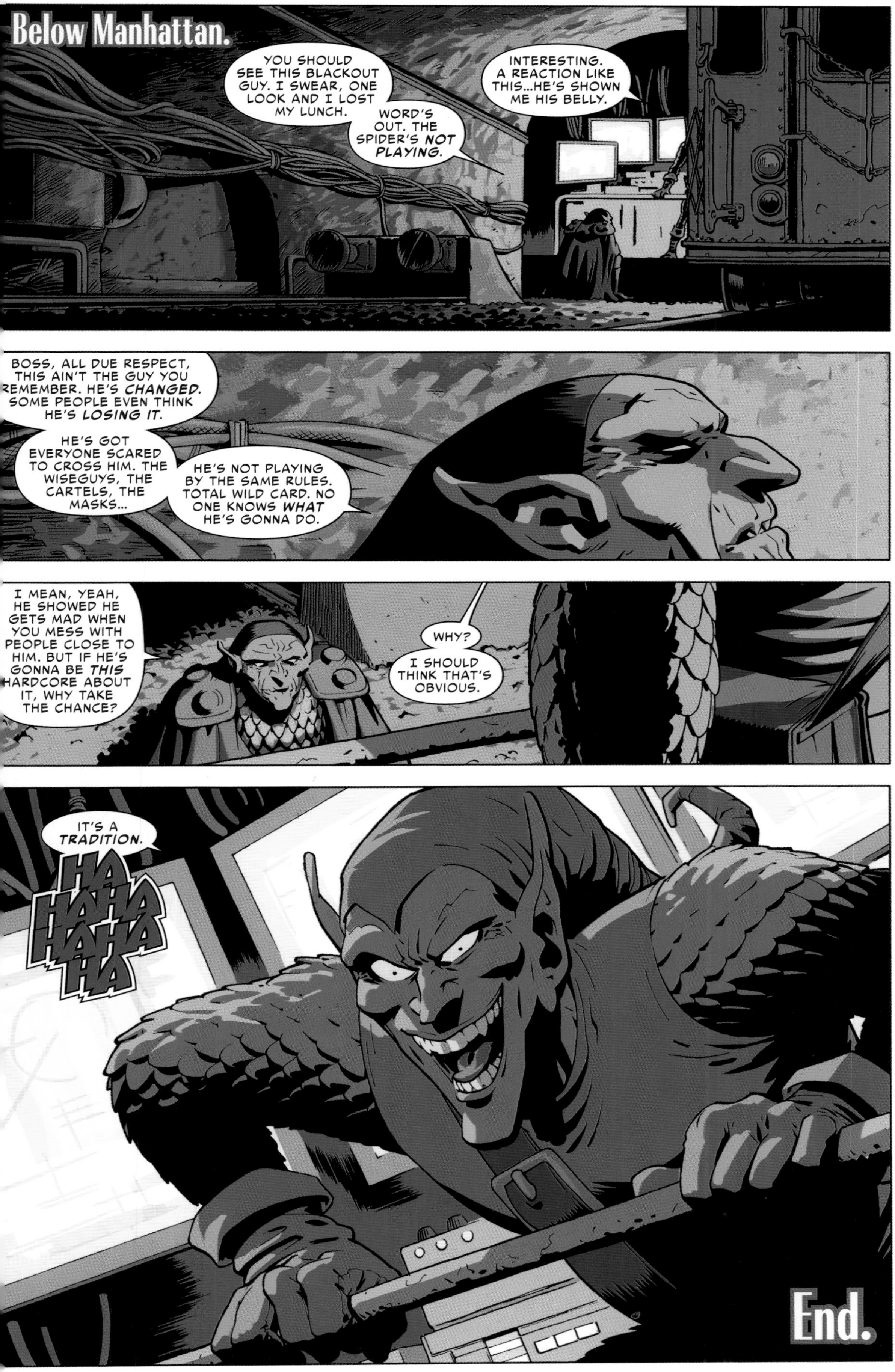
Below Manhattan.
YOU SHOULD SEE THIS BLACKOUT GUY. I SWEAR, ONE LOOK AND I LOST MY LUNCH.
WORD'S OUT. THE SPIDER'S NOT PLAYING.
INTERESTING. A REACTION LIKE THIS...HE'S SHOWN ME HIS BELLY.
BOSS, ALL DUE RESPECT, THIS AIN'T THE GUY YOU REMEMBER. HE'S CHANGED. SOME PEOPLE EVEN THINK HE'S LOSING IT.
HE'S GOT EVERYONE SCARED TO CROSS HIM. THE WISEGUYS, THE CARTELS, THE MASKS...
HE'S NOT PLAYING BY THE SAME RULES. TOTAL WILD CARD. NO ONE KNOWS WHAT HE'S GONNA DO.
I MEAN, YEAH, HE SHOWED HE GETS MAD WHEN YOU MESS WITH PEOPLE CLOSE TO HIM. BUT IF HE'S GONNA BE THIS HARDCORE ABOUT IT, WHY TAKE THE CHANCE?
WHY?
I SHOULD THINK THAT'S OBVIOUS.
IT'S A TRADITION.
HA HAHA HAHA HAHA HA
End.

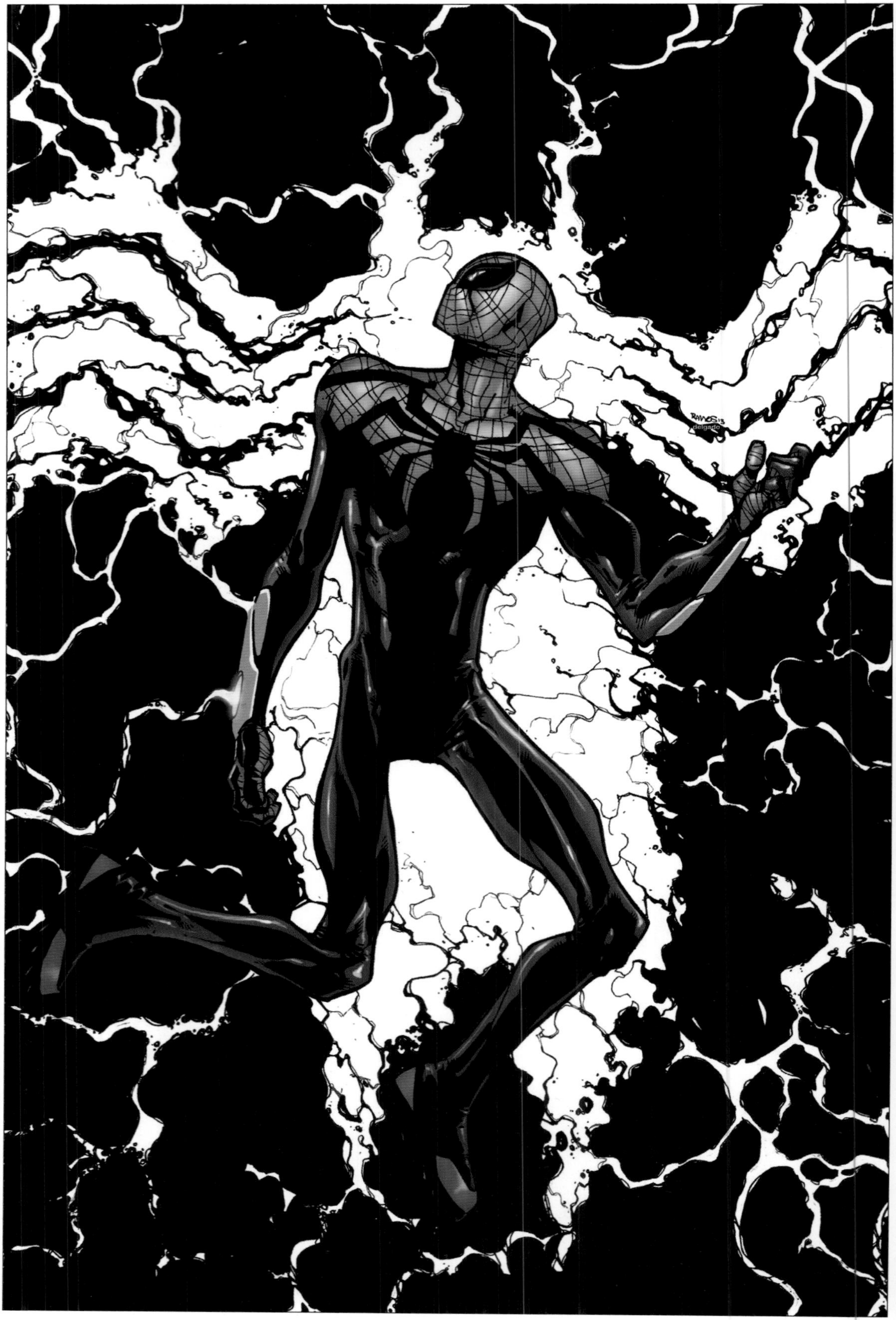
RAMOS 13
delgado

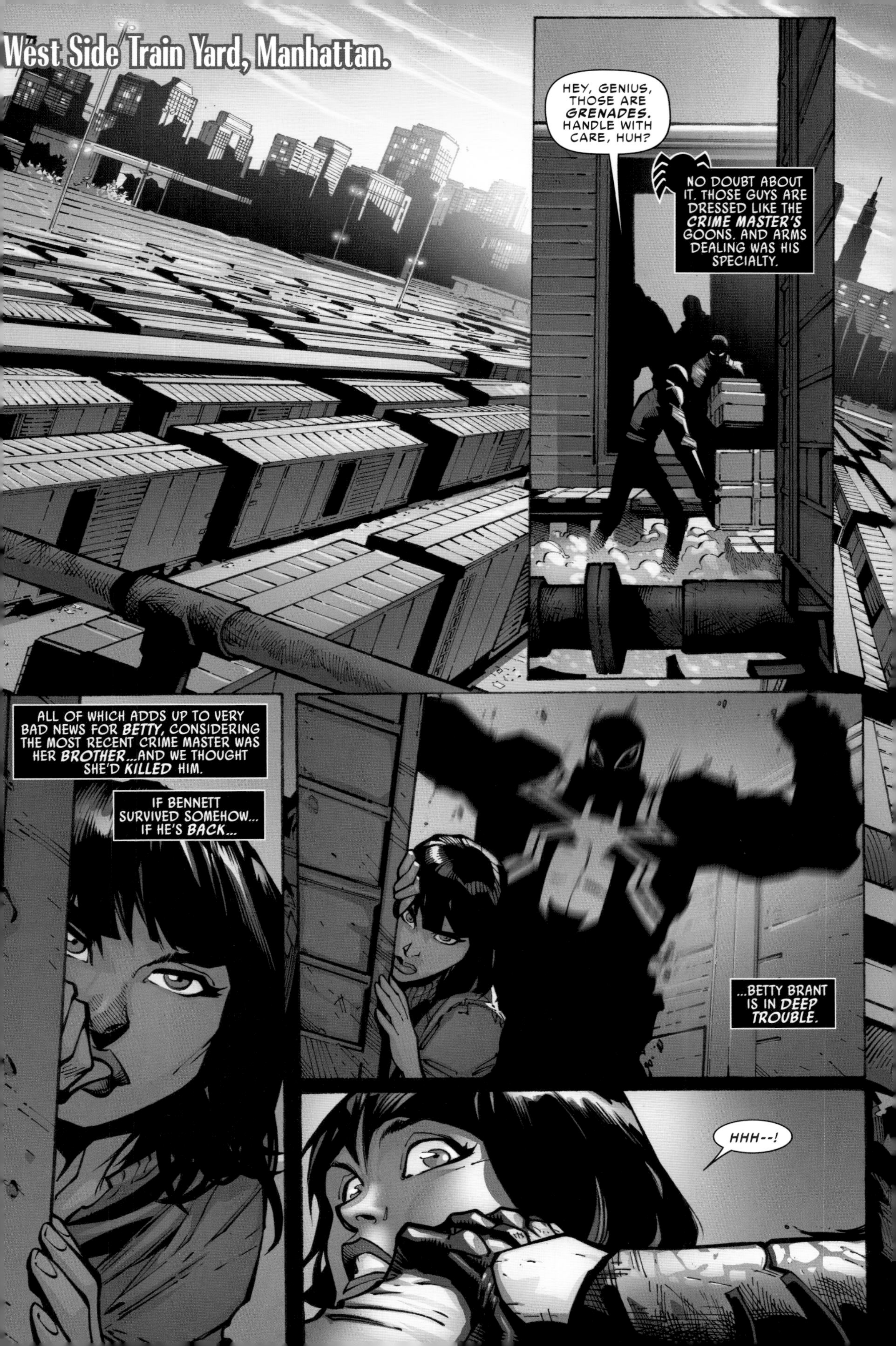
West Side Train Yard, Manhattan.
HEY, GENIUS, THOSE ARE GRENADES. HANDLE WITH CARE, HUH?
NO DOUBT ABOUT IT. THOSE GUYS ARE DRESSED LIKE THE CRIME MASTER'S GOONS. AND ARMS DEALING WAS HIS SPECIALTY.
ALL OF WHICH ADDS UP TO VERY BAD NEWS FOR BETTY, CONSIDERING THE MOST RECENT CRIME MASTER WAS HER BROTHER...AND WE THOUGHT SHE'D KILLED HIM.
IF BENNETT SURVIVED SOMEHOW... IF HE'S BACK...
...BETTY BRANT IS IN DEEP TROUBLE.
HHH--!

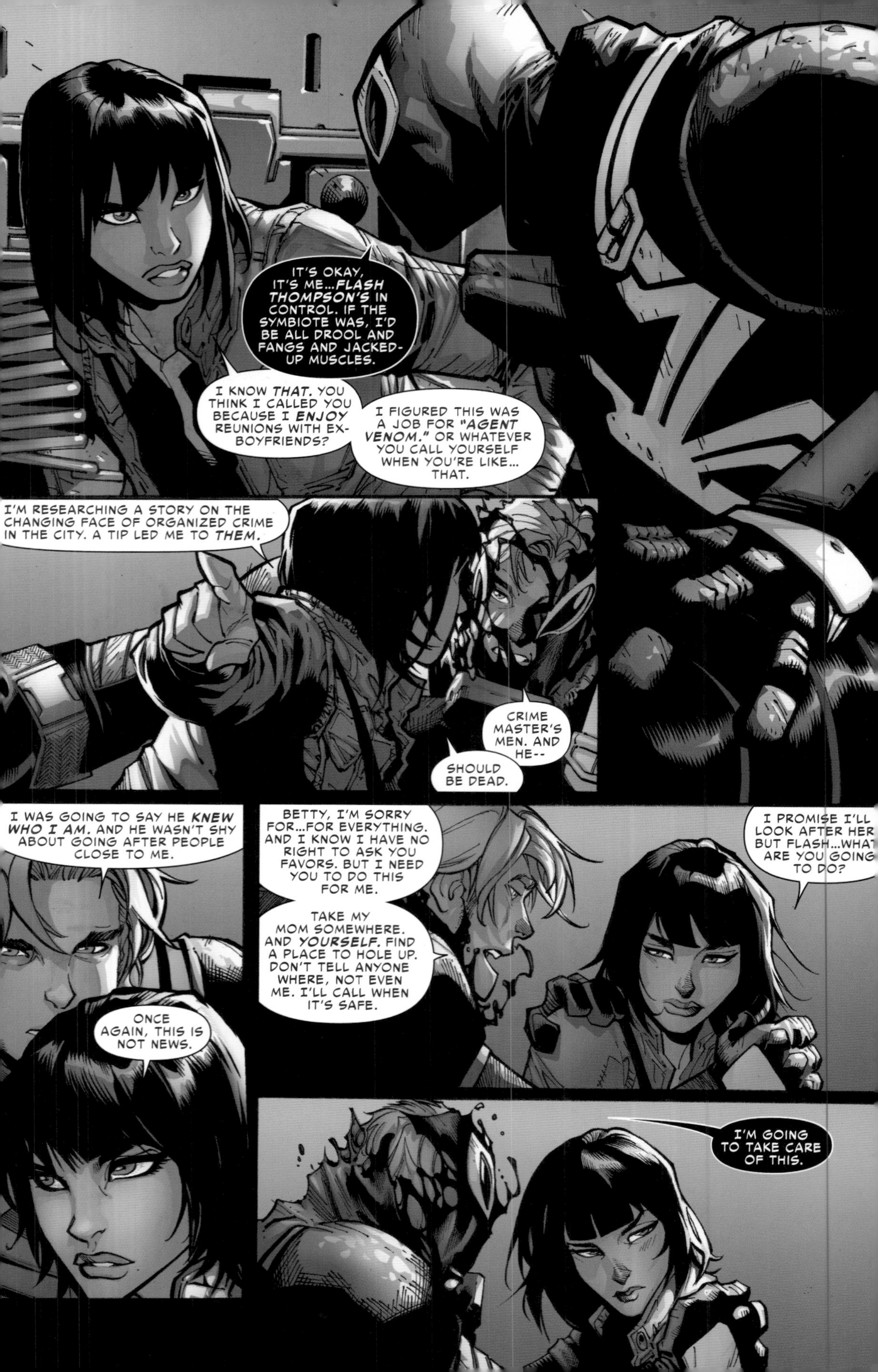
IT'S OKAY, IT'S ME...FLASH THOMPSON'S IN CONTROL. IF THE SYMBIOTE WAS, I'D BE ALL DROOL AND FANGS AND JACKED-UP MUSCLES.
I KNOW THAT. YOU THINK I CALLED YOU BECAUSE I ENJOY REUNIONS WITH EX-BOYFRIENDS?
I FIGURED THIS WAS A JOB FOR "AGENT VENOM." OR WHATEVER YOU CALL YOURSELF WHEN YOU'RE LIKE... THAT.
I'M RESEARCHING A STORY ON THE CHANGING FACE OF ORGANIZED CRIME IN THE CITY. A TIP LED ME TO THEM.
CRIME MASTER'S MEN. AND HE--
SHOULD BE DEAD.
I WAS GOING TO SAY HE KNEW WHO I AM. AND HE WASN'T SHY ABOUT GOING AFTER PEOPLE CLOSE TO ME.
ONCE AGAIN, THIS IS NOT NEWS.
BETTY, I'M SORRY FOR...FOR EVERYTHING. AND I KNOW I HAVE NO RIGHT TO ASK YOU FAVORS. BUT I NEED YOU TO DO THIS FOR ME.
TAKE MY MOM SOMEWHERE. AND YOURSELF. FIND A PLACE TO HOLE UP. DON'T TELL ANYONE WHERE, NOT EVEN ME. I'LL CALL WHEN IT'S SAFE.
I PROMISE I'LL LOOK AFTER HER BUT FLASH...WHAT ARE YOU GOING TO DO?
I'M GOING TO TAKE CARE OF THIS.

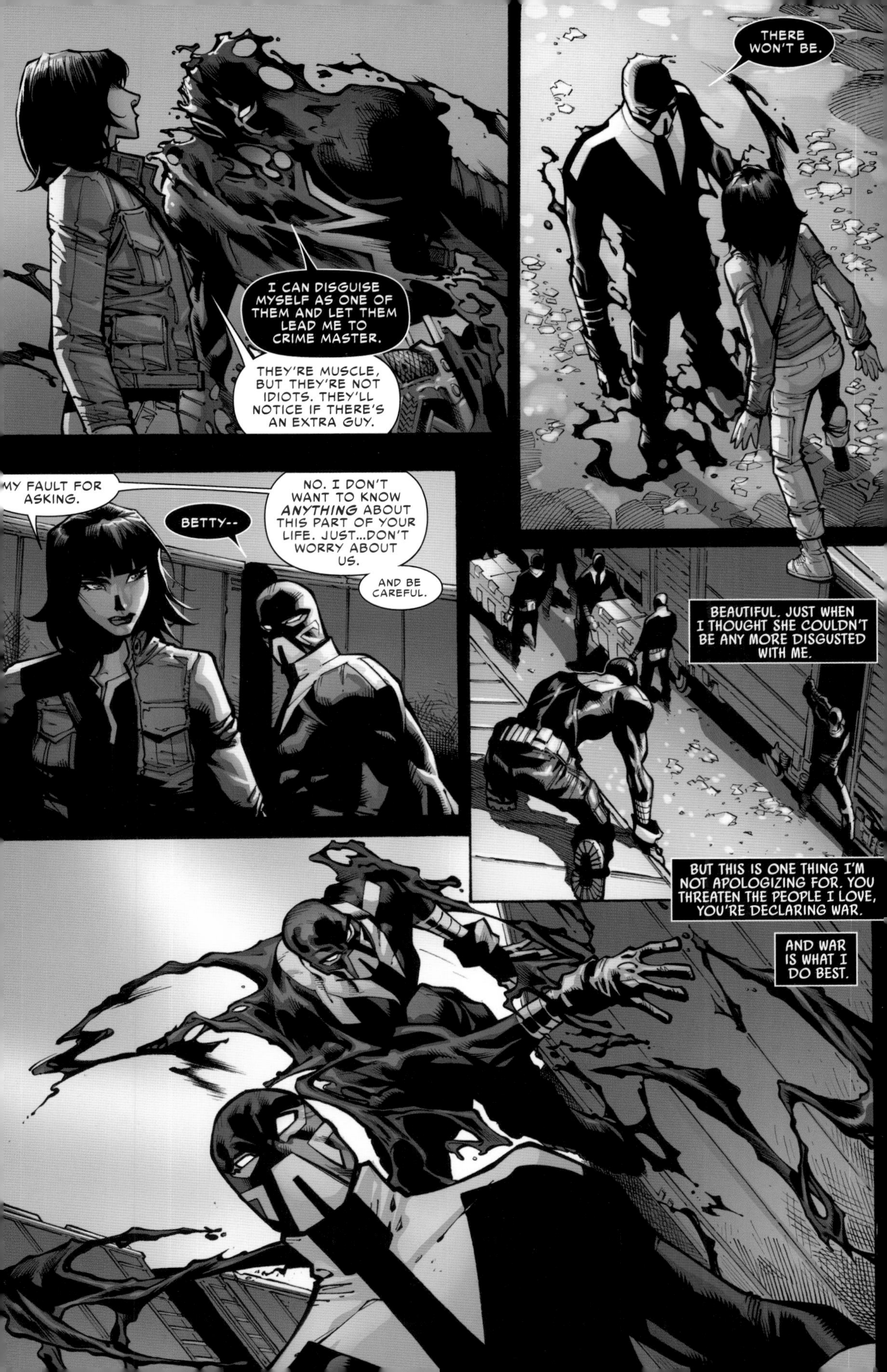
I CAN DISGUISE MYSELF AS ONE OF THEM AND LET THEM LEAD ME TO CRIME MASTER.
THEY'RE MUSCLE, BUT THEY'RE NOT IDIOTS. THEY'LL NOTICE IF THERE'S AN EXTRA GUY.
THERE WON'T BE.
MY FAULT FOR ASKING.
BETTY--
NO. I DON'T WANT TO KNOW *ANYTHING* ABOUT THIS PART OF YOUR LIFE. JUST...DON'T WORRY ABOUT US.
AND BE CAREFUL.
BEAUTIFUL. JUST WHEN I THOUGHT SHE COULDN'T BE ANY MORE DISGUSTED WITH ME.
BUT THIS IS ONE THING I'M NOT APOLOGIZING FOR. YOU THREATEN THE PEOPLE I LOVE, YOU'RE DECLARING WAR.
AND WAR IS WHAT I DO BEST.

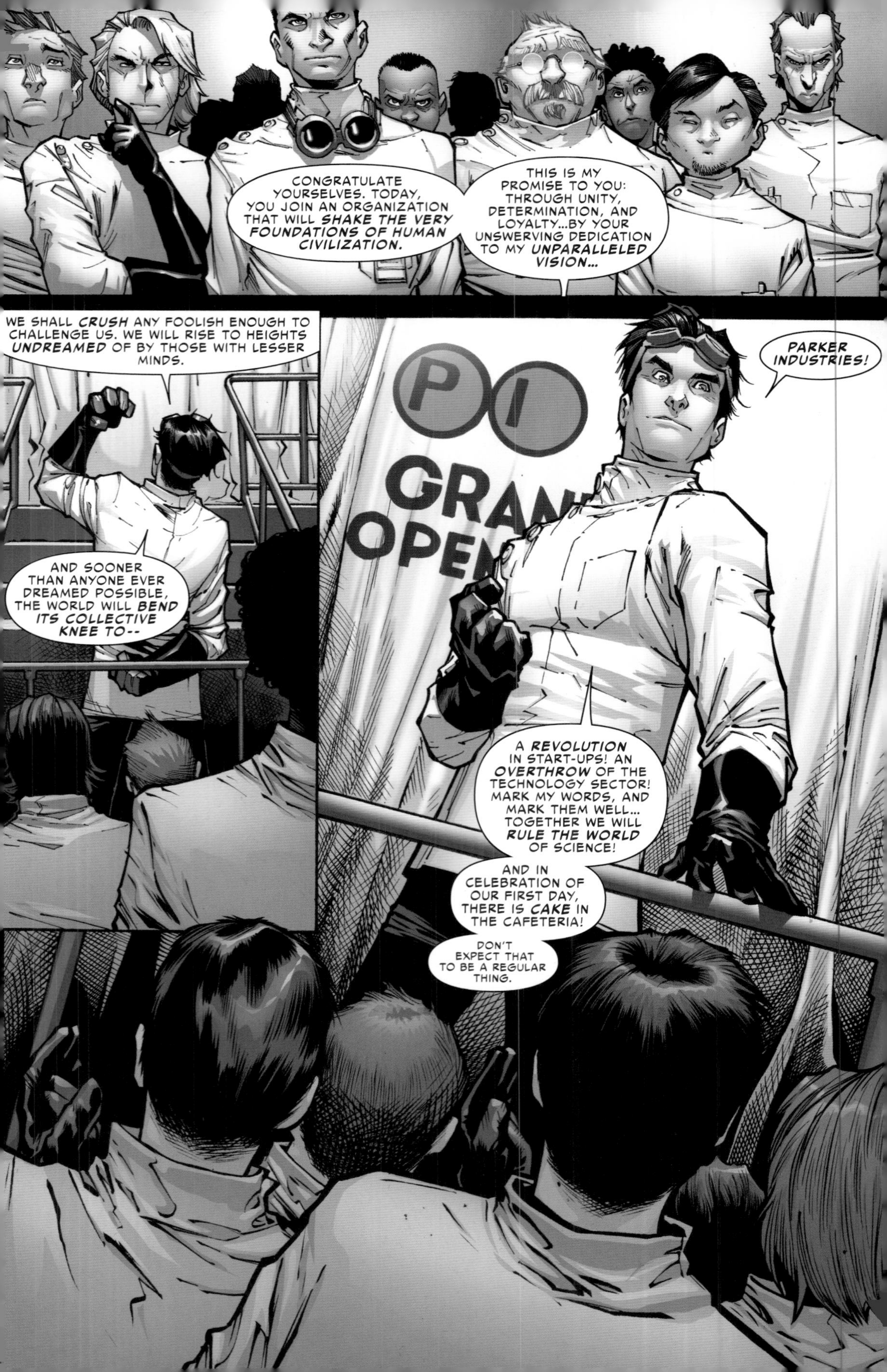
CONGRATULATE YOURSELVES. TODAY, YOU JOIN AN ORGANIZATION THAT WILL SHAKE THE VERY FOUNDATIONS OF HUMAN CIVILIZATION.
THIS IS MY PROMISE TO YOU: THROUGH UNITY, DETERMINATION, AND LOYALTY...BY YOUR UNSWERVING DEDICATION TO MY UNPARALLELED VISION...
WE SHALL CRUSH ANY FOOLISH ENOUGH TO CHALLENGE US. WE WILL RISE TO HEIGHTS UNDREAMED OF BY THOSE WITH LESSER MINDS.
AND SOONER THAN ANYONE EVER DREAMED POSSIBLE, THE WORLD WILL BEND ITS COLLECTIVE KNEE TO--
PARKER INDUSTRIES!
PI
A REVOLUTION IN START-UPS! AN OVERTHROW OF THE TECHNOLOGY SECTOR! MARK MY WORDS, AND MARK THEM WELL... TOGETHER WE WILL RULE THE WORLD OF SCIENCE!
AND IN CELEBRATION OF OUR FIRST DAY, THERE IS CAKE IN THE CAFETERIA!
DON'T EXPECT THAT TO BE A REGULAR THING.

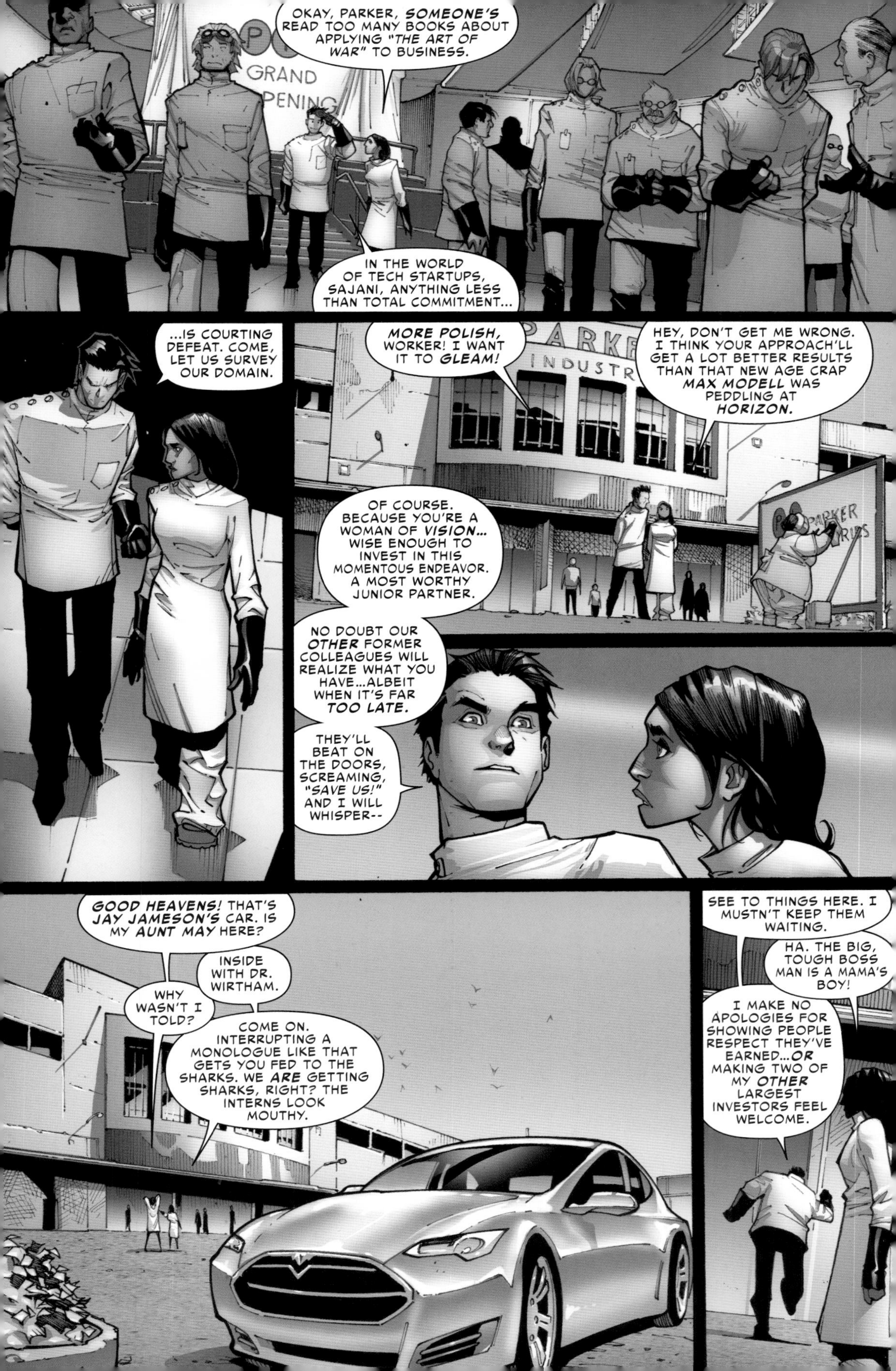
OKAY, PARKER, SOMEONE'S READ TOO MANY BOOKS ABOUT APPLYING "THE ART OF WAR" TO BUSINESS.
GRAND OPENING
IN THE WORLD OF TECH STARTUPS, SAJANI, ANYTHING LESS THAN TOTAL COMMITMENT...
...IS COURTING DEFEAT. COME, LET US SURVEY OUR DOMAIN.
MORE POLISH, WORKER! I WANT IT TO GLEAM!
HEY, DON'T GET ME WRONG. I THINK YOUR APPROACH'LL GET A LOT BETTER RESULTS THAN THAT NEW AGE CRAP MAX MODELL WAS PEDDLING AT HORIZON.
OF COURSE. BECAUSE YOU'RE A WOMAN OF VISION... WISE ENOUGH TO INVEST IN THIS MOMENTOUS ENDEAVOR. A MOST WORTHY JUNIOR PARTNER.
NO DOUBT OUR OTHER FORMER COLLEAGUES WILL REALIZE WHAT YOU HAVE...ALBEIT WHEN IT'S FAR TOO LATE.
THEY'LL BEAT ON THE DOORS, SCREAMING, "SAVE US!" AND I WILL WHISPER--
GOOD HEAVENS! THAT'S JAY JAMESON'S CAR. IS MY AUNT MAY HERE?
INSIDE WITH DR. WIRTHAM.
WHY WASN'T I TOLD?
COME ON. INTERRUPTING A MONOLOGUE LIKE THAT GETS YOU FED TO THE SHARKS. WE ARE GETTING SHARKS, RIGHT? THE INTERNS LOOK MOUTHY.
SEE TO THINGS HERE. I MUSTN'T KEEP THEM WAITING.
HA. THE BIG, TOUGH BOSS MAN IS A MAMA'S BOY!
I MAKE NO APOLOGIES FOR SHOWING PEOPLE RESPECT THEY'VE EARNED...OR MAKING TWO OF MY OTHER LARGEST INVESTORS FEEL WELCOME.

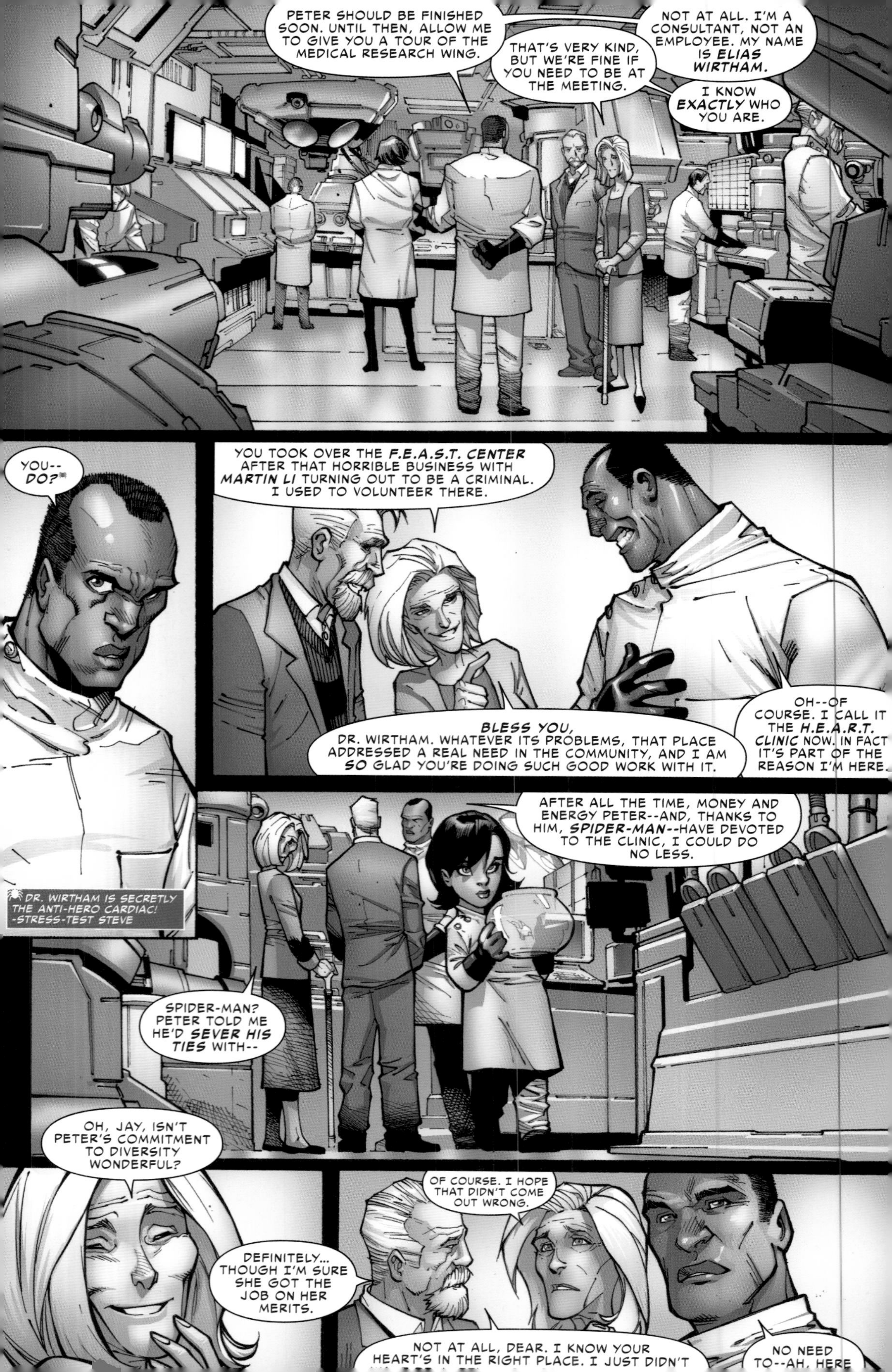
PETER SHOULD BE FINISHED SOON. UNTIL THEN, ALLOW ME TO GIVE YOU A TOUR OF THE MEDICAL RESEARCH WING.
THAT'S VERY KIND, BUT WE'RE FINE IF YOU NEED TO BE AT THE MEETING.
NOT AT ALL. I'M A CONSULTANT, NOT AN EMPLOYEE. MY NAME IS ELIAS WIRTHAM.
I KNOW EXACTLY WHO YOU ARE.
YOU-- DO?
YOU TOOK OVER THE F.E.A.S.T. CENTER AFTER THAT HORRIBLE BUSINESS WITH MARTIN LI TURNING OUT TO BE A CRIMINAL. I USED TO VOLUNTEER THERE.
BLESS YOU, DR. WIRTHAM. WHATEVER ITS PROBLEMS, THAT PLACE ADDRESSED A REAL NEED IN THE COMMUNITY, AND I AM SO GLAD YOU'RE DOING SUCH GOOD WORK WITH IT.
OH--OF COURSE. I CALL IT THE H.E.A.R.T. CLINIC NOW. IN FACT IT'S PART OF THE REASON I'M HERE.
AFTER ALL THE TIME, MONEY AND ENERGY PETER--AND, THANKS TO HIM, SPIDER-MAN--HAVE DEVOTED TO THE CLINIC, I COULD DO NO LESS.
DR. WIRTHAM IS SECRETLY THE ANTI-HERO CARDIAC! -STRESS-TEST STEVE
SPIDER-MAN? PETER TOLD ME HE'D SEVER HIS TIES WITH--
OH, JAY, ISN'T PETER'S COMMITMENT TO DIVERSITY WONDERFUL?
DEFINITELY... THOUGH I'M SURE SHE GOT THE JOB ON HER MERITS.
OF COURSE. I HOPE THAT DIDN'T COME OUT WRONG.
NOT AT ALL, DEAR. I KNOW YOUR HEART'S IN THE RIGHT PLACE. I JUST DIDN'T
NO NEED TO--AH, HERE

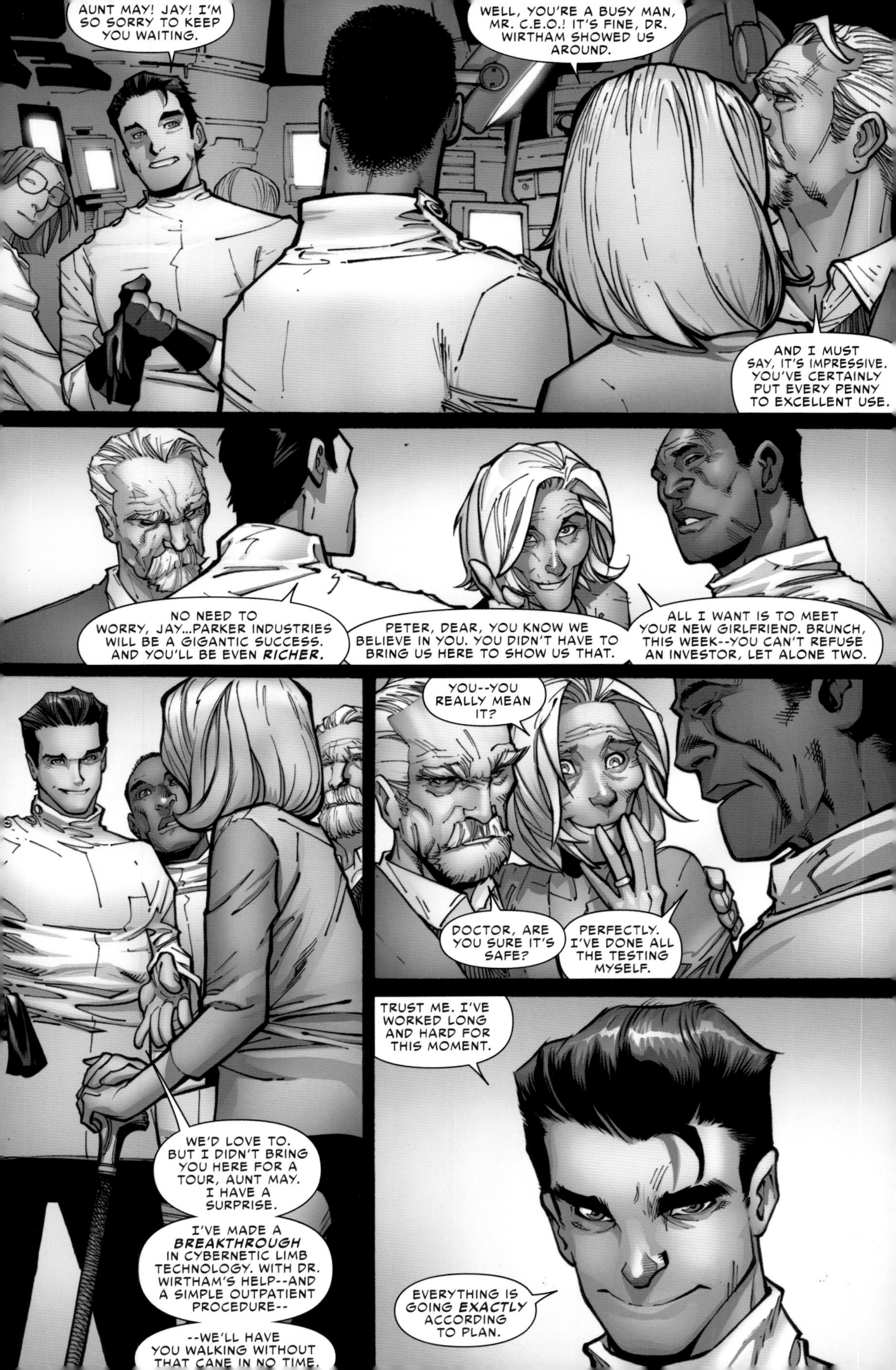
AUNT MAY! JAY! I'M SO SORRY TO KEEP YOU WAITING.
WELL, YOU'RE A BUSY MAN, MR. C.E.O.! IT'S FINE, DR. WIRTHAM SHOWED US AROUND.
AND I MUST SAY, IT'S IMPRESSIVE. YOU'VE CERTAINLY PUT EVERY PENNY TO EXCELLENT USE.
NO NEED TO WORRY, JAY...PARKER INDUSTRIES WILL BE A GIGANTIC SUCCESS. AND YOU'LL BE EVEN *RICHER*.
PETER, DEAR, YOU KNOW WE BELIEVE IN YOU. YOU DIDN'T HAVE TO BRING US HERE TO SHOW US THAT.
ALL I WANT IS TO MEET YOUR NEW GIRLFRIEND. BRUNCH, THIS WEEK--YOU CAN'T REFUSE AN INVESTOR, LET ALONE TWO.
WE'D LOVE TO. BUT I DIDN'T BRING YOU HERE FOR A TOUR, AUNT MAY. I HAVE A SURPRISE.
I'VE MADE A *BREAKTHROUGH* IN CYBERNETIC LIMB TECHNOLOGY. WITH DR. WIRTHAM'S HELP--AND A SIMPLE OUTPATIENT PROCEDURE--
--WE'LL HAVE YOU WALKING WITHOUT THAT CANE IN NO TIME.
YOU--YOU REALLY MEAN IT?
DOCTOR, ARE YOU SURE IT'S SAFE?
PERFECTLY. I'VE DONE ALL THE TESTING MYSELF.
TRUST ME. I'VE WORKED LONG AND HARD FOR THIS MOMENT.
EVERYTHING IS GOING *EXACTLY* ACCORDING TO PLAN.

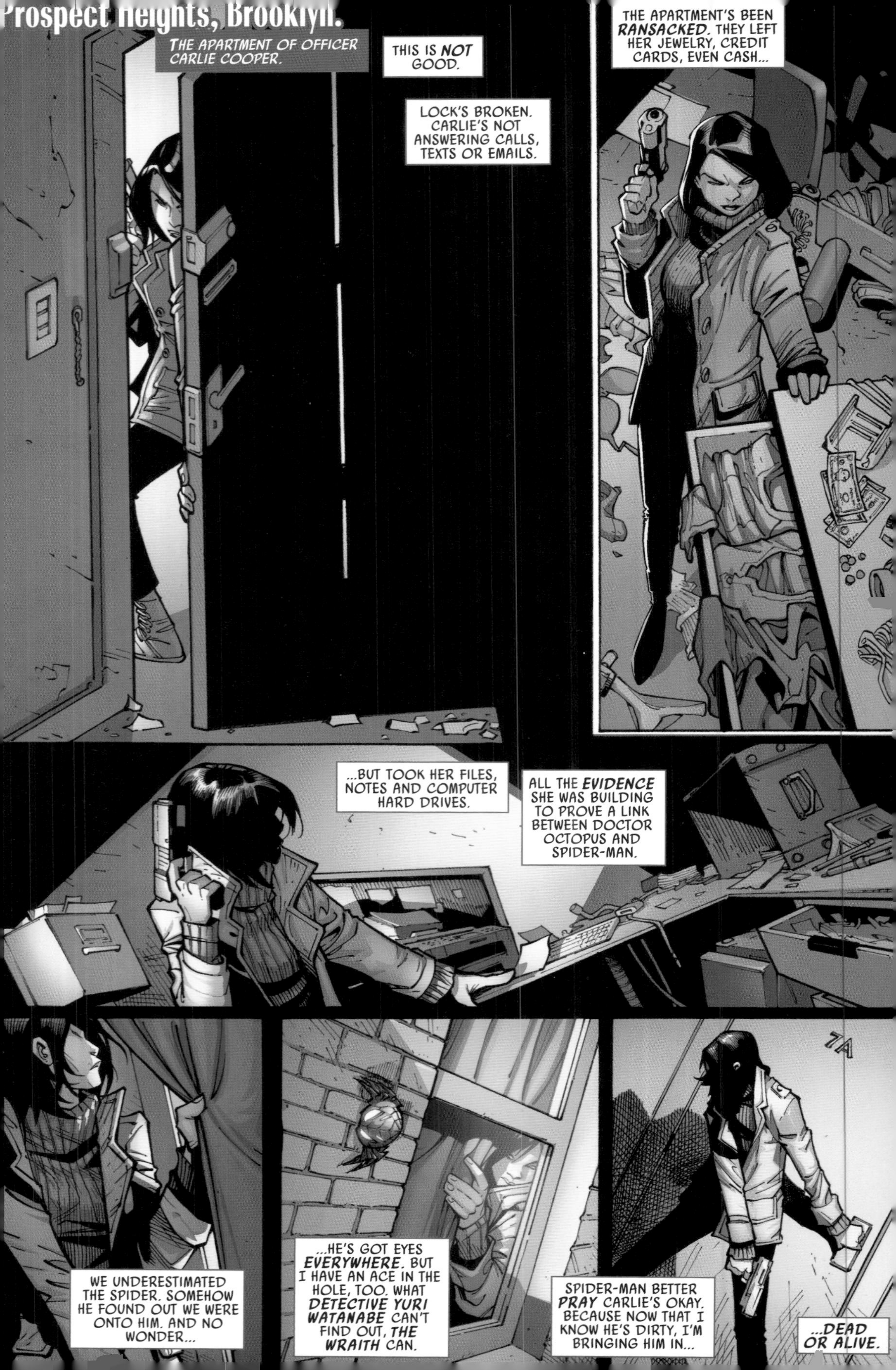
Prospect Heights, Brooklyn.
THE APARTMENT OF OFFICER CARLIE COOPER.
THIS IS NOT GOOD.
LOCK'S BROKEN. CARLIE'S NOT ANSWERING CALLS, TEXTS OR EMAILS.
THE APARTMENT'S BEEN RANSACKED. THEY LEFT HER JEWELRY, CREDIT CARDS, EVEN CASH...
...BUT TOOK HER FILES, NOTES AND COMPUTER HARD DRIVES.
ALL THE EVIDENCE SHE WAS BUILDING TO PROVE A LINK BETWEEN DOCTOR OCTOPUS AND SPIDER-MAN.
WE UNDERESTIMATED THE SPIDER. SOMEHOW HE FOUND OUT WE WERE ONTO HIM. AND NO WONDER...
...HE'S GOT EYES EVERYWHERE. BUT I HAVE AN ACE IN THE HOLE, TOO. WHAT DETECTIVE YURI WATANABE CAN'T FIND OUT, THE WRAITH CAN.
7A
SPIDER-MAN BETTER PRAY CARLIE'S OKAY. BECAUSE NOW THAT I KNOW HE'S DIRTY, I'M BRINGING HIM IN...
...DEAD OR ALIVE.

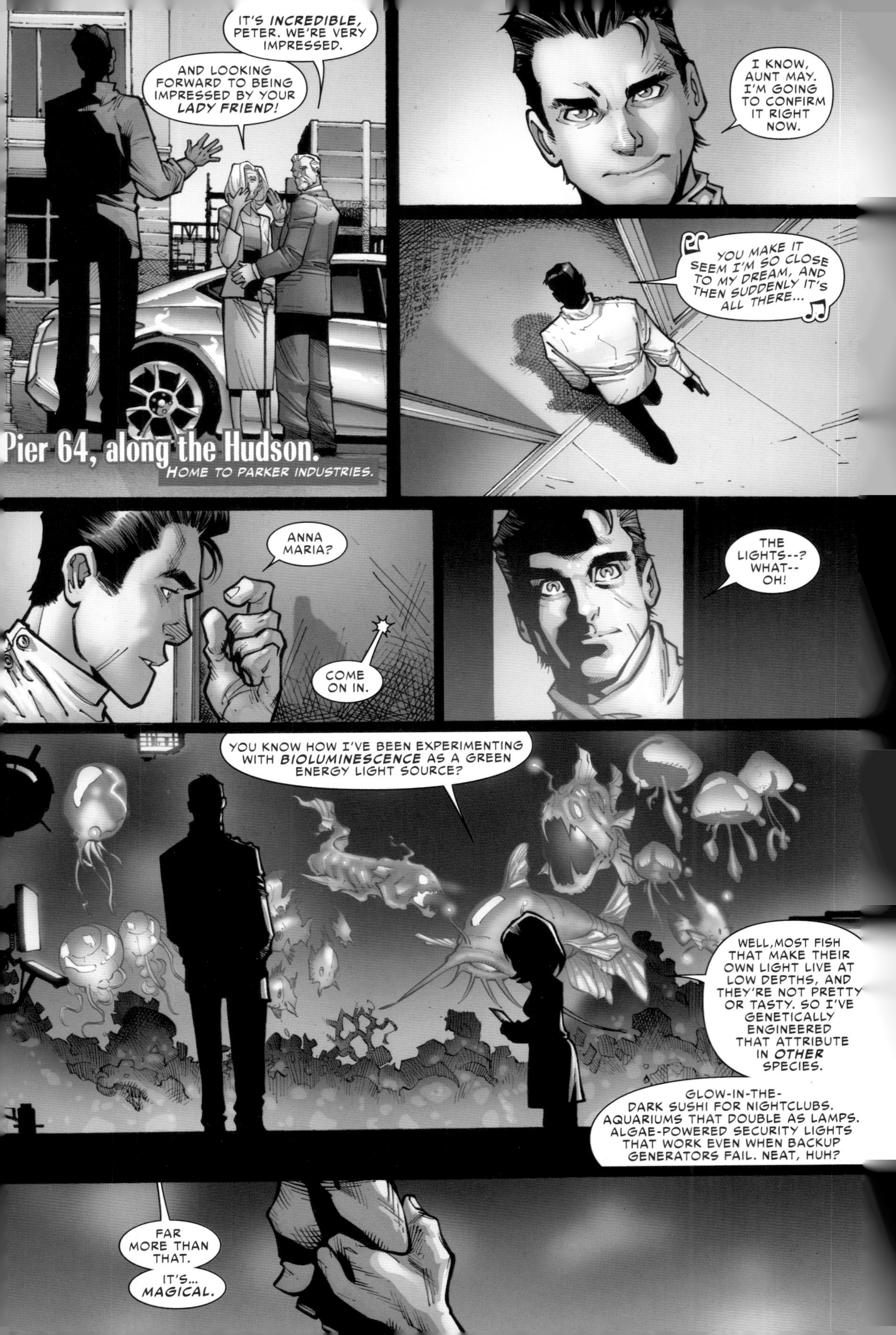
IT'S INCREDIBLE, PETER. WE'RE VERY IMPRESSED.
AND LOOKING FORWARD TO BEING IMPRESSED BY YOUR LADY FRIEND!
Pier 64, along the Hudson.
HOME TO PARKER INDUSTRIES.
I KNOW, AUNT MAY. I'M GOING TO CONFIRM IT RIGHT NOW.
YOU MAKE IT SEEM I'M SO CLOSE TO MY DREAM, AND THEN SUDDENLY IT'S ALL THERE...
ANNA MARIA?
COME ON IN.
THE LIGHTS--? WHAT-- OH!
YOU KNOW HOW I'VE BEEN EXPERIMENTING WITH BIOLUMINESCENCE AS A GREEN ENERGY LIGHT SOURCE?
WELL, MOST FISH THAT MAKE THEIR OWN LIGHT LIVE AT LOW DEPTHS, AND THEY'RE NOT PRETTY OR TASTY. SO I'VE GENETICALLY ENGINEERED THAT ATTRIBUTE IN OTHER SPECIES.
GLOW-IN-THE-DARK SUSHI FOR NIGHTCLUBS. AQUARIUMS THAT DOUBLE AS LAMPS. ALGAE-POWERED SECURITY LIGHTS THAT WORK EVEN WHEN BACKUP GENERATORS FAIL. NEAT, HUH?
FAR MORE THAN THAT.
IT'S... MAGICAL.

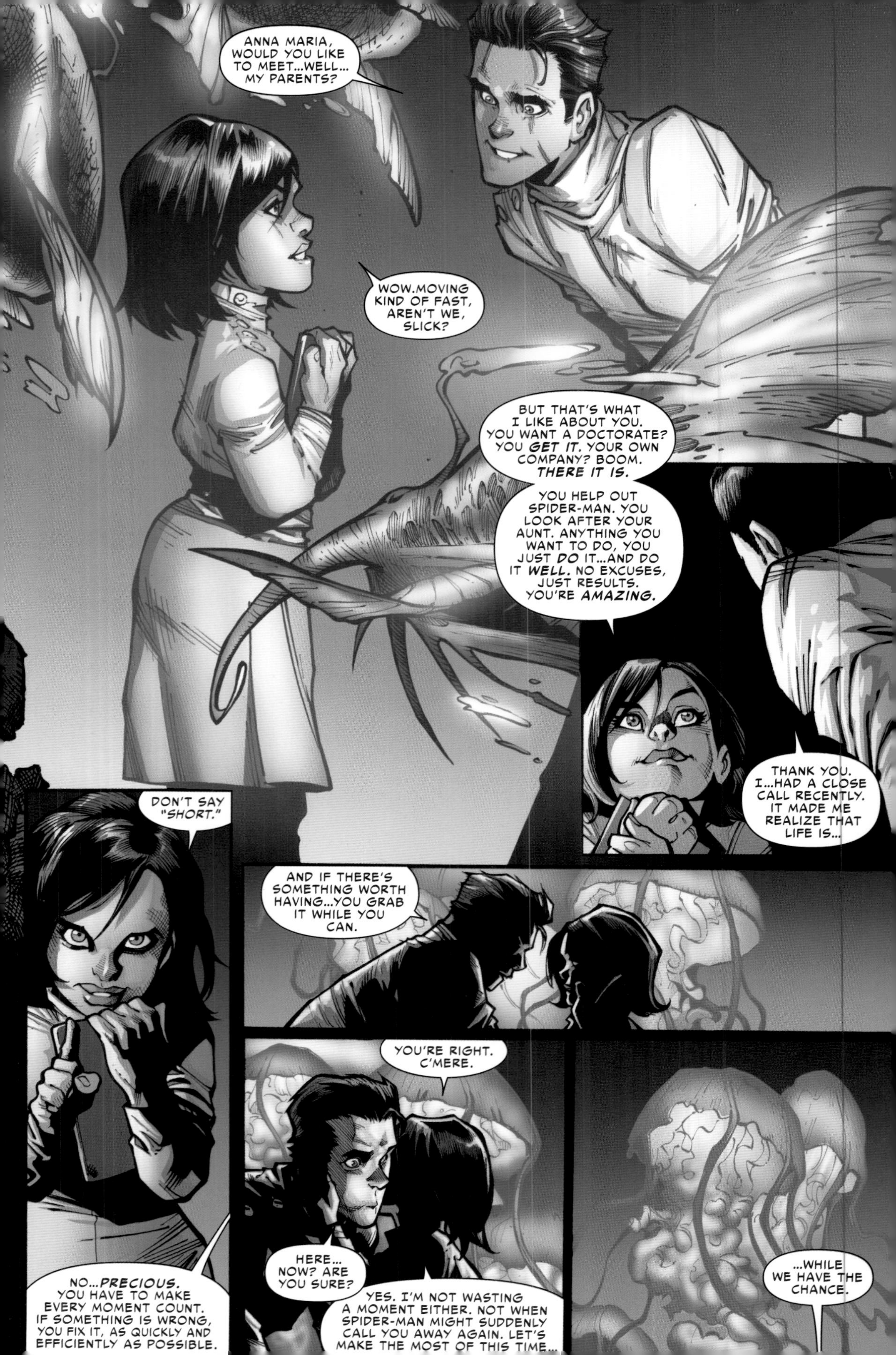
ANNA MARIA, WOULD YOU LIKE TO MEET...WELL... MY PARENTS?
WOW.MOVING KIND OF FAST, AREN'T WE, SLICK?
BUT THAT'S WHAT I LIKE ABOUT YOU. YOU WANT A DOCTORATE? YOU GET IT. YOUR OWN COMPANY? BOOM. THERE IT IS.
YOU HELP OUT SPIDER-MAN. YOU LOOK AFTER YOUR AUNT. ANYTHING YOU WANT TO DO, YOU JUST DO IT...AND DO IT WELL. NO EXCUSES, JUST RESULTS. YOU'RE AMAZING.
THANK YOU. I...HAD A CLOSE CALL RECENTLY. IT MADE ME REALIZE THAT LIFE IS...
DON'T SAY "SHORT."
NO...PRECIOUS. YOU HAVE TO MAKE EVERY MOMENT COUNT. IF SOMETHING IS WRONG, YOU FIX IT, AS QUICKLY AND EFFICIENTLY AS POSSIBLE.
AND IF THERE'S SOMETHING WORTH HAVING...YOU GRAB IT WHILE YOU CAN.
YOU'RE RIGHT. C'MERE.
HERE... NOW? ARE YOU SURE?
YES. I'M NOT WASTING A MOMENT EITHER. NOT WHEN SPIDER-MAN MIGHT SUDDENLY CALL YOU AWAY AGAIN. LET'S MAKE THE MOST OF THIS TIME...
...WHILE WE HAVE THE CHANCE.

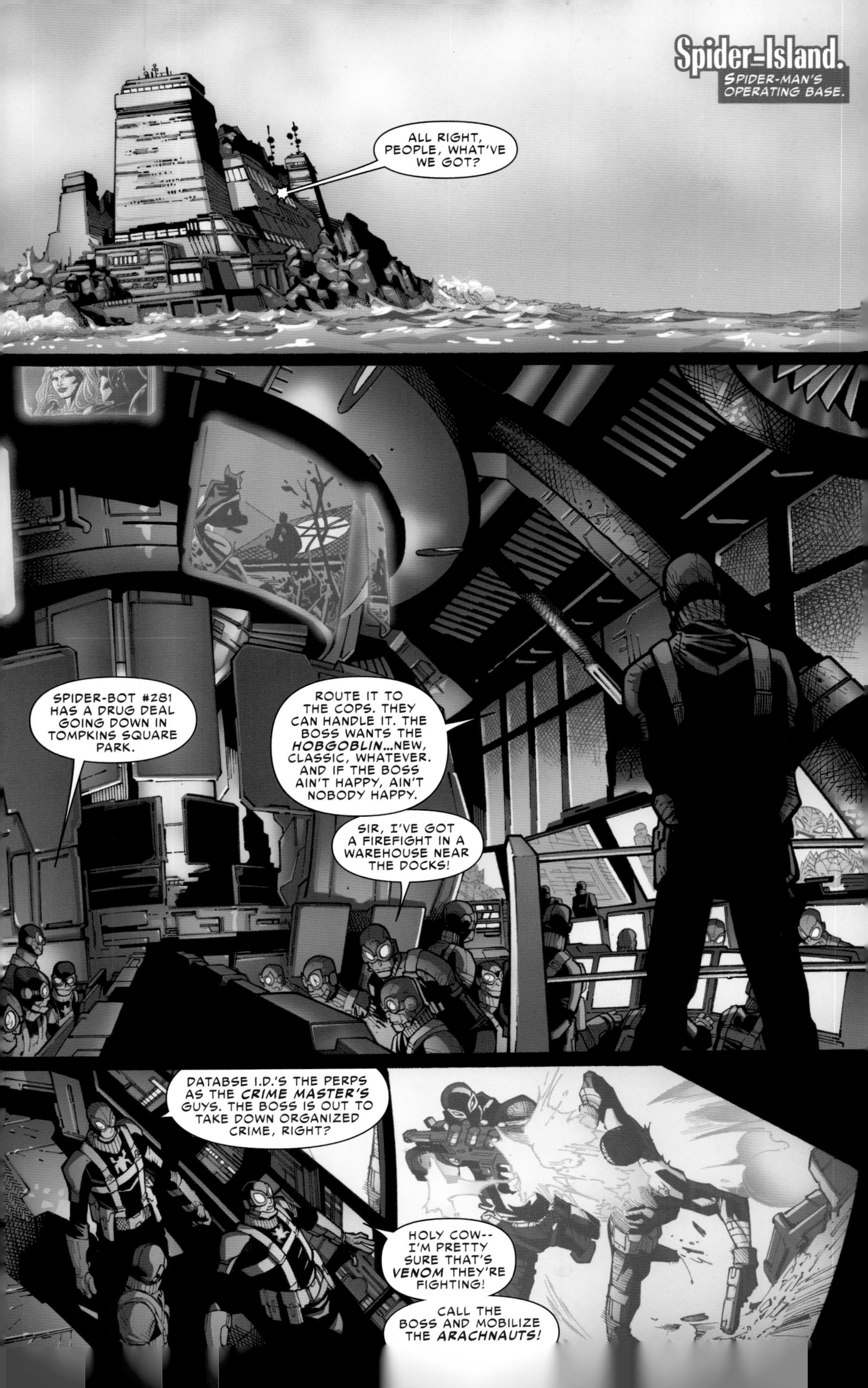
Spider-Island.
SPIDER-MAN'S OPERATING BASE.
ALL RIGHT, PEOPLE, WHAT'VE WE GOT?
SPIDER-BOT #281 HAS A DRUG DEAL GOING DOWN IN TOMPKINS SQUARE PARK.
ROUTE IT TO THE COPS. THEY CAN HANDLE IT. THE BOSS WANTS THE HOBGOBLIN...NEW, CLASSIC, WHATEVER. AND IF THE BOSS AIN'T HAPPY, AIN'T NOBODY HAPPY.
SIR, I'VE GOT A FIREFIGHT IN A WAREHOUSE NEAR THE DOCKS!
DATABSE I.D.'S THE PERPS AS THE CRIME MASTER'S GUYS. THE BOSS IS OUT TO TAKE DOWN ORGANIZED CRIME, RIGHT?
HOLY COW-- I'M PRETTY SURE THAT'S VENOM THEY'RE FIGHTING!
CALL THE BOSS AND MOBILIZE THE ARACHNAUTS!

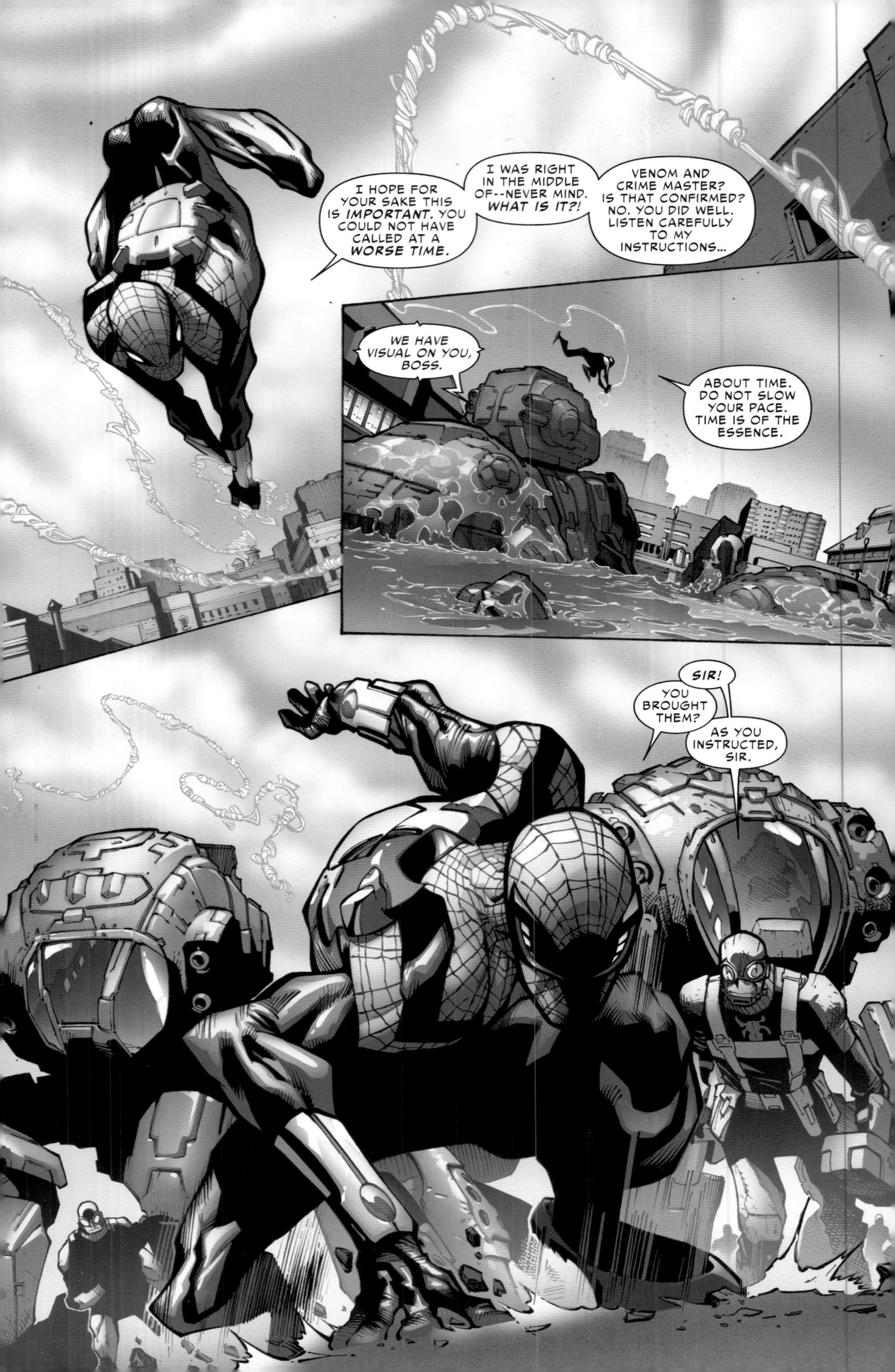
I HOPE FOR YOUR SAKE THIS IS IMPORTANT. YOU COULD NOT HAVE CALLED AT A WORSE TIME.
I WAS RIGHT IN THE MIDDLE OF--NEVER MIND. WHAT IS IT?!
VENOM AND CRIME MASTER? IS THAT CONFIRMED? NO. YOU DID WELL. LISTEN CAREFULLY TO MY INSTRUCTIONS...
WE HAVE VISUAL ON YOU, BOSS.
ABOUT TIME. DO NOT SLOW YOUR PACE. TIME IS OF THE ESSENCE.
SIR!
YOU BROUGHT THEM?
AS YOU INSTRUCTED, SIR.

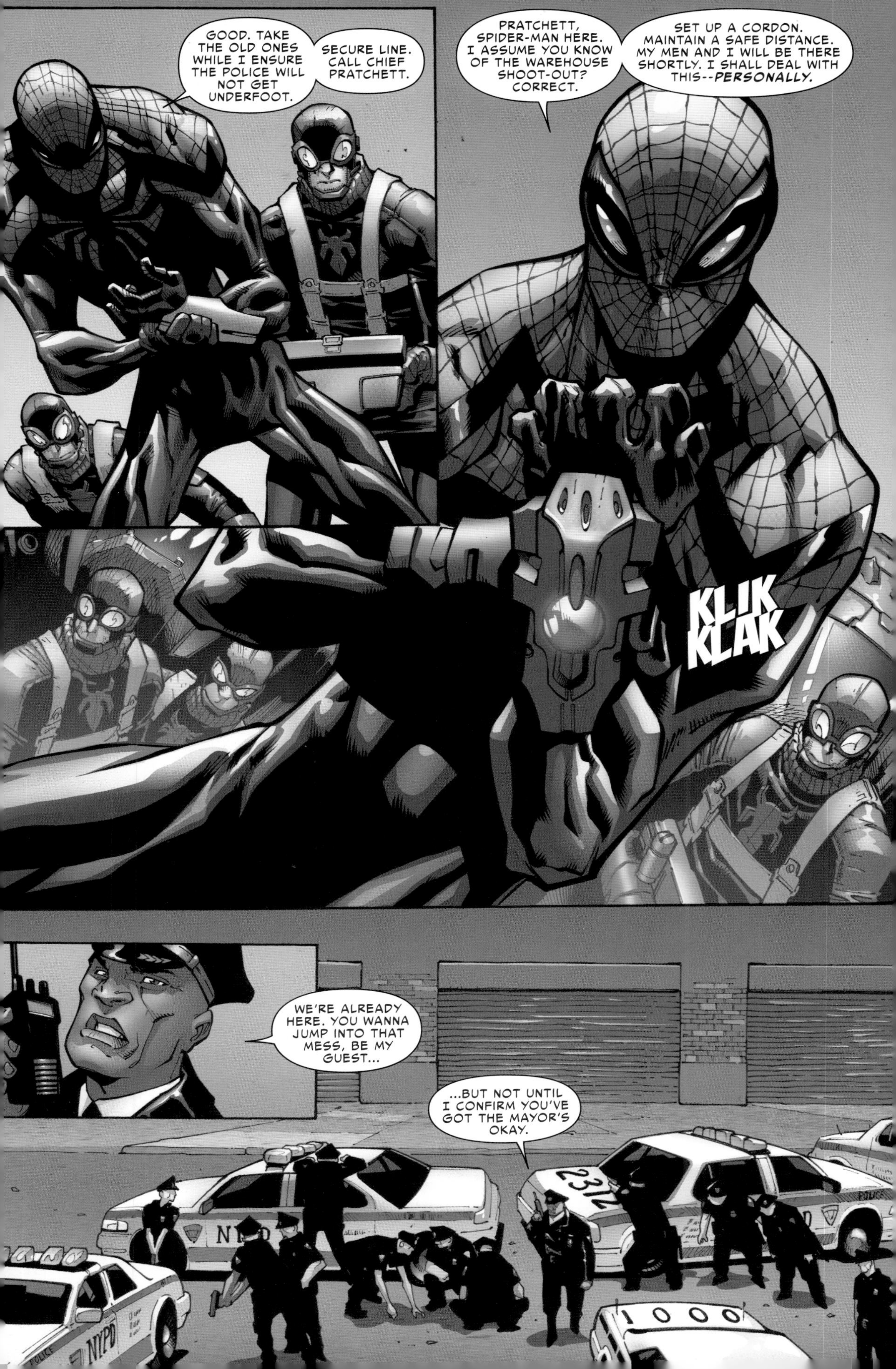
GOOD. TAKE THE OLD ONES WHILE I ENSURE THE POLICE WILL NOT GET UNDERFOOT.
SECURE LINE. CALL CHIEF PRATCHETT.
PRATCHETT, SPIDER-MAN HERE. I ASSUME YOU KNOW OF THE WAREHOUSE SHOOT-OUT? CORRECT.
SET UP A CORDON. MAINTAIN A SAFE DISTANCE. MY MEN AND I WILL BE THERE SHORTLY. I SHALL DEAL WITH THIS--*PERSONALLY.*
KLIK KLAK
WE'RE ALREADY HERE. YOU WANNA JUMP INTO THAT MESS, BE MY GUEST...
...BUT NOT UNTIL I CONFIRM YOU'VE GOT THE MAYOR'S OKAY.
NYPD
POLICE
2312
1000

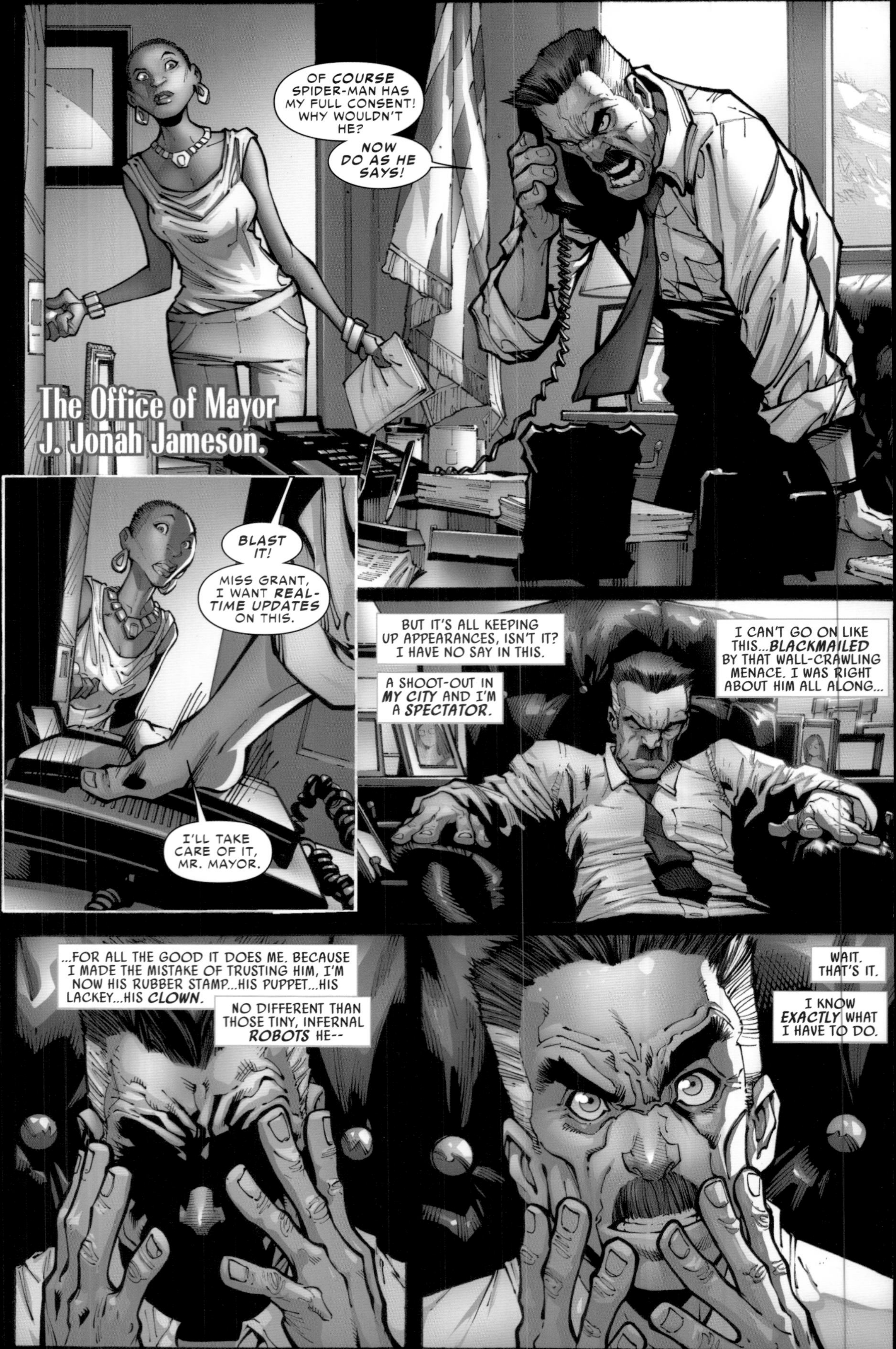

OF COURSE SPIDER-MAN HAS MY FULL CONSENT! WHY WOULDN'T HE?
NOW DO AS HE SAYS!
The Office of Mayor J. Jonah Jameson.
BLAST IT!
MISS GRANT, I WANT REAL-TIME UPDATES ON THIS.
I'LL TAKE CARE OF IT, MR. MAYOR.
BUT IT'S ALL KEEPING UP APPEARANCES, ISN'T IT? I HAVE NO SAY IN THIS.
A SHOOT-OUT IN MY CITY AND I'M A SPECTATOR.
I CAN'T GO ON LIKE THIS...BLACKMAILED BY THAT WALL-CRAWLING MENACE. I WAS RIGHT ABOUT HIM ALL ALONG...
...FOR ALL THE GOOD IT DOES ME. BECAUSE I MADE THE MISTAKE OF TRUSTING HIM, I'M NOW HIS RUBBER STAMP...HIS PUPPET...HIS LACKEY...HIS CLOWN.
NO DIFFERENT THAN THOSE TINY, INFERNAL ROBOTS HE--
WAIT. THAT'S IT.
I KNOW EXACTLY WHAT I HAVE TO DO.

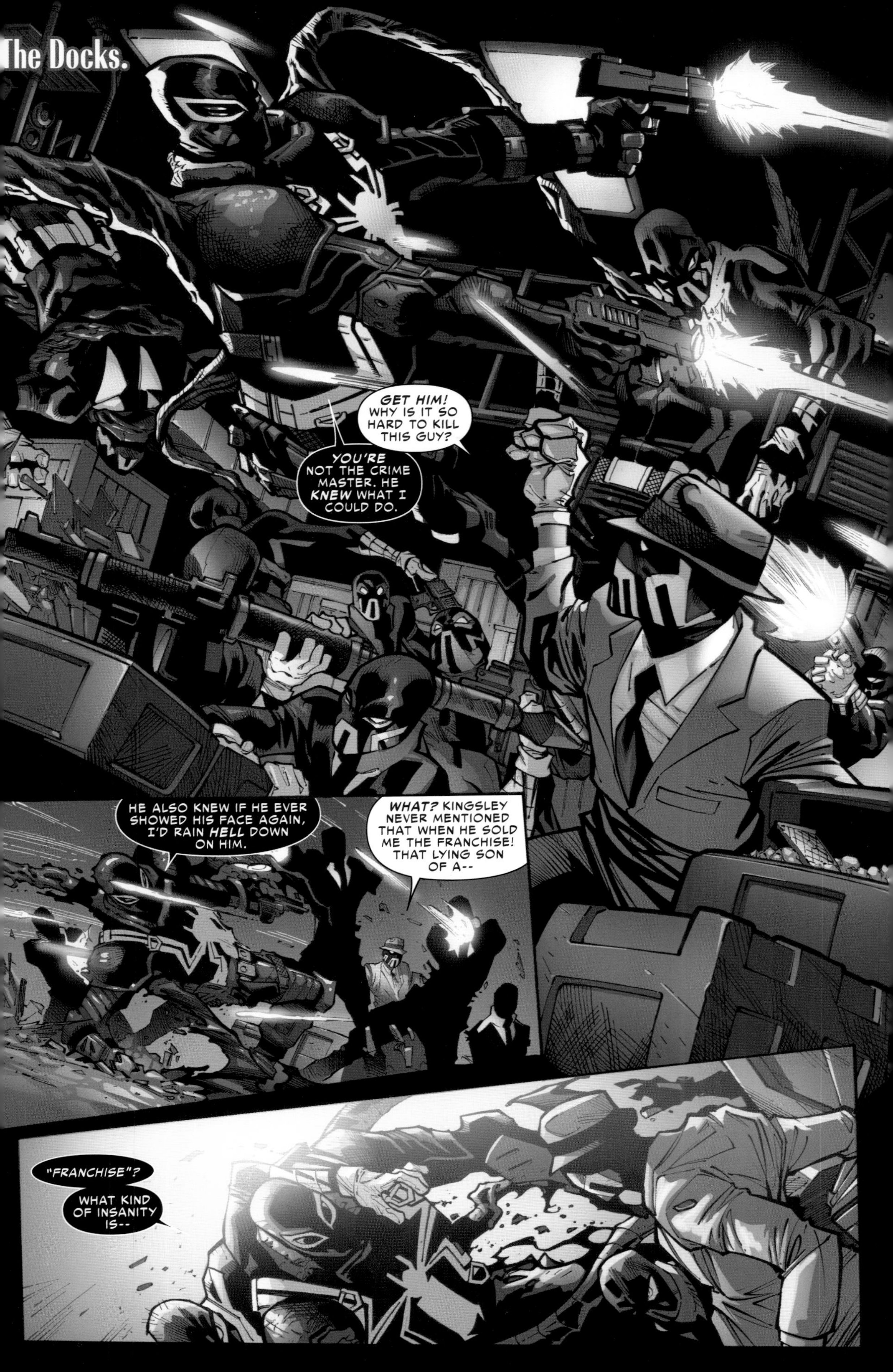
The Docks.
GET HIM! WHY IS IT SO HARD TO KILL THIS GUY?
YOU'RE NOT THE CRIME MASTER. HE KNEW WHAT I COULD DO.
HE ALSO KNEW IF HE EVER SHOWED HIS FACE AGAIN, I'D RAIN HELL DOWN ON HIM.
WHAT? KINGSLEY NEVER MENTIONED THAT WHEN HE SOLD ME THE FRANCHISE! THAT LYING SON OF A--
"FRANCHISE"?
WHAT KIND OF INSANITY IS--

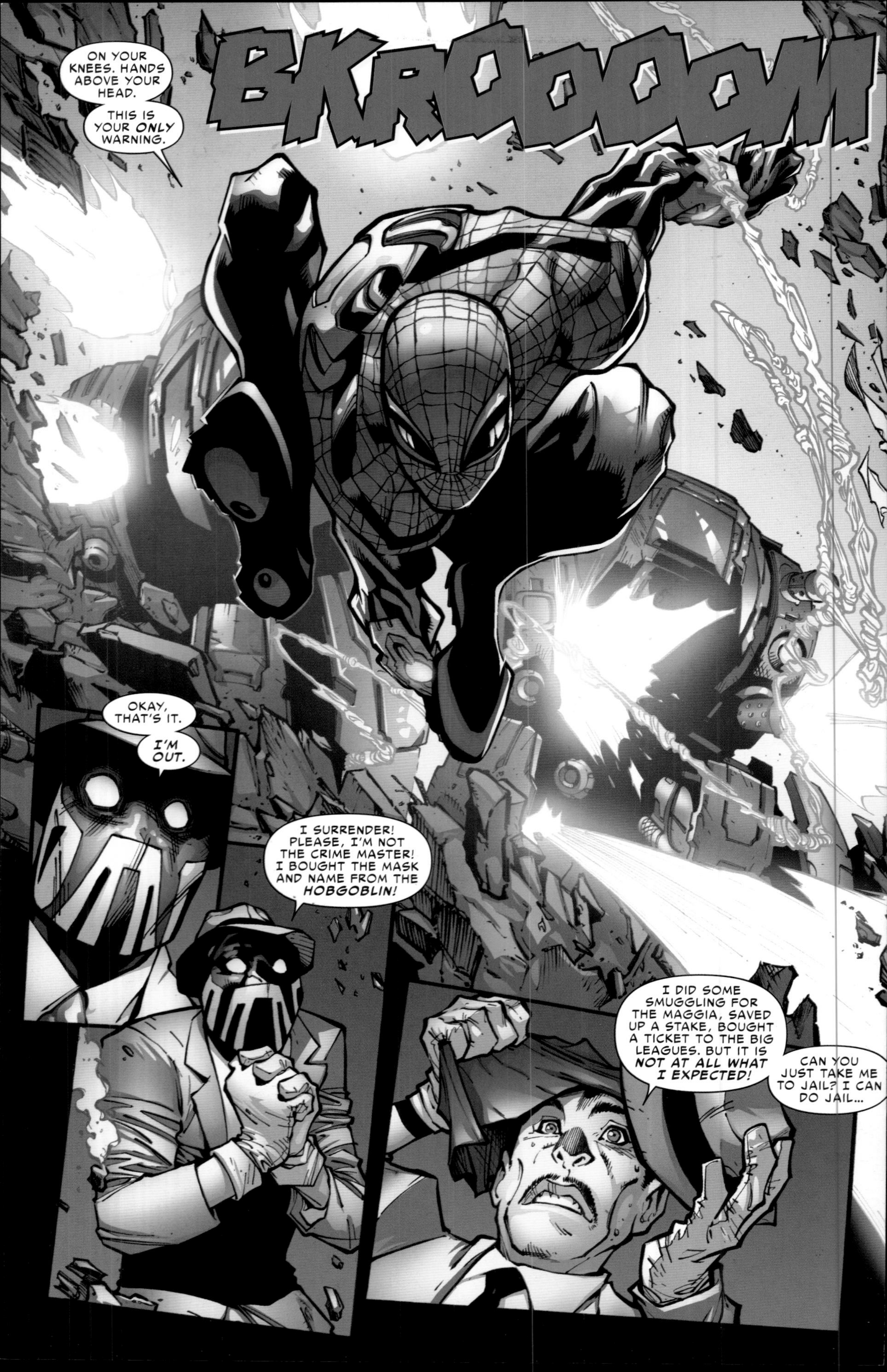

BKROOOOM
ON YOUR KNEES. HANDS ABOVE YOUR HEAD.
THIS IS YOUR ONLY WARNING.
OKAY, THAT'S IT.
I'M OUT.
I SURRENDER! PLEASE, I'M NOT THE CRIME MASTER! I BOUGHT THE MASK AND NAME FROM THE HOBGOBLIN!
I DID SOME SMUGGLING FOR THE MAGGIA, SAVED UP A STAKE, BOUGHT A TICKET TO THE BIG LEAGUES. BUT IT IS NOT AT ALL WHAT I EXPECTED!
CAN YOU JUST TAKE ME TO JAIL? I CAN DO JAIL...

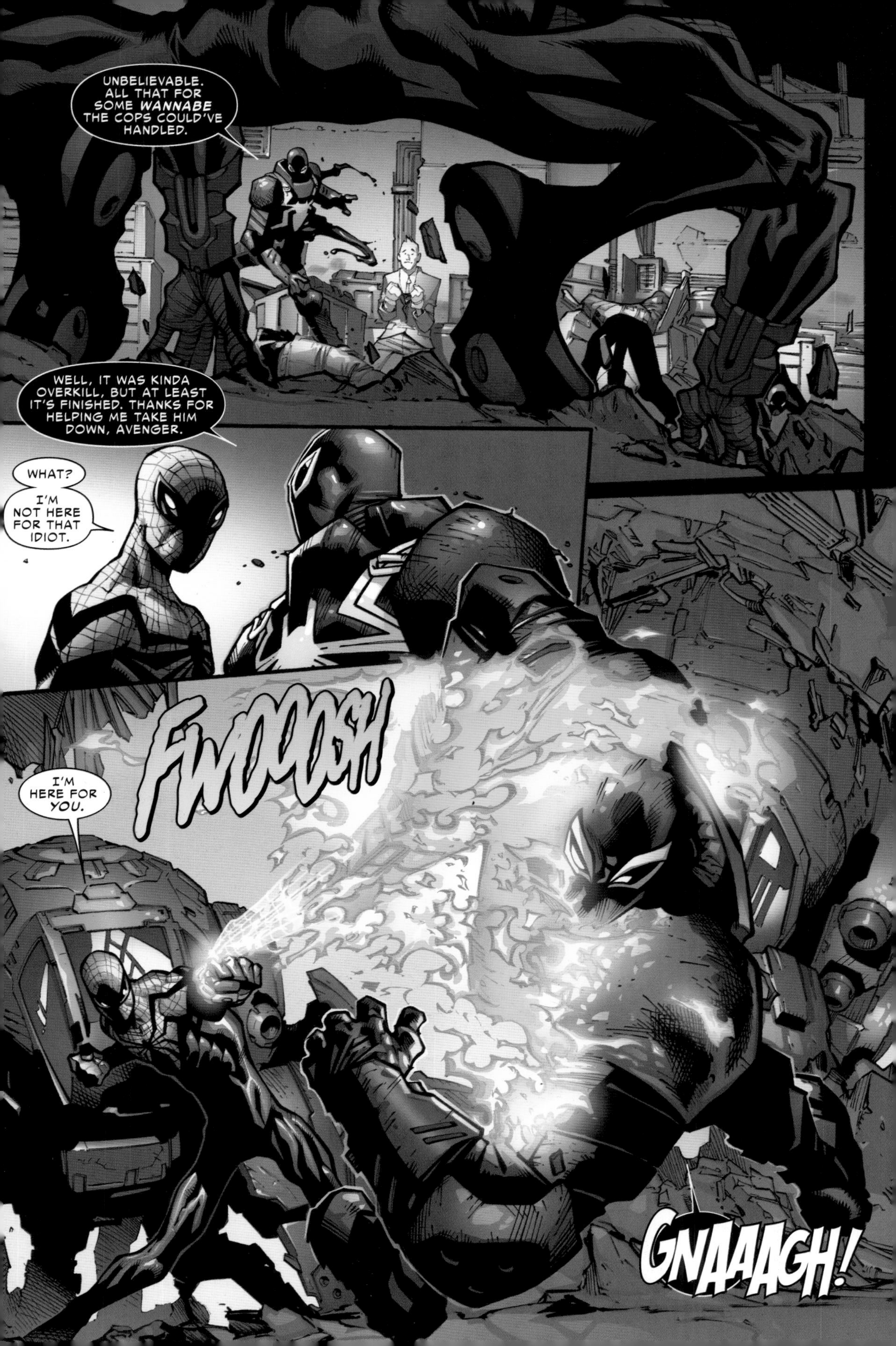
UNBELIEVABLE. ALL THAT FOR SOME WANNABE THE COPS COULD'VE HANDLED.
WELL, IT WAS KINDA OVERKILL, BUT AT LEAST IT'S FINISHED. THANKS FOR HELPING ME TAKE HIM DOWN, AVENGER.
WHAT?
I'M NOT HERE FOR THAT IDIOT.
FWOOOSH
I'M HERE FOR YOU.
GNAAAGH!

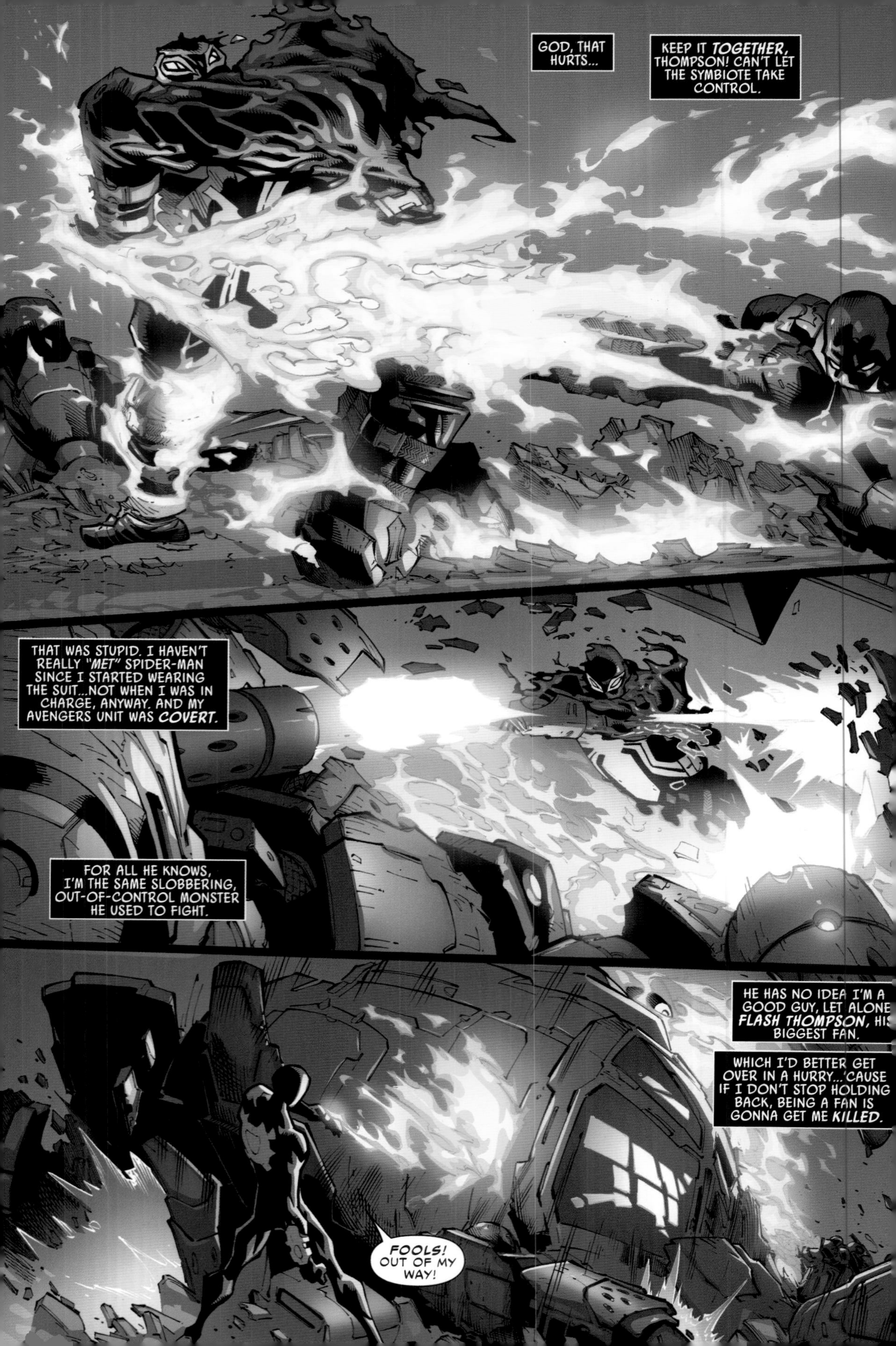
GOD, THAT HURTS...
KEEP IT TOGETHER, THOMPSON! CAN'T LET THE SYMBIOTE TAKE CONTROL.
THAT WAS STUPID. I HAVEN'T REALLY "MET" SPIDER-MAN SINCE I STARTED WEARING THE SUIT...NOT WHEN I WAS IN CHARGE, ANYWAY. AND MY AVENGERS UNIT WAS COVERT.
FOR ALL HE KNOWS, I'M THE SAME SLOBBERING, OUT-OF-CONTROL MONSTER HE USED TO FIGHT.
HE HAS NO IDEA I'M A GOOD GUY, LET ALONE FLASH THOMPSON, HIS BIGGEST FAN.
WHICH I'D BETTER GET OVER IN A HURRY...'CAUSE IF I DON'T STOP HOLDING BACK, BEING A FAN IS GONNA GET ME KILLED.
FOOLS! OUT OF MY WAY!

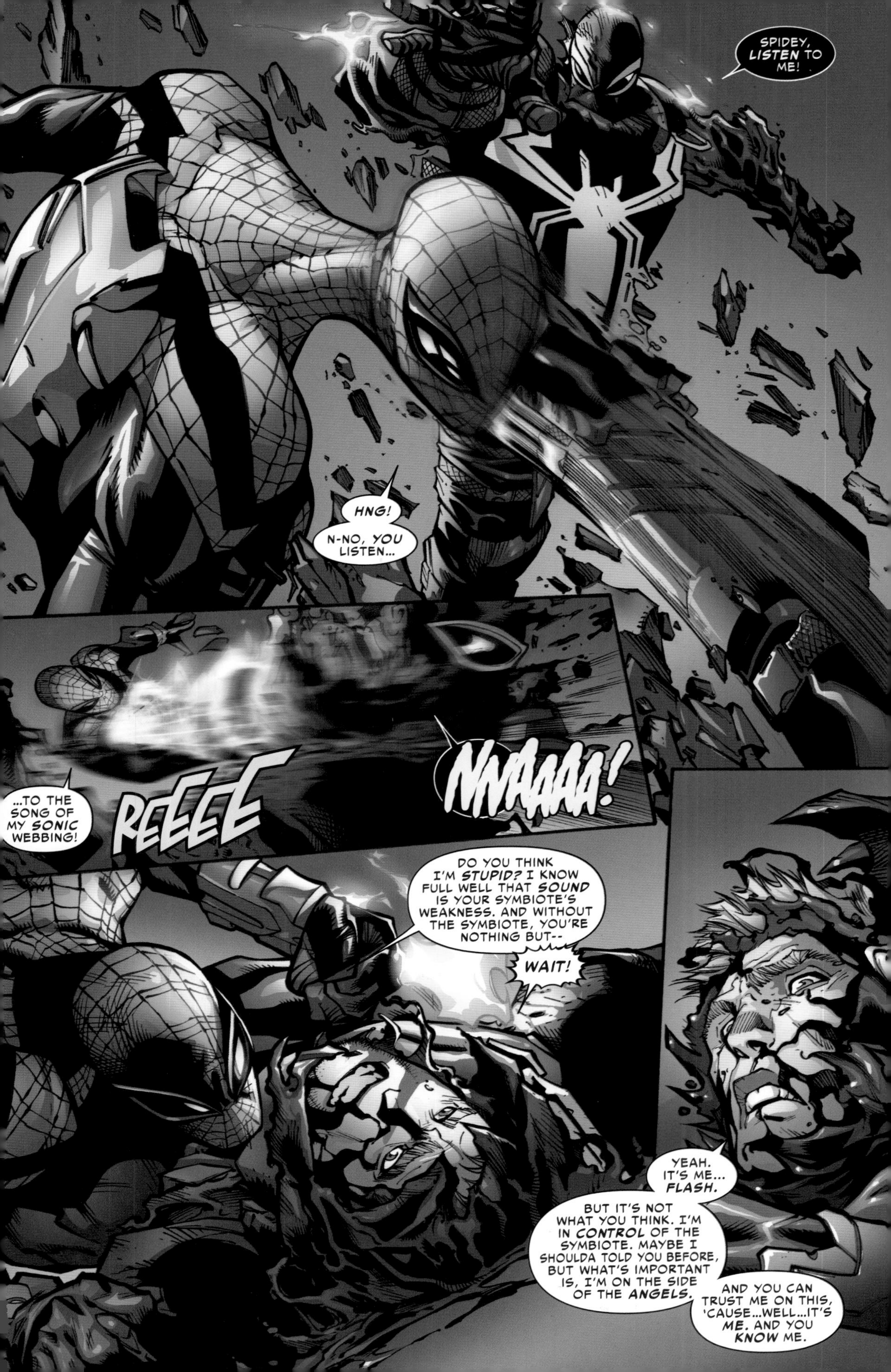
SPIDEY, LISTEN TO ME!
HNG!
N-NO, YOU LISTEN...
...TO THE SONG OF MY SONIC WEBBING!
REEEE
NNAAAAA!
DO YOU THINK I'M STUPID? I KNOW FULL WELL THAT SOUND IS YOUR SYMBIOTE'S WEAKNESS. AND WITHOUT THE SYMBIOTE, YOU'RE NOTHING BUT--
WAIT!
YEAH. IT'S ME... FLASH.
BUT IT'S NOT WHAT YOU THINK. I'M IN CONTROL OF THE SYMBIOTE. MAYBE I SHOULDA TOLD YOU BEFORE, BUT WHAT'S IMPORTANT IS, I'M ON THE SIDE OF THE ANGELS.
AND YOU CAN TRUST ME ON THIS, 'CAUSE...WELL...IT'S ME. AND YOU KNOW ME.

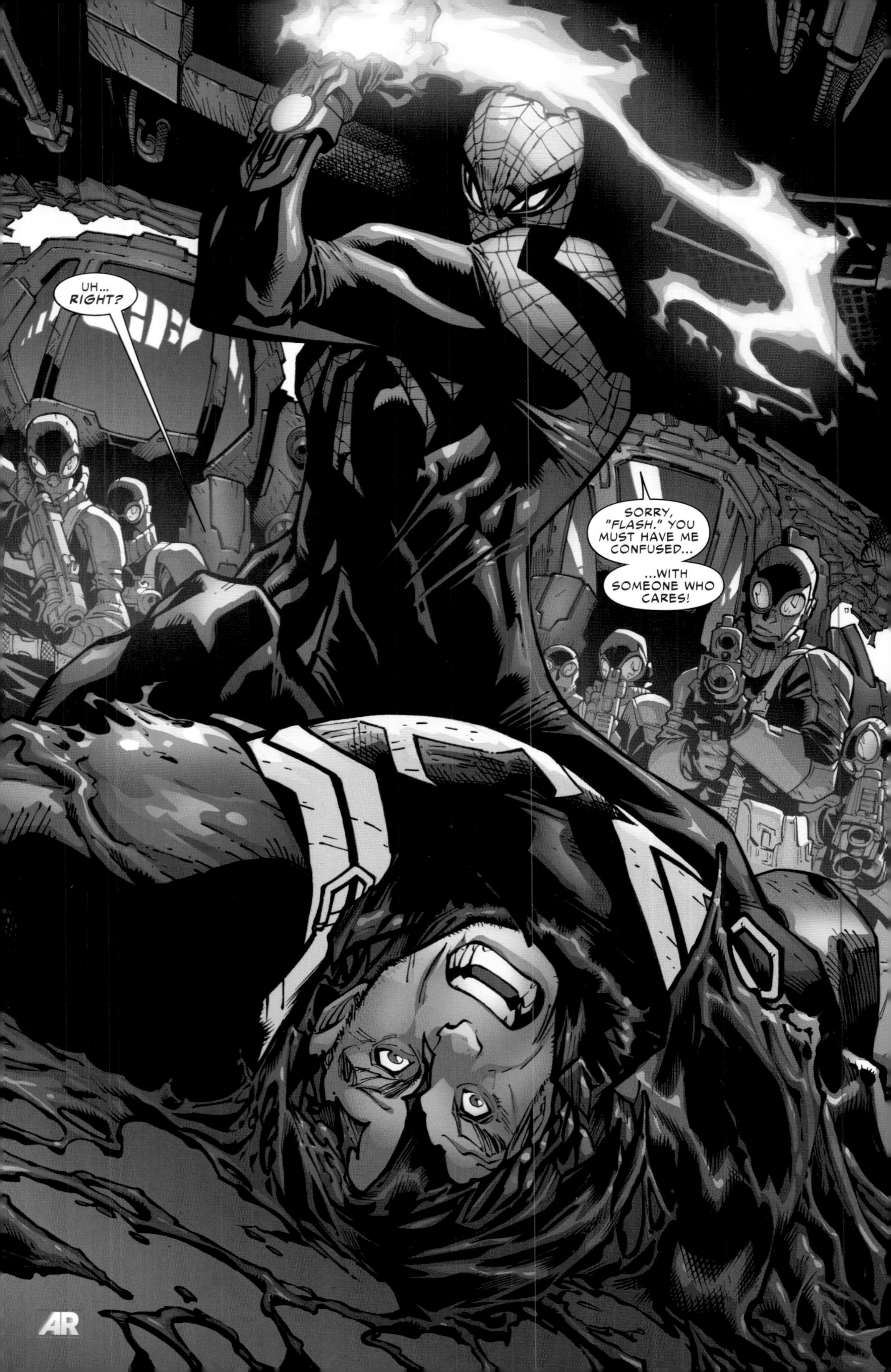
UH... RIGHT?
SORRY, "FLASH." YOU MUST HAVE ME CONFUSED...
...WITH SOMEONE WHO CARES!

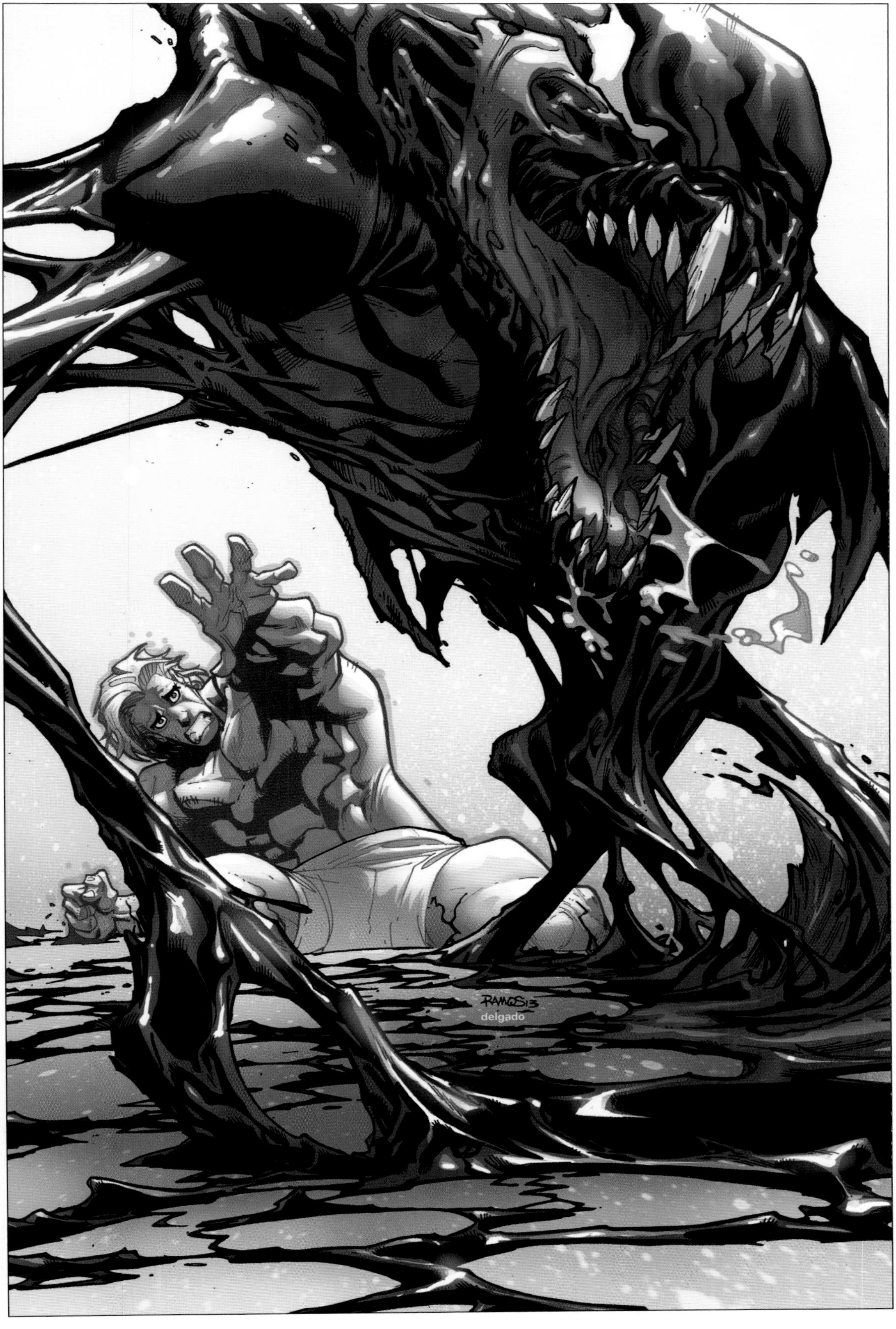
RAMOS13
delgado

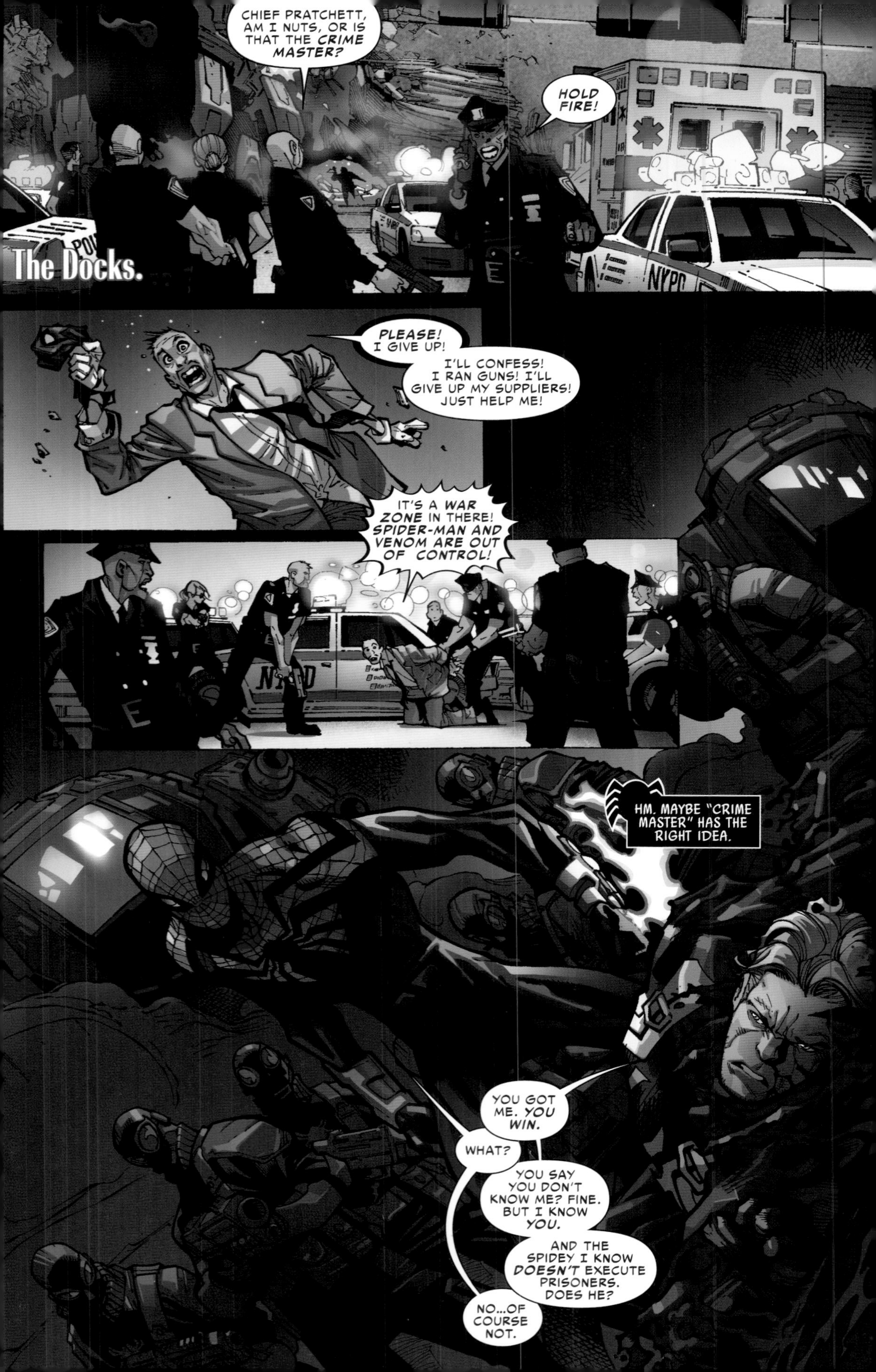
CHIEF PRATCHETT, AM I NUTS, OR IS THAT THE CRIME MASTER?
HOLD FIRE!
The Docks.
PLEASE! I GIVE UP!
I'LL CONFESS! I RAN GUNS! I'LL GIVE UP MY SUPPLIERS! JUST HELP ME!
IT'S A WAR ZONE IN THERE! SPIDER-MAN AND VENOM ARE OUT OF CONTROL!
HM. MAYBE "CRIME MASTER" HAS THE RIGHT IDEA.
YOU GOT ME. YOU WIN.
WHAT?
YOU SAY YOU DON'T KNOW ME? FINE. BUT I KNOW YOU.
AND THE SPIDEY I KNOW DOESN'T EXECUTE PRISONERS. DOES HE?
NO...OF COURSE NOT.

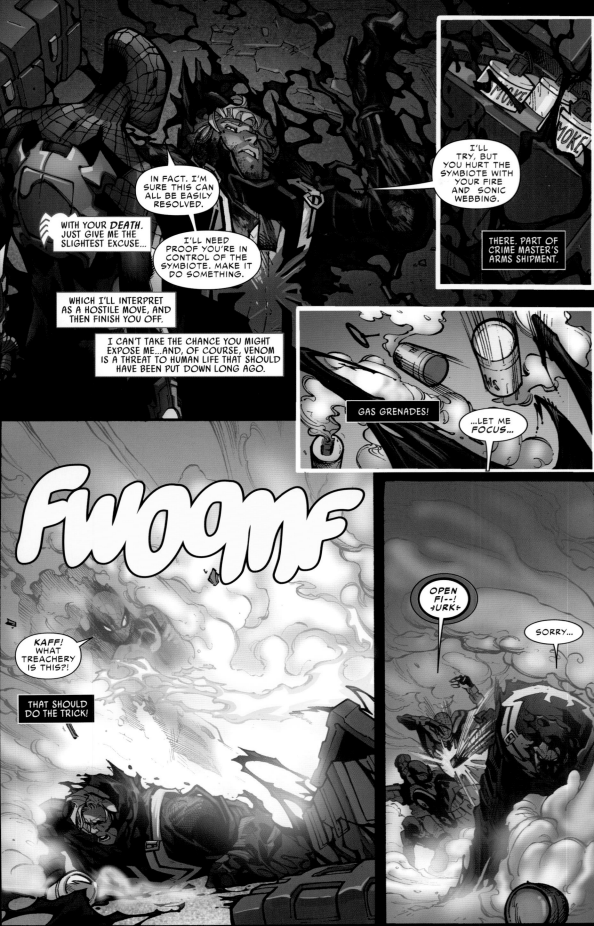

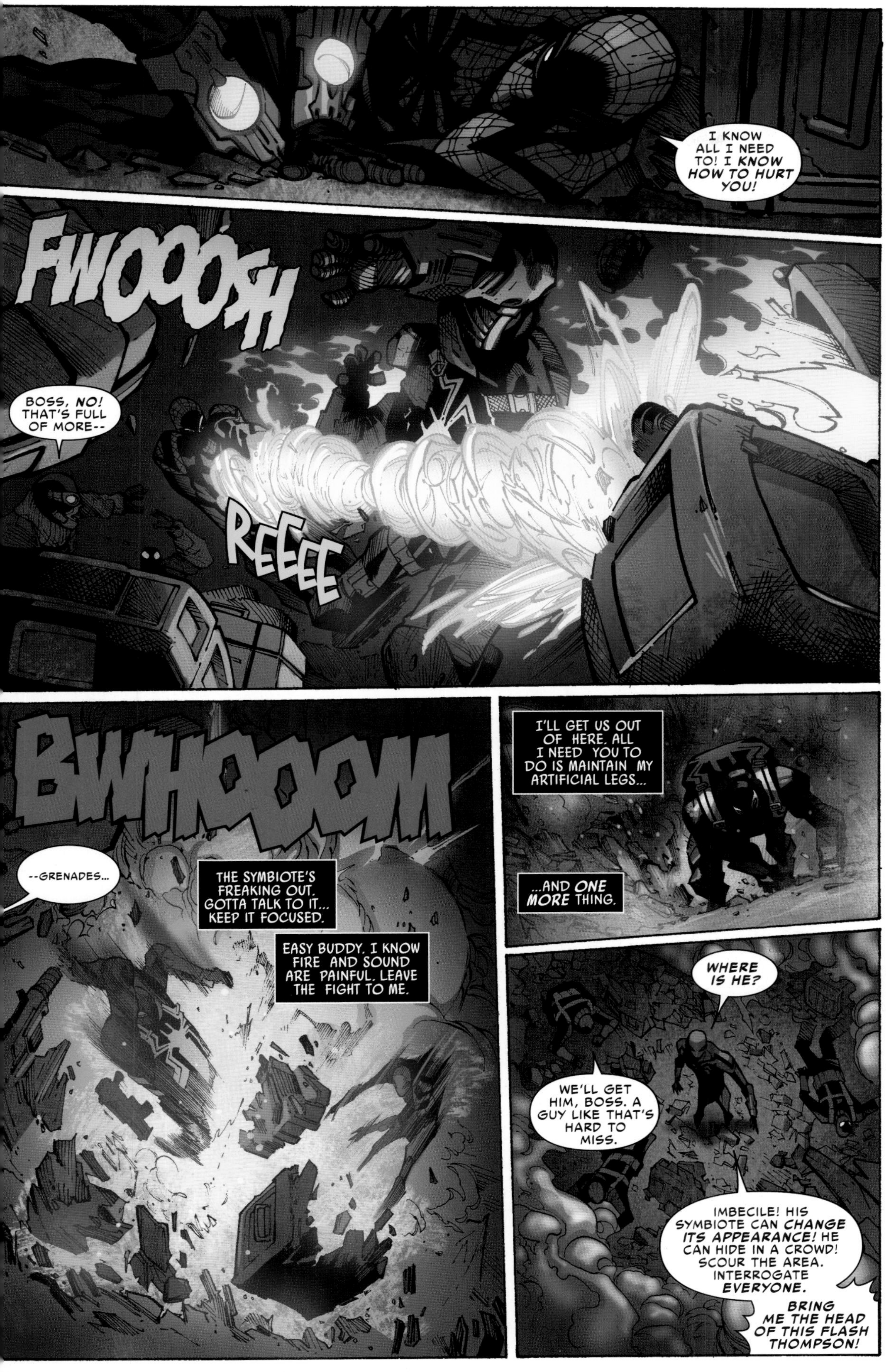
I KNOW ALL I NEED TO! I KNOW HOW TO HURT YOU!
FWOOOSH
BOSS, NO! THAT'S FULL OF MORE--
REEEEE
BWHOOOM
--GRENADES...
THE SYMBIOTE'S FREAKING OUT. GOTTA TALK TO IT... KEEP IT FOCUSED.
EASY BUDDY. I KNOW FIRE AND SOUND ARE PAINFUL. LEAVE THE FIGHT TO ME.
I'LL GET US OUT OF HERE. ALL I NEED YOU TO DO IS MAINTAIN MY ARTIFICIAL LEGS...
...AND ONE MORE THING.
WHERE IS HE?
WE'LL GET HIM, BOSS. A GUY LIKE THAT'S HARD TO MISS.
IMBECILE! HIS SYMBIOTE CAN CHANGE ITS APPEARANCE! HE CAN HIDE IN A CROWD! SCOUR THE AREA. INTERROGATE EVERYONE.
BRING ME THE HEAD OF THIS FLASH THOMPSON!

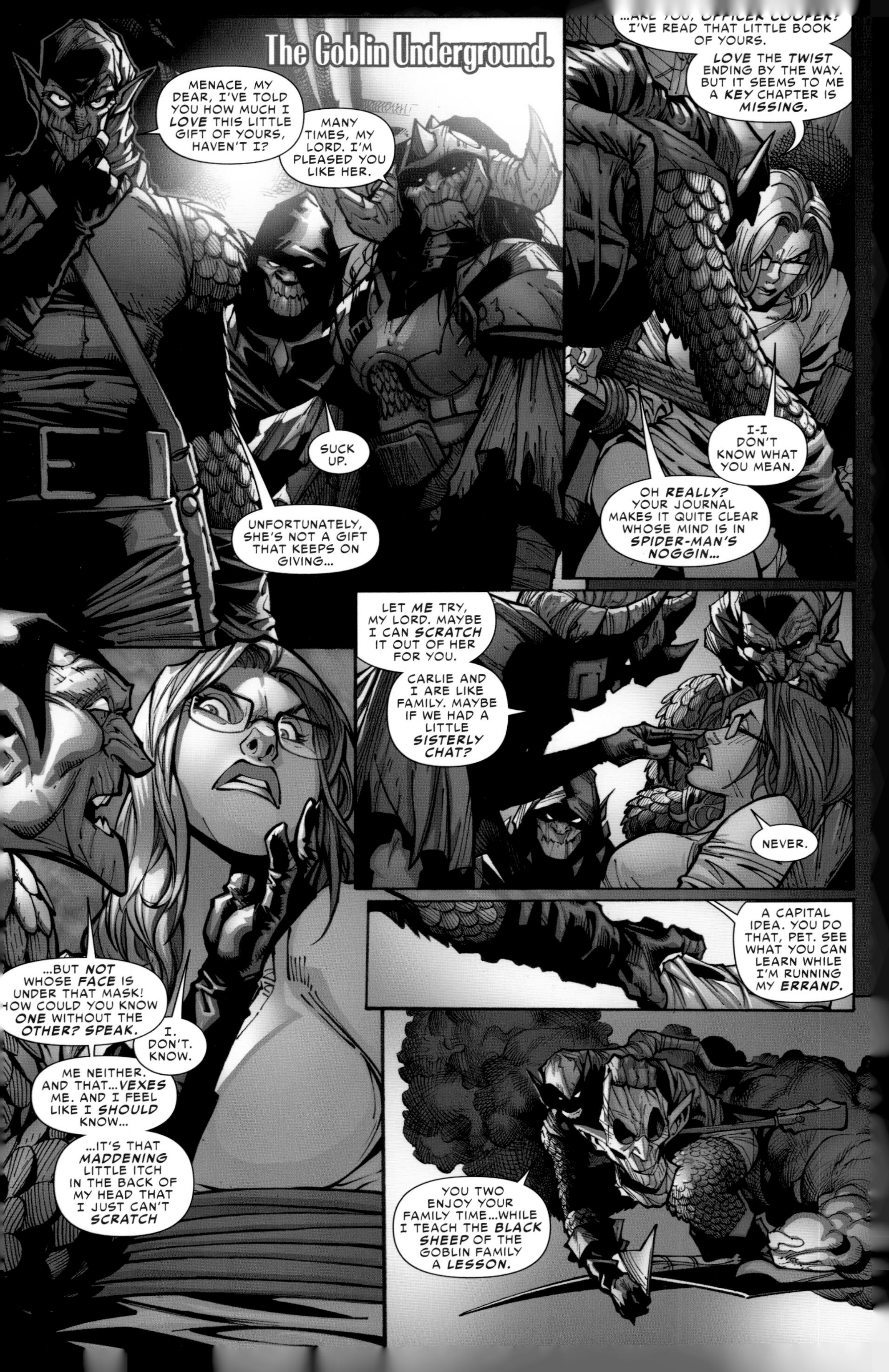

The Goblin Underground.
MENACE, MY DEAR, I'VE TOLD YOU HOW MUCH I LOVE THIS LITTLE GIFT OF YOURS, HAVEN'T I?
MANY TIMES, MY LORD. I'M PLEASED YOU LIKE HER.
SUCK UP.
UNFORTUNATELY, SHE'S NOT A GIFT THAT KEEPS ON GIVING...
...ARE YOU, OFFICER COOPER? I'VE READ THAT LITTLE BOOK OF YOURS.
LOVE THE TWIST ENDING BY THE WAY. BUT IT SEEMS TO ME A KEY CHAPTER IS MISSING.
I-I DON'T KNOW WHAT YOU MEAN.
OH REALLY? YOUR JOURNAL MAKES IT QUITE CLEAR WHOSE MIND IS IN SPIDER-MAN'S NOGGIN...
...BUT NOT WHOSE FACE IS UNDER THAT MASK! HOW COULD YOU KNOW ONE WITHOUT THE OTHER? SPEAK.
I. DON'T. KNOW.
ME NEITHER. AND THAT...VEXES ME. AND I FEEL LIKE I SHOULD KNOW...
...IT'S THAT MADDENING LITTLE ITCH IN THE BACK OF MY HEAD THAT I JUST CAN'T SCRATCH
LET ME TRY, MY LORD. MAYBE I CAN SCRATCH IT OUT OF HER FOR YOU.
CARLIE AND I ARE LIKE FAMILY. MAYBE IF WE HAD A LITTLE SISTERLY CHAT?
NEVER.
A CAPITAL IDEA. YOU DO THAT, PET. SEE WHAT YOU CAN LEARN WHILE I'M RUNNING MY ERRAND.
YOU TWO ENJOY YOUR FAMILY TIME...WHILE I TEACH THE BLACK SHEEP OF THE GOBLIN FAMILY A LESSON.

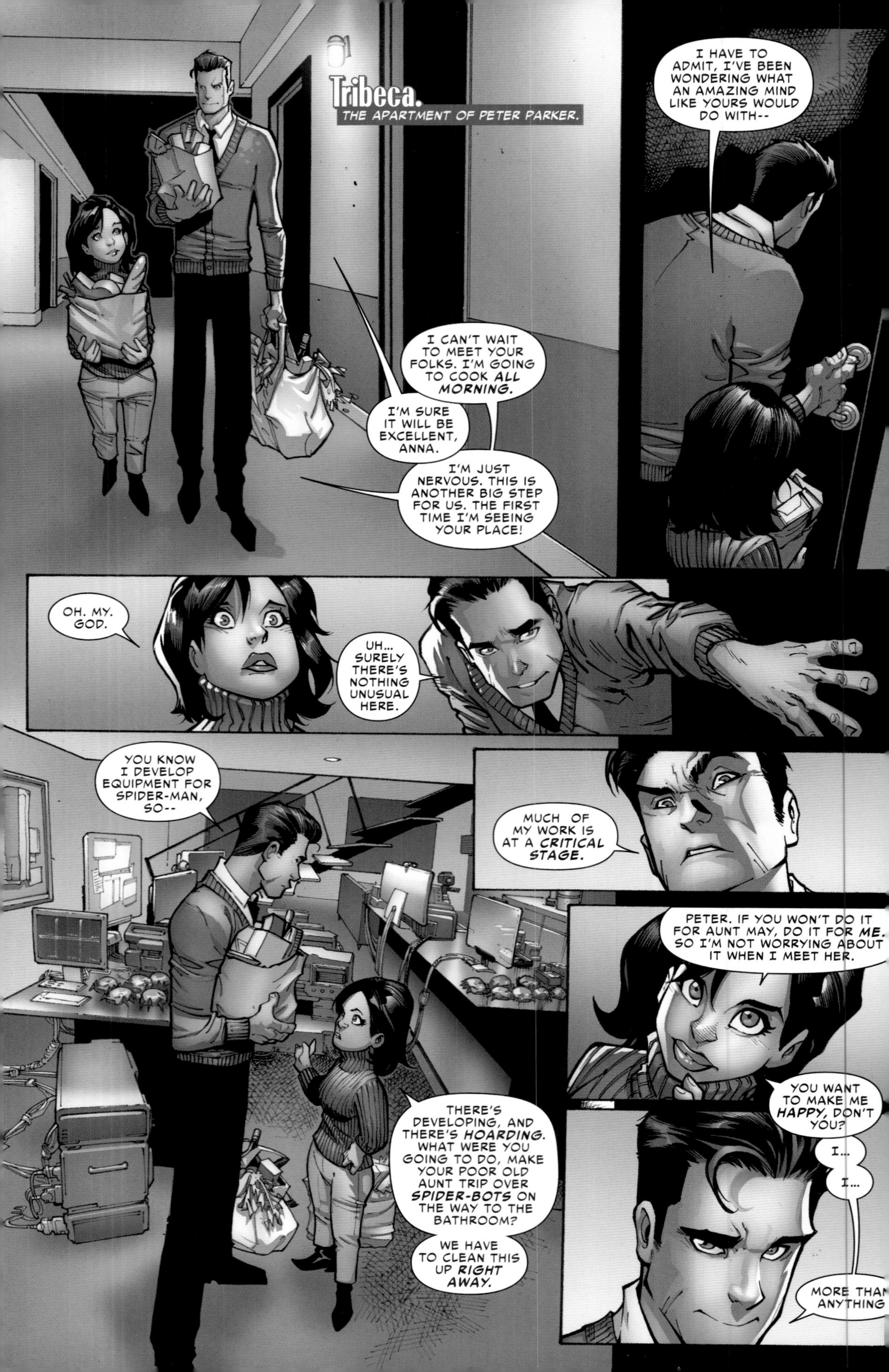
Tribeca.
THE APARTMENT OF PETER PARKER.
I CAN'T WAIT TO MEET YOUR FOLKS. I'M GOING TO COOK ALL MORNING.
I'M SURE IT WILL BE EXCELLENT, ANNA.
I'M JUST NERVOUS. THIS IS ANOTHER BIG STEP FOR US. THE FIRST TIME I'M SEEING YOUR PLACE!
I HAVE TO ADMIT, I'VE BEEN WONDERING WHAT AN AMAZING MIND LIKE YOURS WOULD DO WITH--
OH. MY. GOD.
UH... SURELY THERE'S NOTHING UNUSUAL HERE.
YOU KNOW I DEVELOP EQUIPMENT FOR SPIDER-MAN, SO--
THERE'S DEVELOPING, AND THERE'S HOARDING. WHAT WERE YOU GOING TO DO, MAKE YOUR POOR OLD AUNT TRIP OVER SPIDER-BOTS ON THE WAY TO THE BATHROOM?
WE HAVE TO CLEAN THIS UP RIGHT AWAY.
MUCH OF MY WORK IS AT A CRITICAL STAGE.
PETER. IF YOU WON'T DO IT FOR AUNT MAY, DO IT FOR ME. SO I'M NOT WORRYING ABOUT IT WHEN I MEET HER.
YOU WANT TO MAKE ME HAPPY, DON'T YOU?
I...
I...
MORE THAN ANYTHING

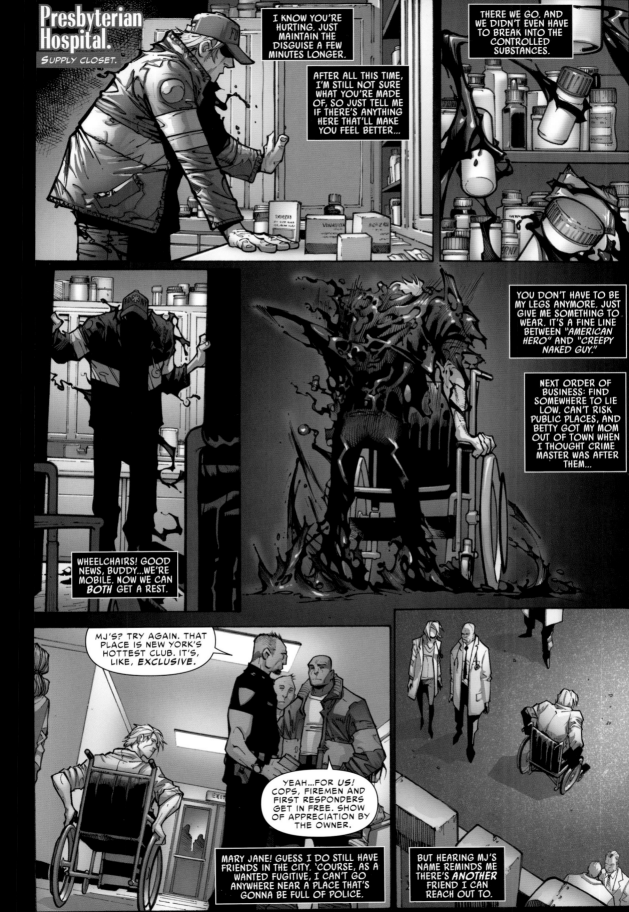

Presbyterian Hospital.
SUPPLY CLOSET.

I KNOW YOU'RE HURTING. JUST MAINTAIN THE DISGUISE A FEW MINUTES LONGER.

AFTER ALL THIS TIME, I'M STILL NOT SURE WHAT YOU'RE MADE OF, SO JUST TELL ME IF THERE'S ANYTHING HERE THAT'LL MAKE YOU FEEL BETTER...

THERE WE GO. AND WE DIDN'T EVEN HAVE TO BREAK INTO THE CONTROLLED SUBSTANCES.

YOU DON'T HAVE TO BE MY LEGS ANYMORE. JUST GIVE ME SOMETHING TO WEAR. IT'S A FINE LINE BETWEEN "AMERICAN HERO" AND "CREEPY NAKED GUY."

NEXT ORDER OF BUSINESS: FIND SOMEWHERE TO LIE LOW. CAN'T RISK PUBLIC PLACES, AND BETTY GOT MY MOM OUT OF TOWN WHEN I THOUGHT CRIME MASTER WAS AFTER THEM...

WHEELCHAIRS! GOOD NEWS, BUDDY...WE'RE MOBILE. NOW WE CAN *BOTH* GET A REST.

MJ'S? TRY AGAIN. THAT PLACE IS NEW YORK'S HOTTEST CLUB. IT'S, LIKE, *EXCLUSIVE.*

YEAH...FOR *US!* COPS, FIREMEN AND FIRST RESPONDERS GET IN FREE. SHOW OF APPRECIATION BY THE OWNER.

MARY JANE! GUESS I DO STILL HAVE FRIENDS IN THE CITY. 'COURSE, AS A WANTED FUGITIVE, I CAN'T GO ANYWHERE NEAR A PLACE THAT'S GONNA BE FULL OF POLICE.

BUT HEARING MJ'S NAME REMINDS ME THERE'S *ANOTHER* FRIEND I CAN REACH OUT TO.

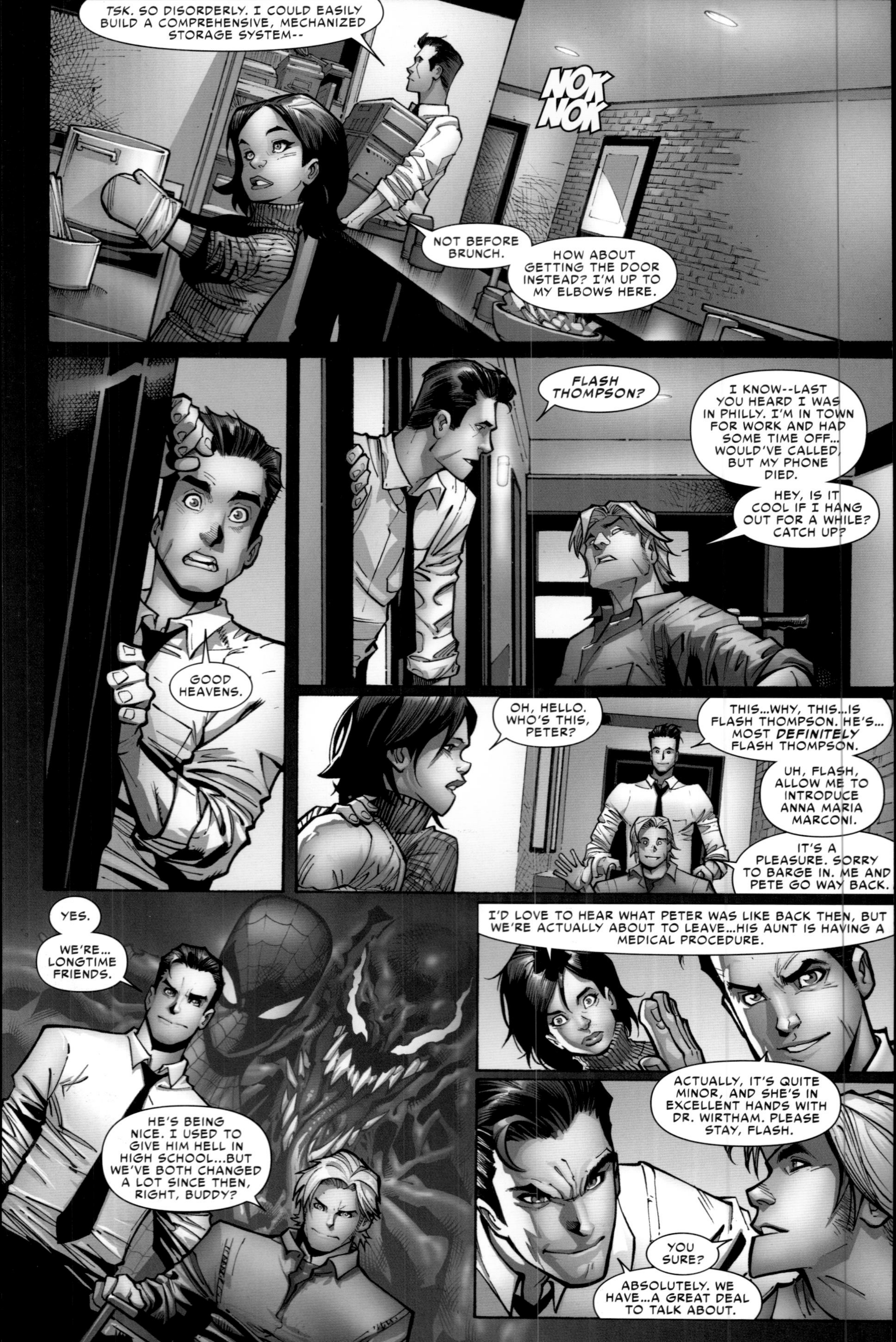
TSK. SO DISORDERLY. I COULD EASILY BUILD A COMPREHENSIVE, MECHANIZED STORAGE SYSTEM--
NOK NOK
NOT BEFORE BRUNCH.
HOW ABOUT GETTING THE DOOR INSTEAD? I'M UP TO MY ELBOWS HERE.
GOOD HEAVENS.
FLASH THOMPSON?
I KNOW--LAST YOU HEARD I WAS IN PHILLY. I'M IN TOWN FOR WORK AND HAD SOME TIME OFF... WOULD'VE CALLED, BUT MY PHONE DIED.
HEY, IS IT COOL IF I HANG OUT FOR A WHILE? CATCH UP?
OH, HELLO. WHO'S THIS, PETER?
THIS...WHY, THIS...IS FLASH THOMPSON. HE'S... MOST DEFINITELY FLASH THOMPSON.
UH, FLASH, ALLOW ME TO INTRODUCE ANNA MARIA MARCONI.
IT'S A PLEASURE. SORRY TO BARGE IN. ME AND PETE GO WAY BACK.
YES.
WE'RE... LONGTIME FRIENDS.
HE'S BEING NICE. I USED TO GIVE HIM HELL IN HIGH SCHOOL....BUT WE'VE BOTH CHANGED A LOT SINCE THEN, RIGHT, BUDDY?
I'D LOVE TO HEAR WHAT PETER WAS LIKE BACK THEN, BUT WE'RE ACTUALLY ABOUT TO LEAVE...HIS AUNT IS HAVING A MEDICAL PROCEDURE.
ACTUALLY, IT'S QUITE MINOR, AND SHE'S IN EXCELLENT HANDS WITH DR. WIRTHAM. PLEASE STAY, FLASH.
YOU SURE?
ABSOLUTELY. WE HAVE...A GREAT DEAL TO TALK ABOUT.

THAT SHOULD DO IT, MRS. JAMESON. THE CYBERNETICS HAVE REPLACED THE DAMAGED PORTIONS OF YOUR LEG, AND THEY SEEM TO HAVE CONNECTED NICELY WITH YOUR NERVOUS SYSTEM.

IT'S NANOTECH. MICROSCOPIC. THERE SHOULD BE NO DISCOMFORT WHATSOEVER. YOUR NEPHEW REALLY IS A GENIUS.

WHY, THAT BARELY TOOK FIVE MINUTES. YOU DIDN'T MAKE AN INCISION...OR EVEN USE ANESTHESIA!

AN *ABSENT* GENIUS. HE DID TEXT TO MAKE SURE IT WENT WELL, BUT AFTER HOW ATTENTIVE HE'S BEEN TO YOU LATELY, DEAR...

...WELL, I'D HATE TO THINK HE'S BACKSLIDING TO HIS OLD THOUGHTLESS WAYS.

HUSH UP, JAY. PETER HAS THIS ENTIRE COMPANY TO RUN. AND WE'RE MEETING HIS NEW GIRLFRIEND IN JUST A COUPLE HOURS. I'M QUITE HAPPY WITH HOW HE'S BEEN DOING.

THAT'S NOT ALL YOU SHOULD BE HAPPY ABOUT.

OH...?

OH! MY CANE...

YOU WALKED ON YOUR OWN. NO LIMP, NO PAIN.

NOW I *AM* A LITTLE UPSET PETER WASN'T HERE. THIS IS TRULY A MIRACLE.

IT'S THIS WORKAHOLIC MENTALITY NOWADAYS MY SON DIDN'T MAKE I EITHER. I REALIZE HE'S THE MAYOR...

...BUT I'D LOVE TO KNOW WHAT H CONSIDERS MORE IMPORTANT THAN FAMILY.

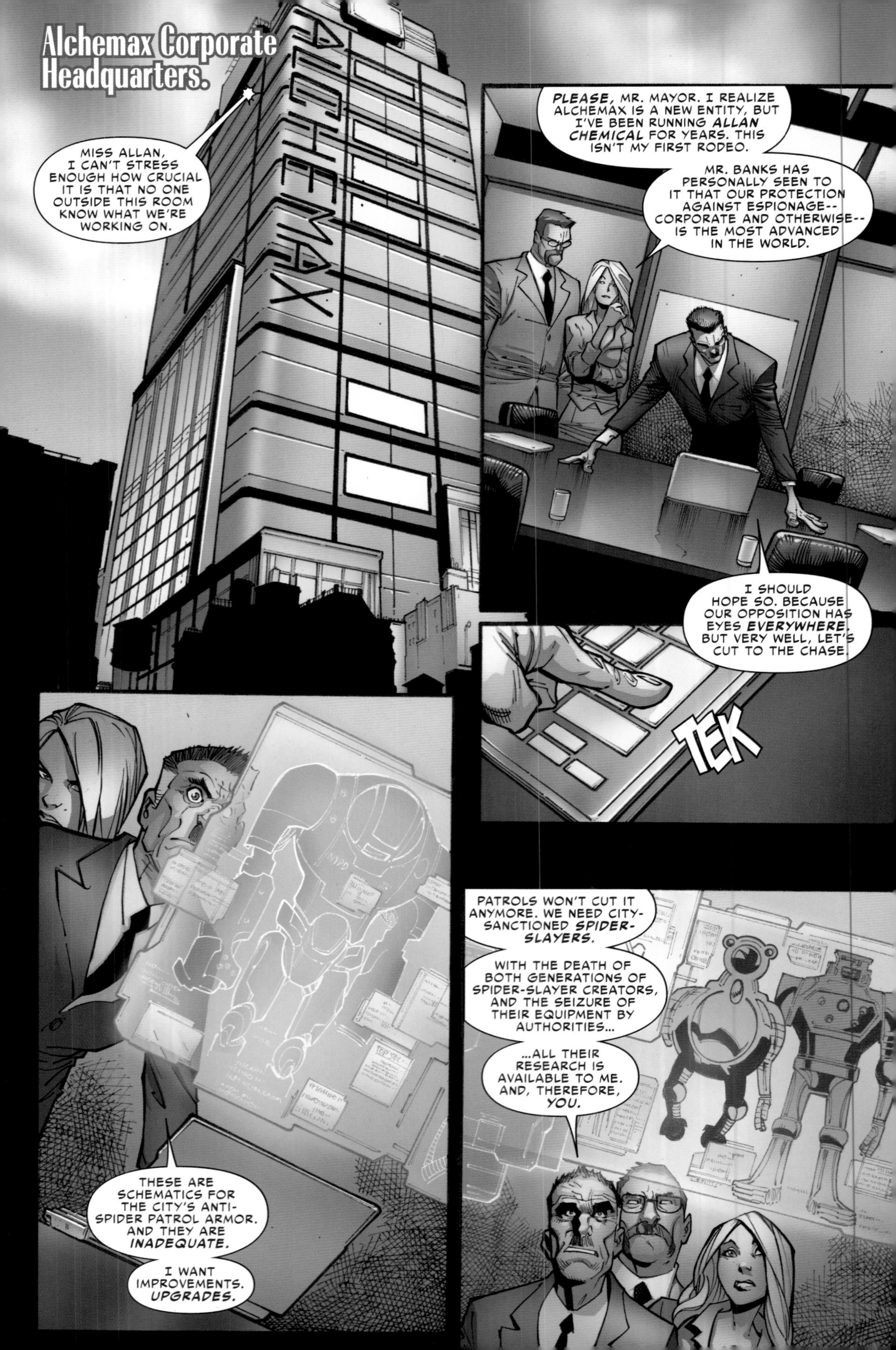
Alchemax Corporate Headquarters.
MISS ALLAN, I CAN'T STRESS ENOUGH HOW CRUCIAL IT IS THAT NO ONE OUTSIDE THIS ROOM KNOW WHAT WE'RE WORKING ON.
PLEASE, MR. MAYOR. I REALIZE ALCHEMAX IS A NEW ENTITY, BUT I'VE BEEN RUNNING ALLAN CHEMICAL FOR YEARS. THIS ISN'T MY FIRST RODEO.
MR. BANKS HAS PERSONALLY SEEN TO IT THAT OUR PROTECTION AGAINST ESPIONAGE-- CORPORATE AND OTHERWISE-- IS THE MOST ADVANCED IN THE WORLD.
I SHOULD HOPE SO. BECAUSE OUR OPPOSITION HAS EYES EVERYWHERE. BUT VERY WELL, LET'S CUT TO THE CHASE.
TEK
THESE ARE SCHEMATICS FOR THE CITY'S ANTI-SPIDER PATROL ARMOR. AND THEY ARE INADEQUATE.
I WANT IMPROVEMENTS. UPGRADES.
PATROLS WON'T CUT IT ANYMORE. WE NEED CITY-SANCTIONED SPIDER-SLAYERS.
WITH THE DEATH OF BOTH GENERATIONS OF SPIDER-SLAYER CREATORS, AND THE SEIZURE OF THEIR EQUIPMENT BY AUTHORITIES...
...ALL THEIR RESEARCH IS AVAILABLE TO ME. AND, THEREFORE, YOU.

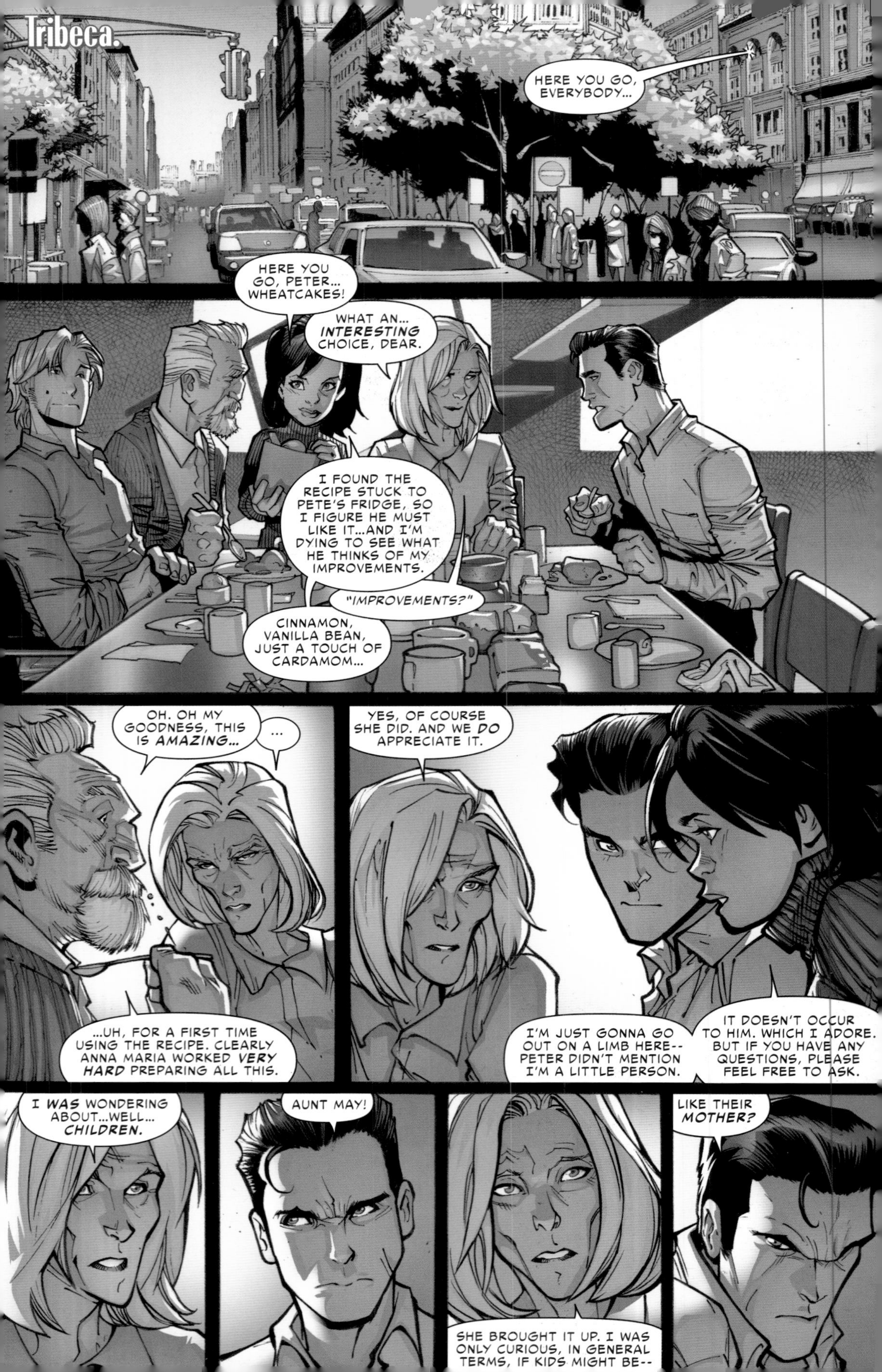
Tribeca.
HERE YOU GO, EVERYBODY...
HERE YOU GO, PETER... WHEATCAKES!
WHAT AN... INTERESTING CHOICE, DEAR.
I FOUND THE RECIPE STUCK TO PETE'S FRIDGE, SO I FIGURE HE MUST LIKE IT...AND I'M DYING TO SEE WHAT HE THINKS OF MY IMPROVEMENTS.
"IMPROVEMENTS?"
CINNAMON, VANILLA BEAN, JUST A TOUCH OF CARDAMOM...
OH. OH MY GOODNESS, THIS IS AMAZING...
...
...UH, FOR A FIRST TIME USING THE RECIPE. CLEARLY ANNA MARIA WORKED VERY HARD PREPARING ALL THIS.
YES, OF COURSE SHE DID. AND WE DO APPRECIATE IT.
I'M JUST GONNA GO OUT ON A LIMB HERE-- PETER DIDN'T MENTION I'M A LITTLE PERSON.
IT DOESN'T OCCUR TO HIM. WHICH I ADORE. BUT IF YOU HAVE ANY QUESTIONS, PLEASE FEEL FREE TO ASK.
I WAS WONDERING ABOUT...WELL... CHILDREN.
AUNT MAY!
SHE BROUGHT IT UP. I WAS ONLY CURIOUS, IN GENERAL TERMS, IF KIDS MIGHT BE--
LIKE THEIR MOTHER?

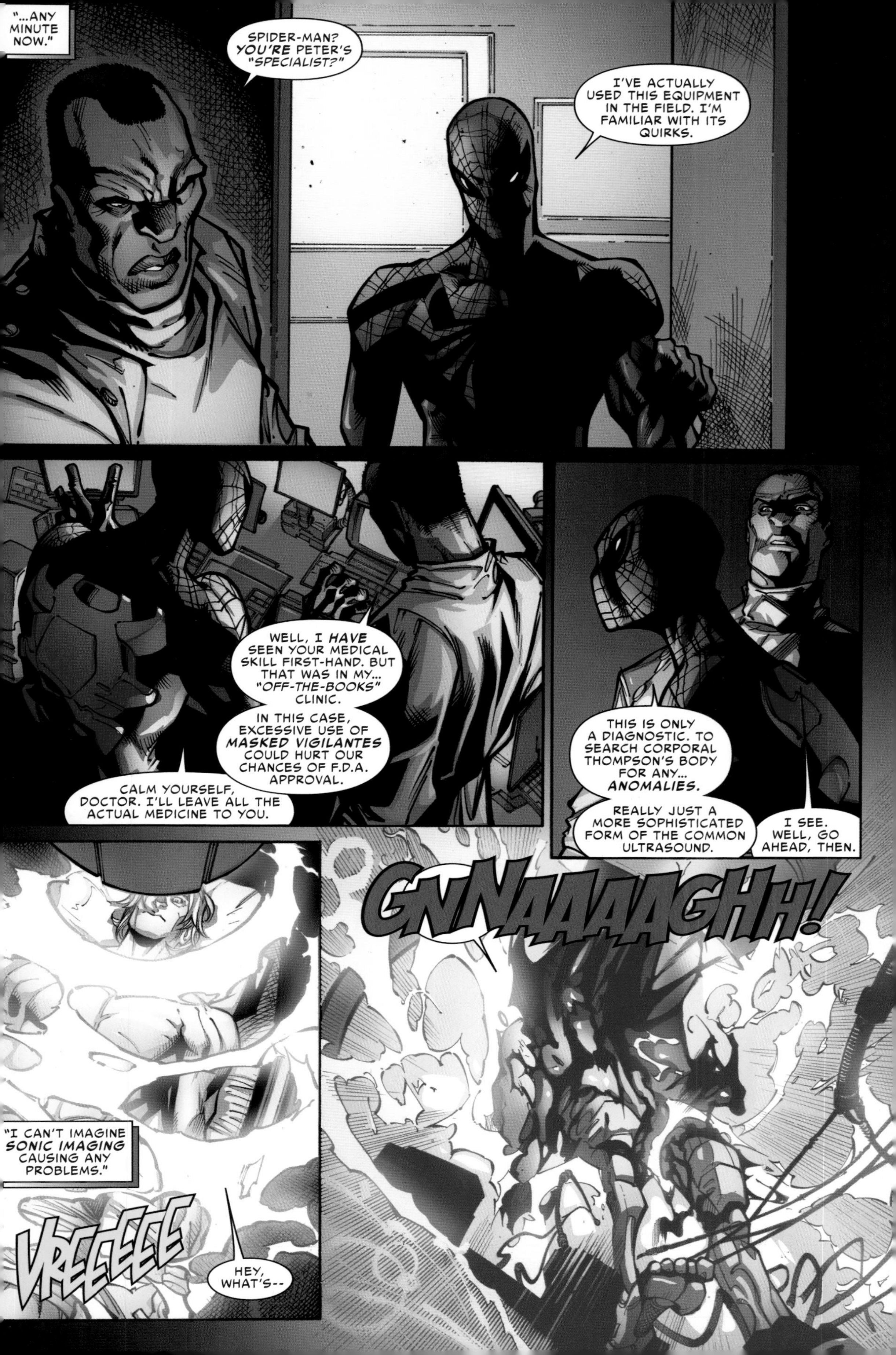

"...ANY MINUTE NOW."
SPIDER-MAN? YOU'RE PETER'S "SPECIALIST?"
I'VE ACTUALLY USED THIS EQUIPMENT IN THE FIELD. I'M FAMILIAR WITH ITS QUIRKS.
WELL, I HAVE SEEN YOUR MEDICAL SKILL FIRST-HAND. BUT THAT WAS IN MY... "OFF-THE-BOOKS" CLINIC.
IN THIS CASE, EXCESSIVE USE OF MASKED VIGILANTES COULD HURT OUR CHANCES OF F.D.A. APPROVAL.
CALM YOURSELF, DOCTOR. I'LL LEAVE ALL THE ACTUAL MEDICINE TO YOU.
THIS IS ONLY A DIAGNOSTIC. TO SEARCH CORPORAL THOMPSON'S BODY FOR ANY... ANOMALIES.
REALLY JUST A MORE SOPHISTICATED FORM OF THE COMMON ULTRASOUND.
I SEE. WELL, GO AHEAD, THEN.
"I CAN'T IMAGINE SONIC IMAGING CAUSING ANY PROBLEMS."
VREEEEE
HEY, WHAT'S--
GNNAAAAAGHH!

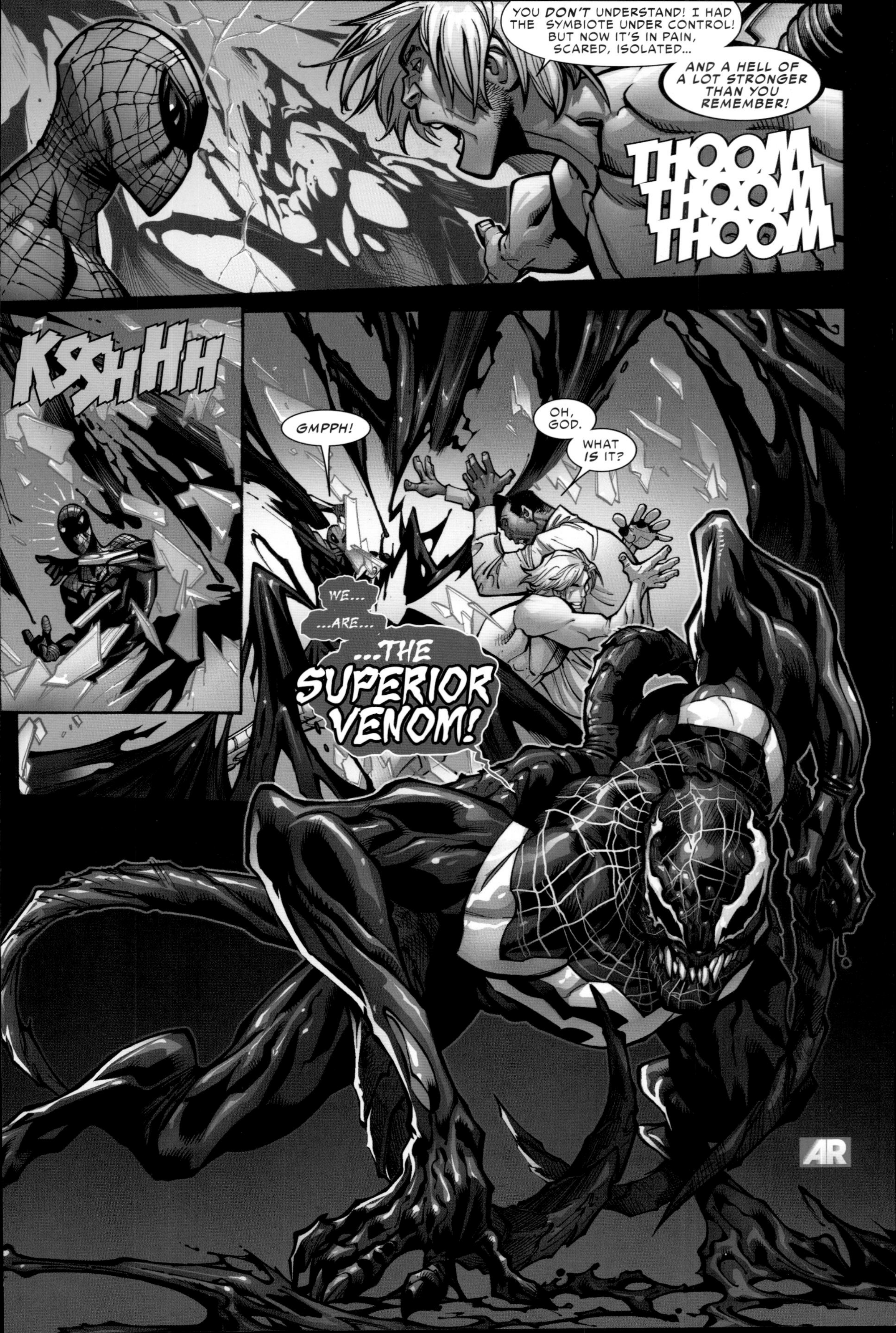
YOU DON'T UNDERSTAND! I HAD THE SYMBIOTE UNDER CONTROL! BUT NOW IT'S IN PAIN, SCARED, ISOLATED...
AND A HELL OF A LOT STRONGER THAN YOU REMEMBER!
THOOM THOOM THOOM
KSSHHH
GMPPH!
OH, GOD.
WHAT IS IT?
WE...
...ARE...
...THE SUPERIOR VENOM!
AR

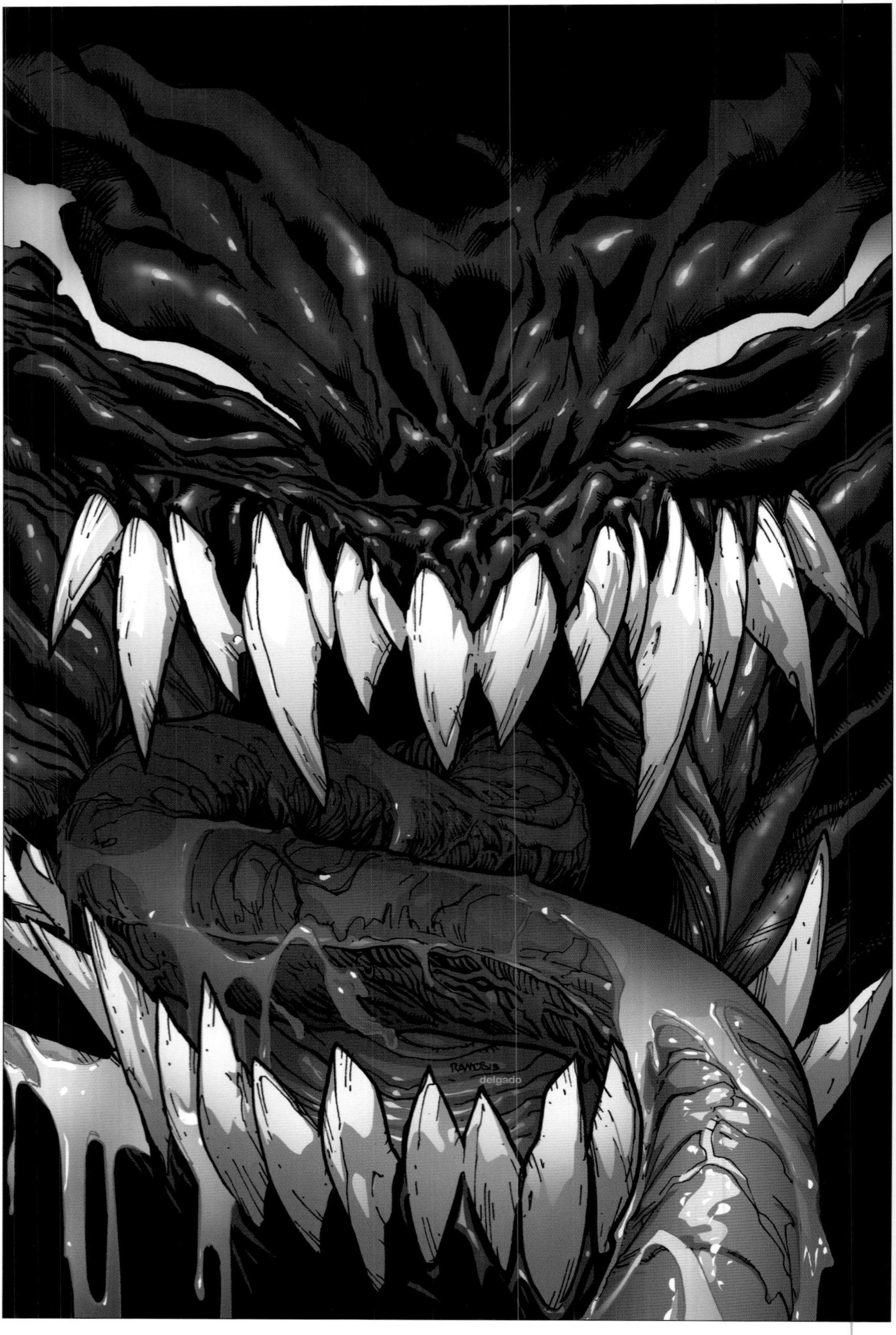
RAMOS'13
delgado

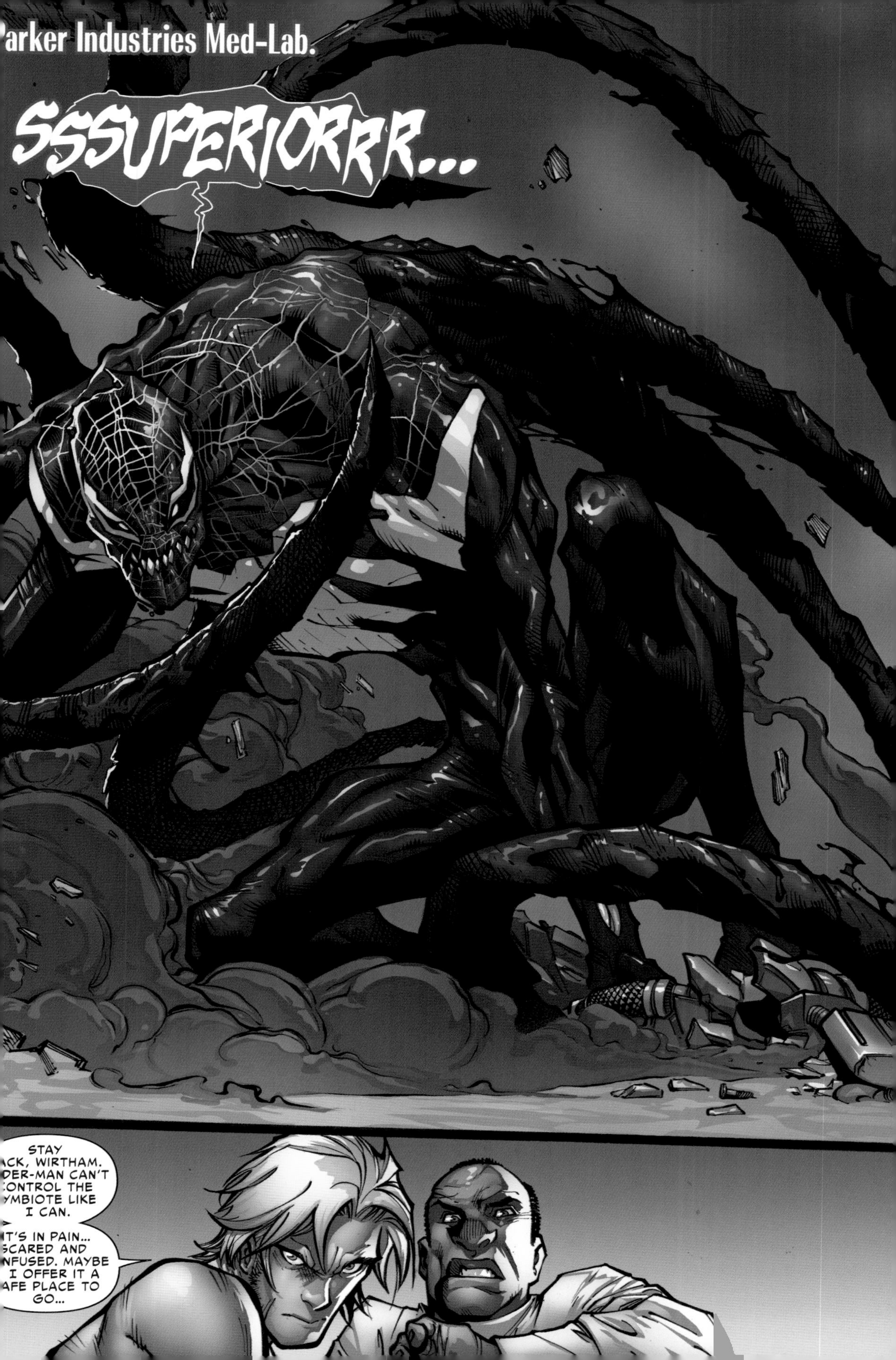
arker Industries Med-Lab.
SSSUPERIORRRR...
STAY ACK, WIRTHAM. DER-MAN CAN'T CONTROL THE YMBIOTE LIKE I CAN.
T'S IN PAIN... SCARED AND NFUSED. MAYBE I OFFER IT A AFE PLACE TO GO...

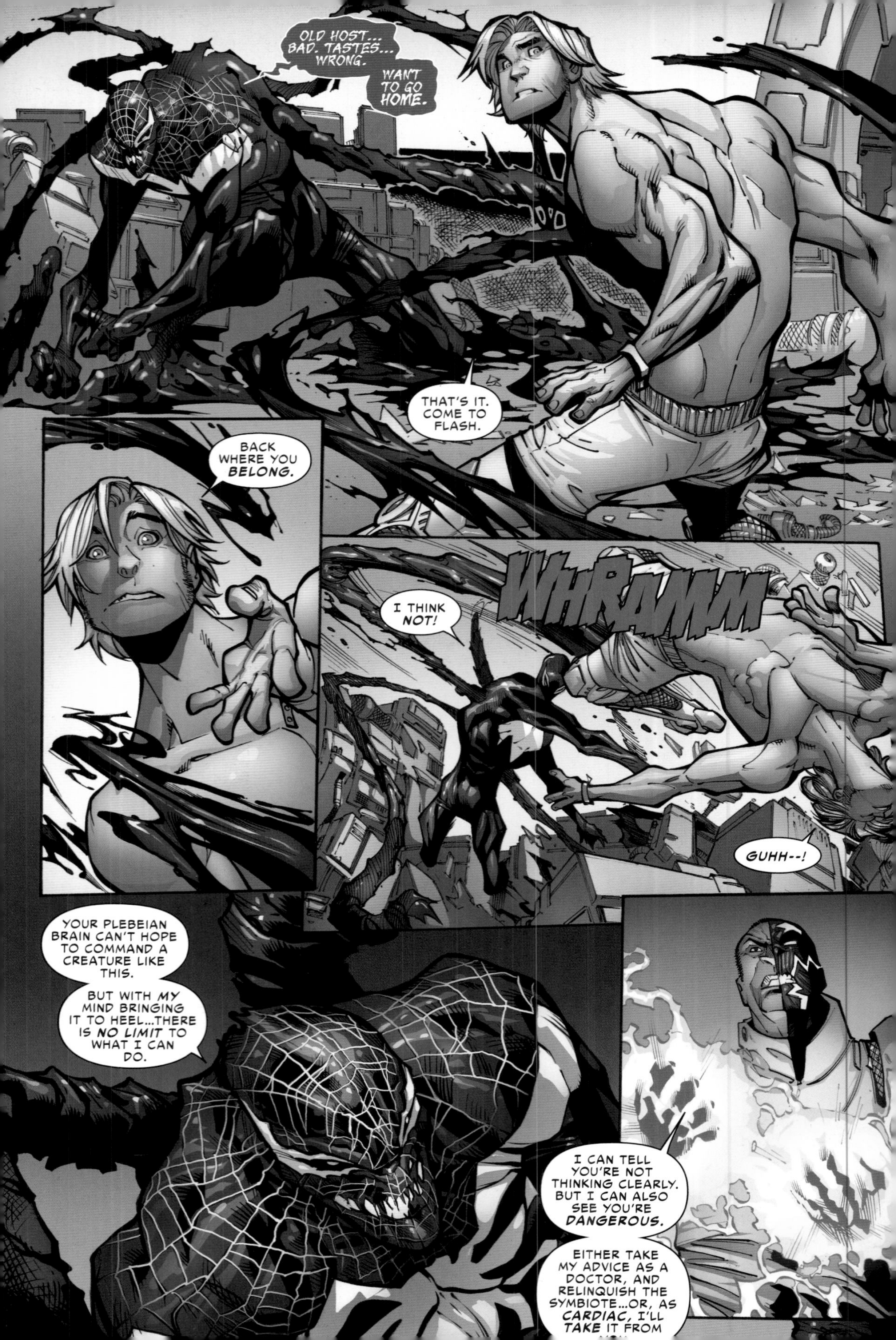
OLD HOST... BAD. TASTES... WRONG.
WANT TO GO HOME.
THAT'S IT. COME TO FLASH.
BACK WHERE YOU BELONG.
WHRAMM
I THINK NOT!
GUHH--!
YOUR PLEBEIAN BRAIN CAN'T HOPE TO COMMAND A CREATURE LIKE THIS.
BUT WITH MY MIND BRINGING IT TO HEEL...THERE IS NO LIMIT TO WHAT I CAN DO.
I CAN TELL YOU'RE NOT THINKING CLEARLY. BUT I CAN ALSO SEE YOU'RE DANGEROUS.
EITHER TAKE MY ADVICE AS A DOCTOR, AND RELINQUISH THE SYMBIOTE...OR, AS CARDIAC, I'LL TAKE IT FROM

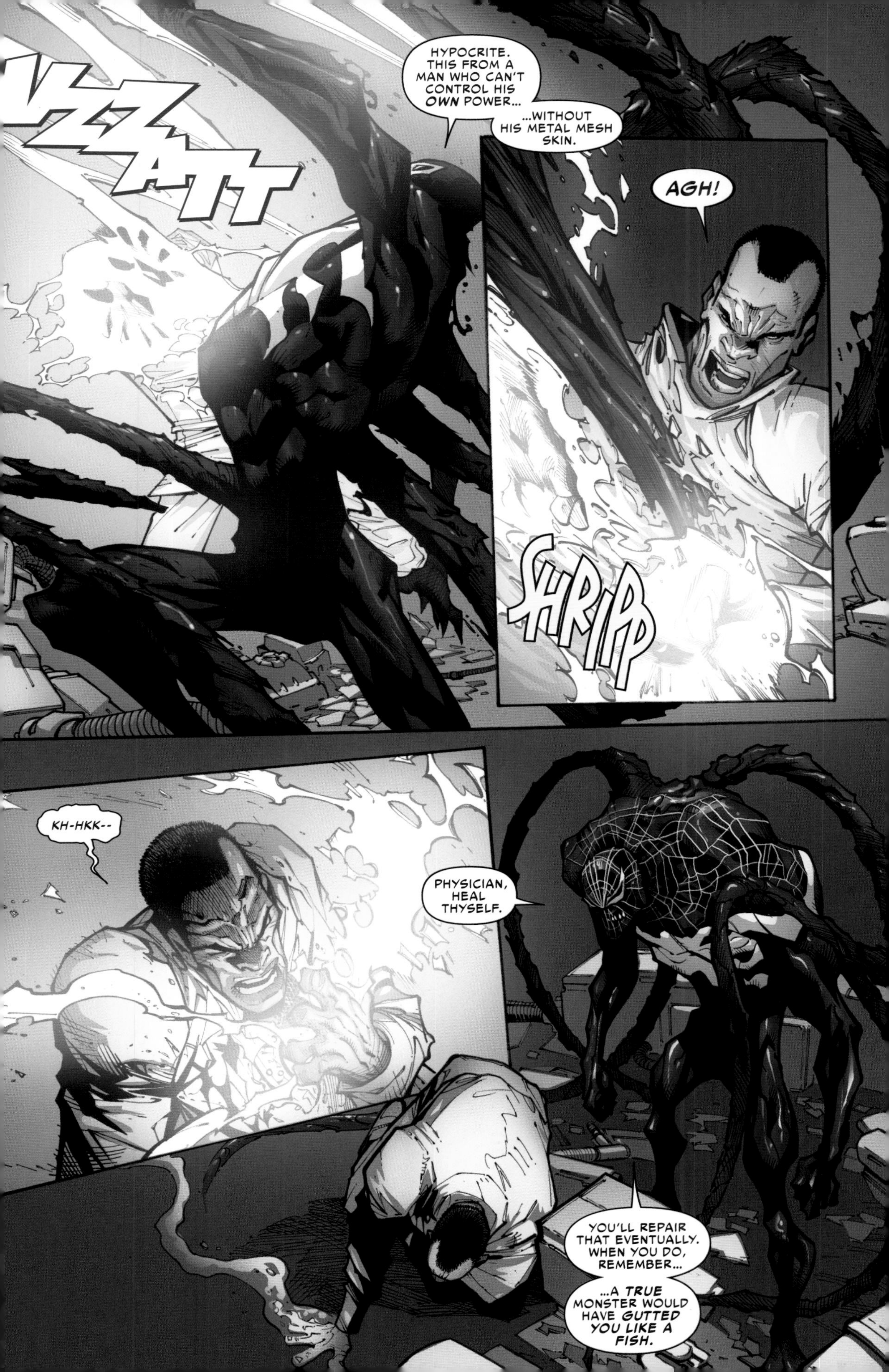
ZZATT
HYPOCRITE. THIS FROM A MAN WHO CAN'T CONTROL HIS *OWN* POWER...
...WITHOUT HIS METAL MESH SKIN.
AGH!
SHRIPP
KH-HKK--
PHYSICIAN, HEAL THYSELF.
YOU'LL REPAIR THAT EVENTUALLY. WHEN YOU DO, REMEMBER...
...A *TRUE* MONSTER WOULD HAVE *GUTTED* YOU LIKE A *FISH*.

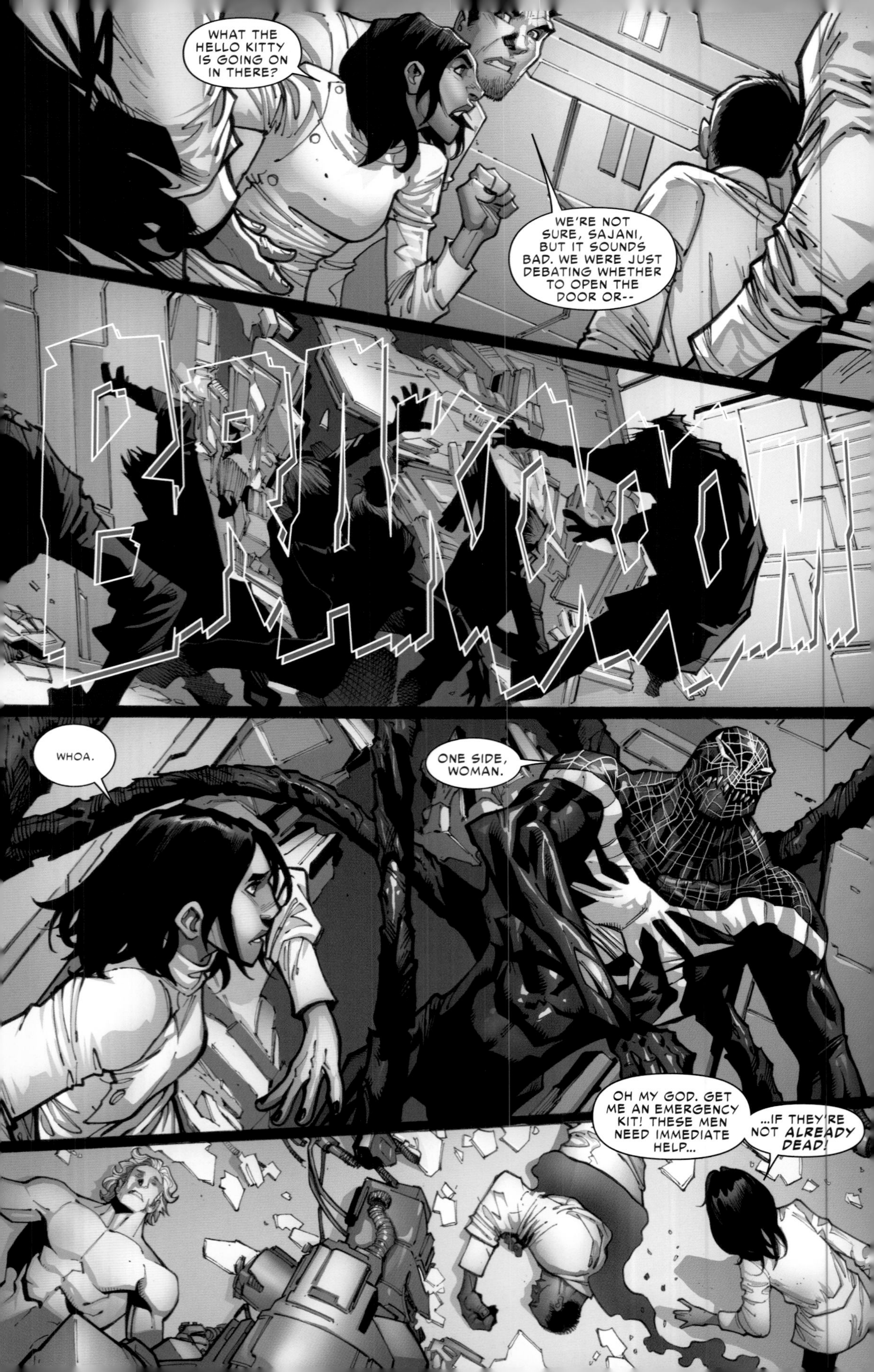
WHAT THE HELLO KITTY IS GOING ON IN THERE?
WE'RE NOT SURE, SAJANI, BUT IT SOUNDS BAD. WE WERE JUST DEBATING WHETHER TO OPEN THE DOOR OR--
WHOA.
ONE SIDE, WOMAN.
OH MY GOD. GET ME AN EMERGENCY KIT! THESE MEN NEED IMMEDIATE HELP...
...IF THEY'RE NOT *ALREADY DEAD!*

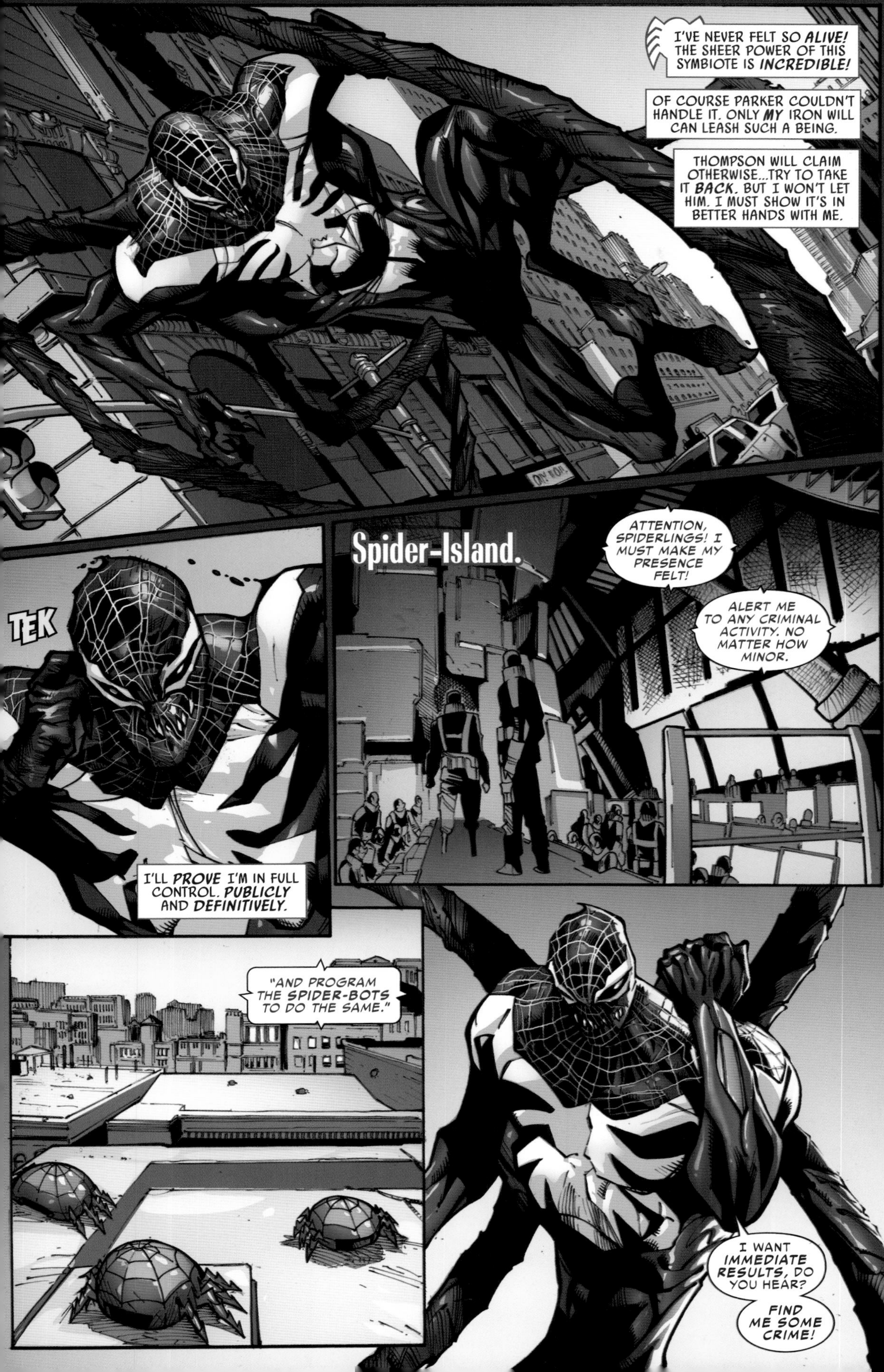

I'VE NEVER FELT SO ALIVE! THE SHEER POWER OF THIS SYMBIOTE IS INCREDIBLE!
OF COURSE PARKER COULDN'T HANDLE IT. ONLY MY IRON WILL CAN LEASH SUCH A BEING.
THOMPSON WILL CLAIM OTHERWISE...TRY TO TAKE IT BACK. BUT I WON'T LET HIM. I MUST SHOW IT'S IN BETTER HANDS WITH ME.
TEK
I'LL PROVE I'M IN FULL CONTROL. PUBLICLY AND DEFINITIVELY.
Spider-Island.
ATTENTION, SPIDERLINGS! I MUST MAKE MY PRESENCE FELT!
ALERT ME TO ANY CRIMINAL ACTIVITY. NO MATTER HOW MINOR.
"AND PROGRAM THE SPIDER-BOTS TO DO THE SAME."
I WANT IMMEDIATE RESULTS, DO YOU HEAR?
FIND ME SOME CRIME!

Parker Industries.

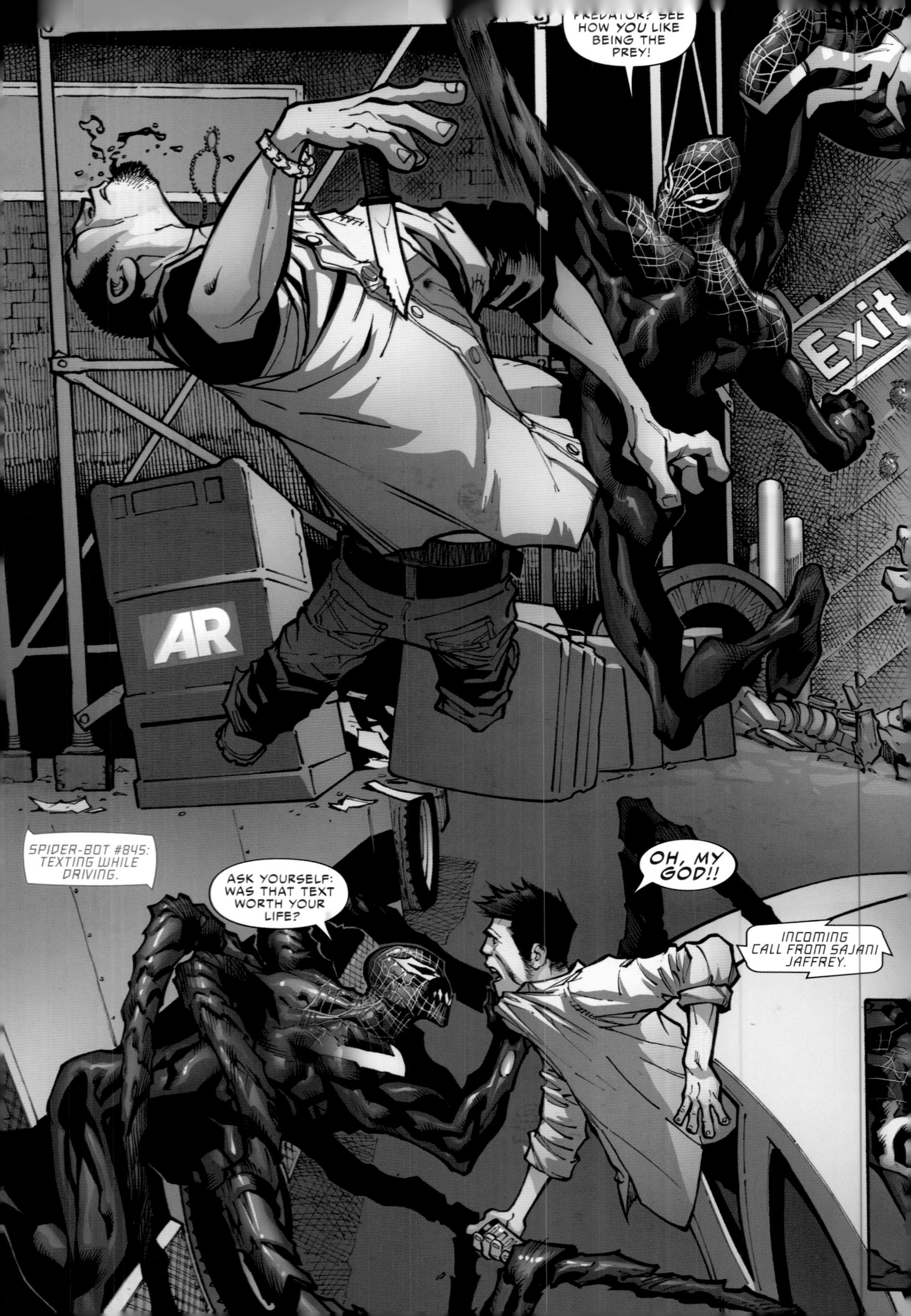
HOW YOU LIKE BEING THE PREY!
Exit
AR
SPIDER-BOT #845: TEXTING WHILE DRIVING.
ASK YOURSELF: WAS THAT TEXT WORTH YOUR LIFE?
OH, MY GOD!!
INCOMING CALL FROM SAJANI JAFFREY.

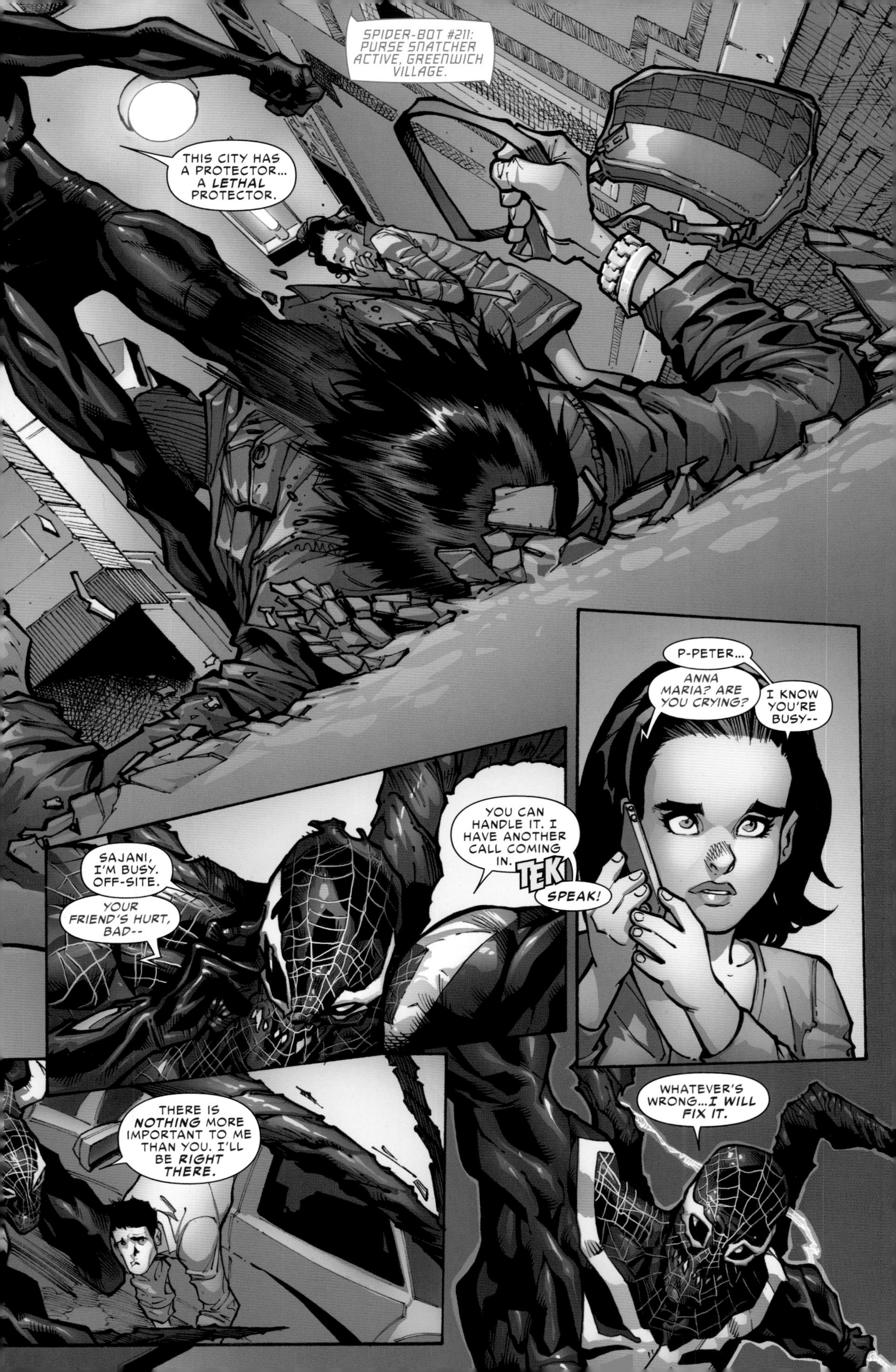
SPIDER-BOT #211: PURSE SNATCHER ACTIVE, GREENWICH VILLAGE.
THIS CITY HAS A PROTECTOR... A LETHAL PROTECTOR.
P-PETER...
ANNA MARIA? ARE YOU CRYING?
I KNOW YOU'RE BUSY--
SAJANI, I'M BUSY. OFF-SITE.
YOUR FRIEND'S HURT, BAD--
YOU CAN HANDLE IT. I HAVE ANOTHER CALL COMING IN.
TEK!
SPEAK!
THERE IS NOTHING MORE IMPORTANT TO ME THAN YOU. I'LL BE RIGHT THERE.
WHATEVER'S WRONG...I WILL FIX IT.

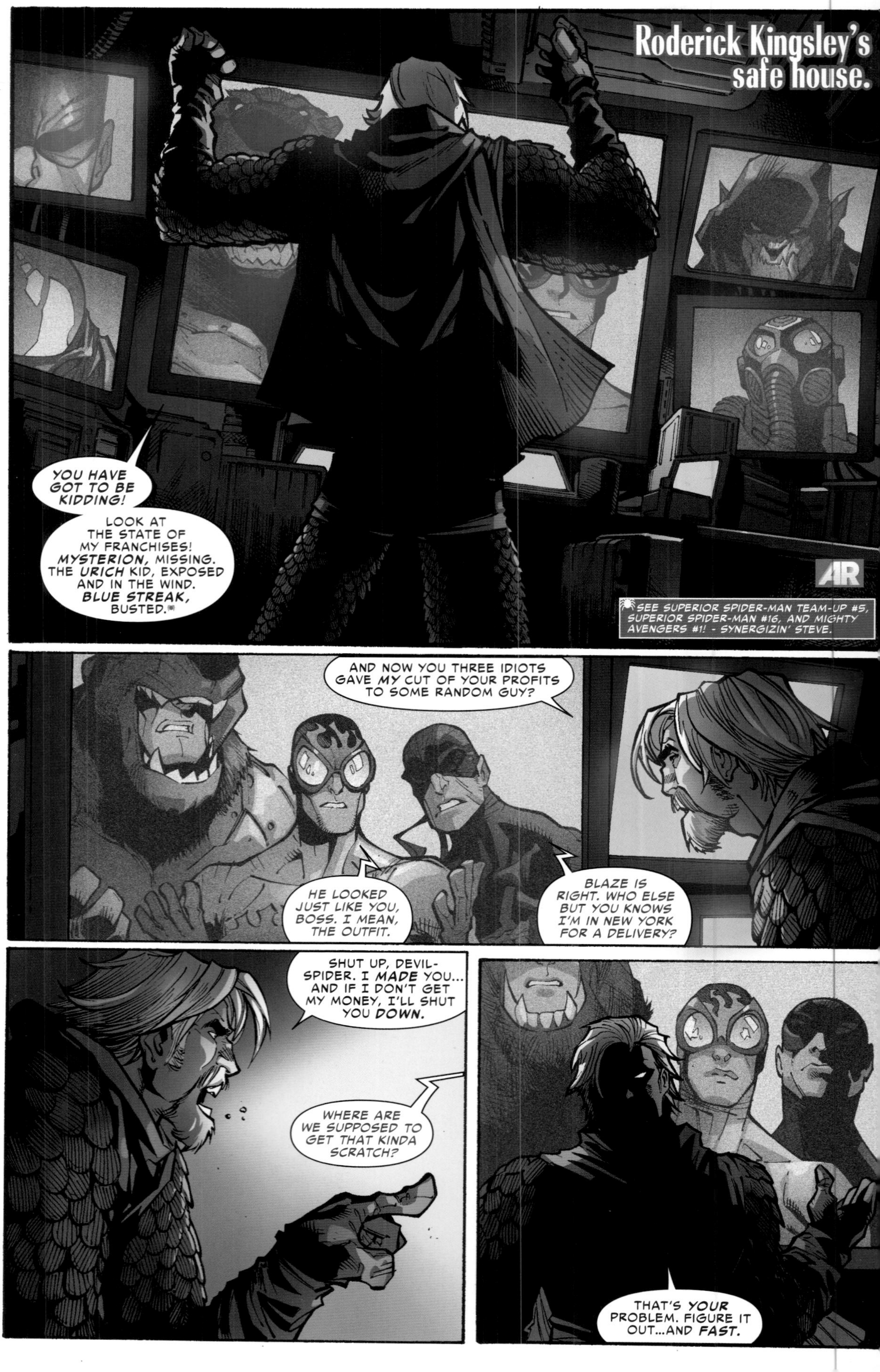
Roderick Kingsley's safe house.
YOU HAVE GOT TO BE KIDDING!
LOOK AT THE STATE OF MY FRANCHISES! MYSTERION, MISSING. THE URICH KID, EXPOSED AND IN THE WIND. BLUE STREAK, BUSTED.*
*SEE SUPERIOR SPIDER-MAN TEAM-UP #5, SUPERIOR SPIDER-MAN #16, AND MIGHTY AVENGERS #1! - SYNERGIZIN' STEVE.
AND NOW YOU THREE IDIOTS GAVE MY CUT OF YOUR PROFITS TO SOME RANDOM GUY?
HE LOOKED JUST LIKE YOU, BOSS. I MEAN, THE OUTFIT.
BLAZE IS RIGHT. WHO ELSE BUT YOU KNOWS I'M IN NEW YORK FOR A DELIVERY?
SHUT UP, DEVIL-SPIDER. I MADE YOU... AND IF I DON'T GET MY MONEY, I'LL SHUT YOU DOWN.
WHERE ARE WE SUPPOSED TO GET THAT KINDA SCRATCH?
THAT'S YOUR PROBLEM. FIGURE IT OUT...AND FAST.

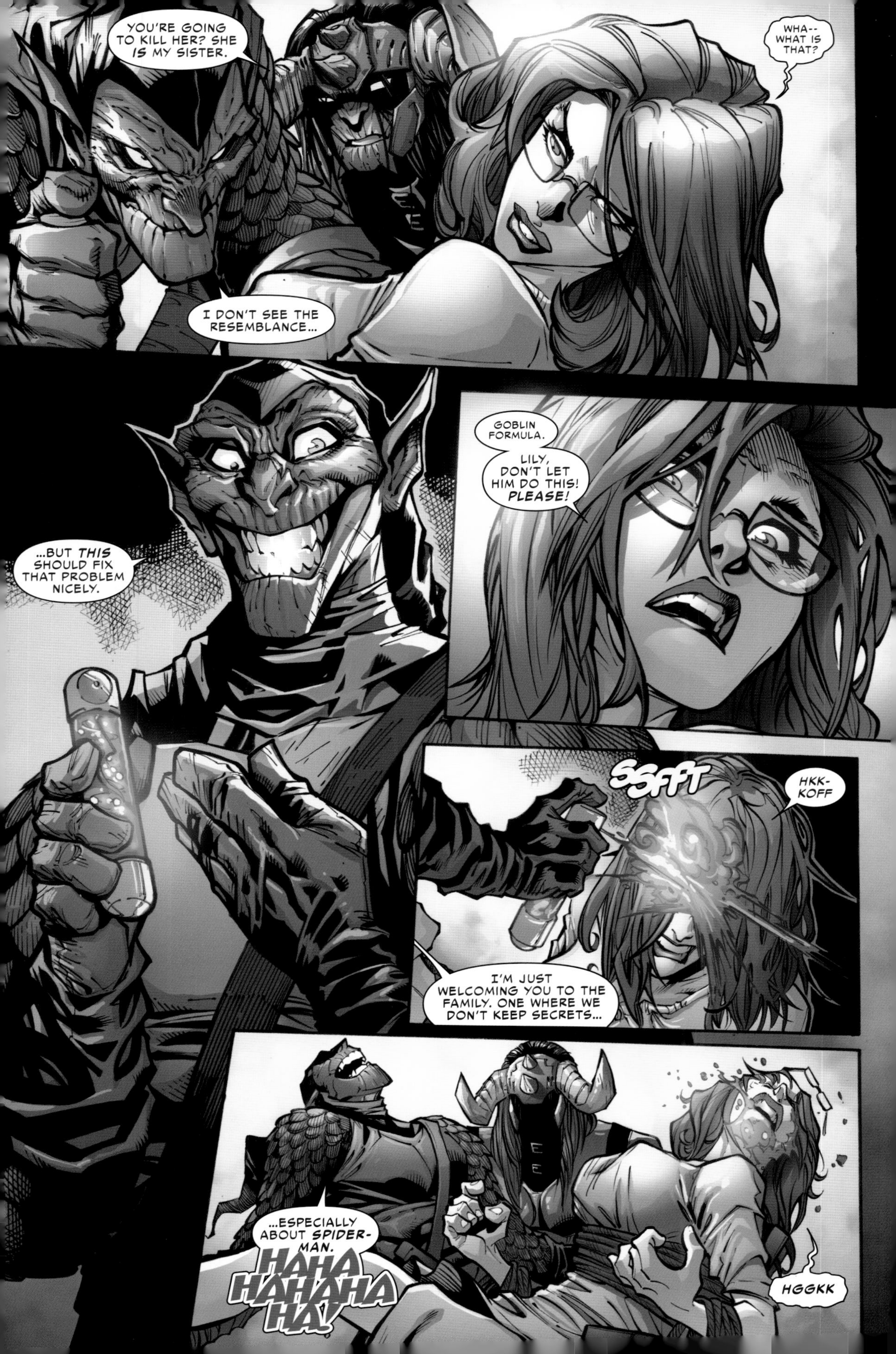
YOU'RE GOING TO KILL HER? SHE IS MY SISTER.
WHA-- WHAT IS THAT?
I DON'T SEE THE RESEMBLANCE...
...BUT THIS SHOULD FIX THAT PROBLEM NICELY.
GOBLIN FORMULA.
LILY, DON'T LET HIM DO THIS! PLEASE!
SSFFT
HKK-KOFF
I'M JUST WELCOMING YOU TO THE FAMILY. ONE WHERE WE DON'T KEEP SECRETS...
...ESPECIALLY ABOUT SPIDER-MAN.
HAHA HAHAHAHA HA!
HGGKK

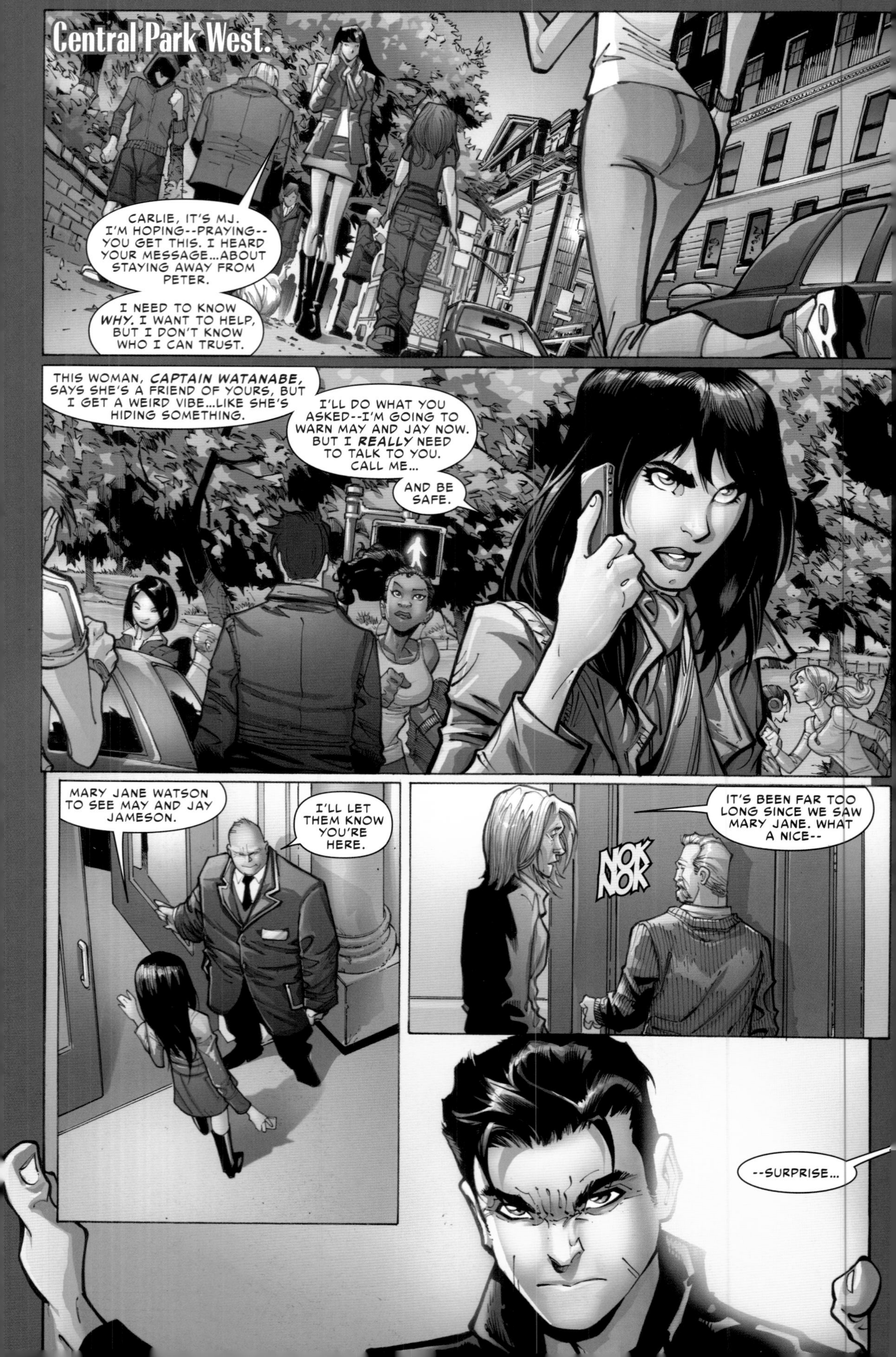
Central Park West.
CARLIE, IT'S MJ. I'M HOPING--PRAYING--YOU GET THIS. I HEARD YOUR MESSAGE...ABOUT STAYING AWAY FROM PETER.
I NEED TO KNOW WHY. I WANT TO HELP, BUT I DON'T KNOW WHO I CAN TRUST.
THIS WOMAN, CAPTAIN WATANABE, SAYS SHE'S A FRIEND OF YOURS, BUT I GET A WEIRD VIBE...LIKE SHE'S HIDING SOMETHING.
I'LL DO WHAT YOU ASKED--I'M GOING TO WARN MAY AND JAY NOW. BUT I REALLY NEED TO TALK TO YOU. CALL ME...
AND BE SAFE.
MARY JANE WATSON TO SEE MAY AND JAY JAMESON.
I'LL LET THEM KNOW YOU'RE HERE.
IT'S BEEN FAR TOO LONG SINCE WE SAW MARY JANE. WHAT A NICE--
NOK NOK
--SURPRISE...

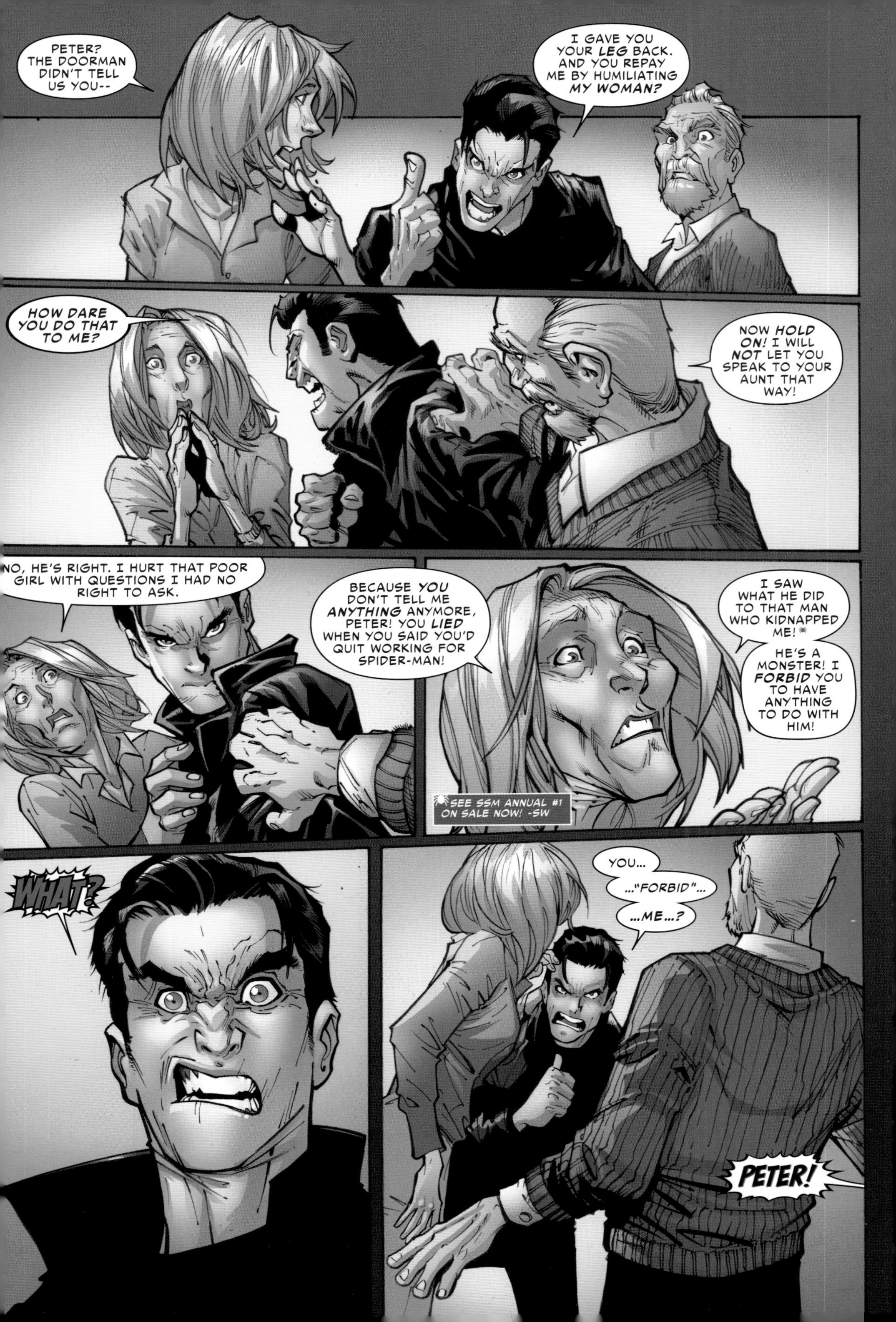
PETER? THE DOORMAN DIDN'T TELL US YOU--
I GAVE YOU YOUR LEG BACK. AND YOU REPAY ME BY HUMILIATING MY WOMAN?
HOW DARE YOU DO THAT TO ME?
NOW HOLD ON! I WILL NOT LET YOU SPEAK TO YOUR AUNT THAT WAY!
NO, HE'S RIGHT. I HURT THAT POOR GIRL WITH QUESTIONS I HAD NO RIGHT TO ASK.
BECAUSE YOU DON'T TELL ME ANYTHING ANYMORE, PETER! YOU LIED WHEN YOU SAID YOU'D QUIT WORKING FOR SPIDER-MAN!
I SAW WHAT HE DID TO THAT MAN WHO KIDNAPPED ME!
HE'S A MONSTER! I FORBID YOU TO HAVE ANYTHING TO DO WITH HIM!
SEE SSM ANNUAL #1 ON SALE NOW! -SW
WHAT?
YOU...
..."FORBID"...
...ME...?
PETER!

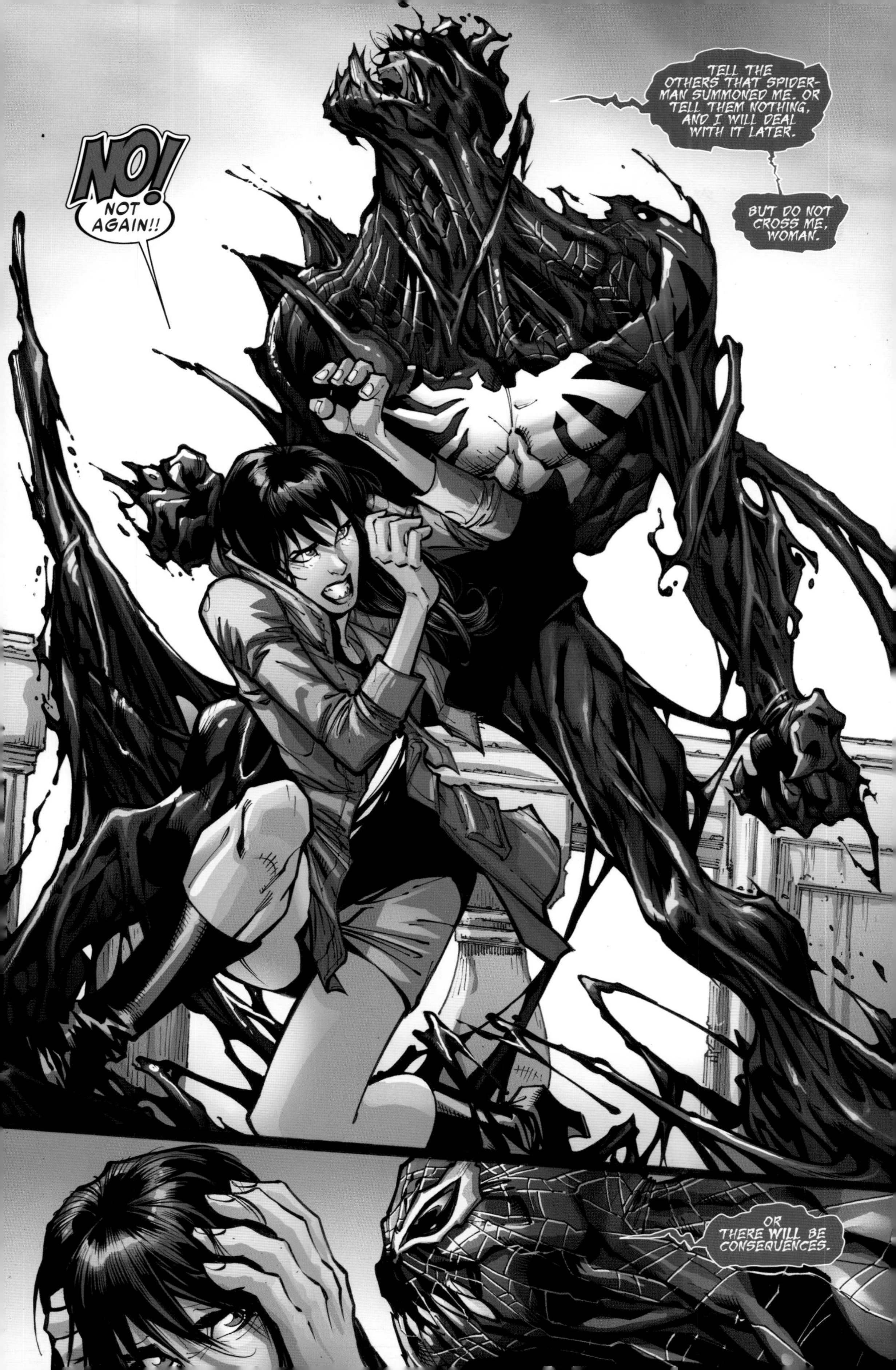
NO!
NOT AGAIN!!
TELL THE OTHERS THAT SPIDER-MAN SUMMONED ME. OR TELL THEM NOTHING, AND I WILL DEAL WITH IT LATER.
BUT DO NOT CROSS ME, WOMAN.
OR THERE WILL BE CONSEQUENCES.

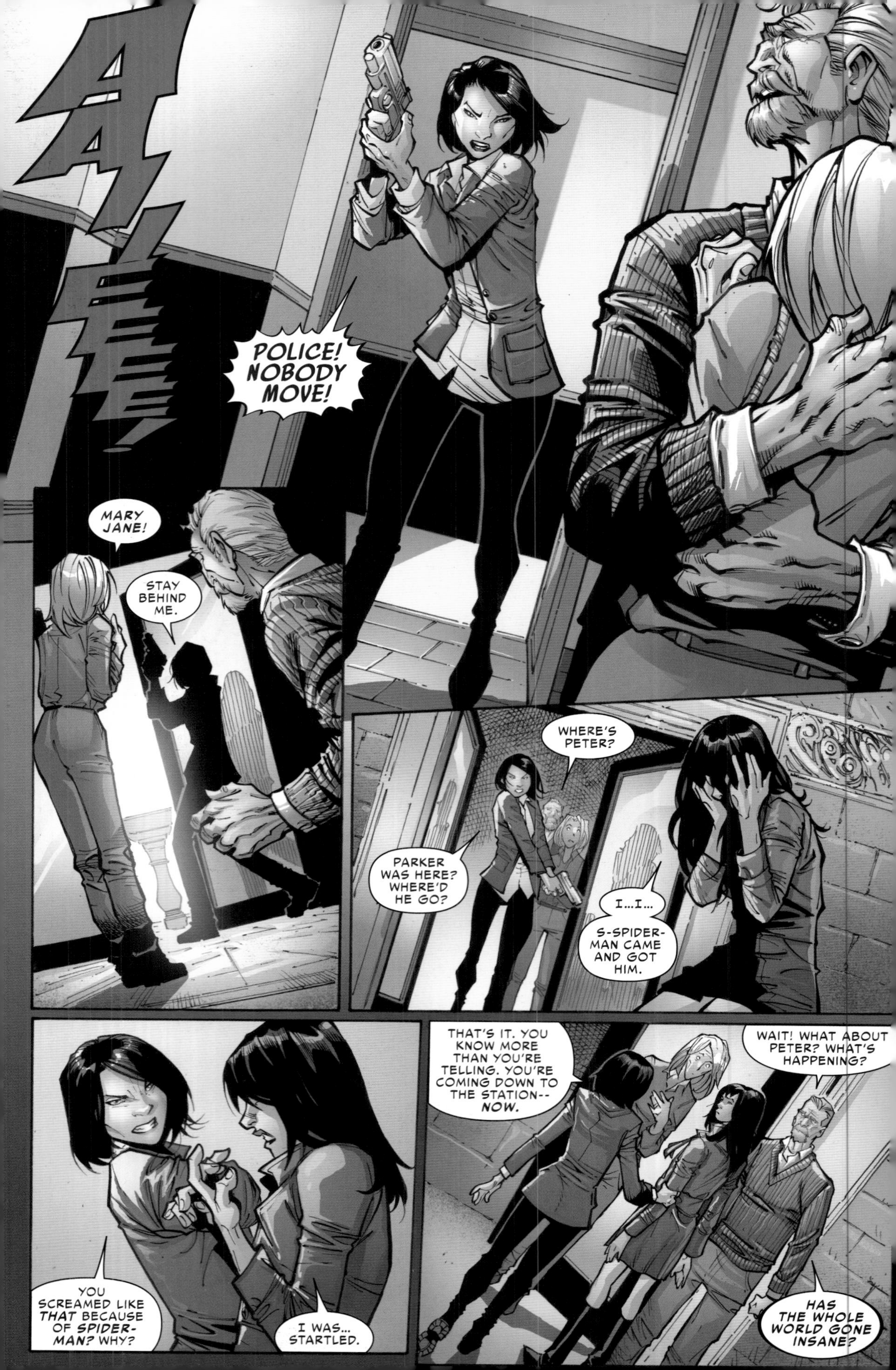
AAIEEE!
POLICE! NOBODY MOVE!
MARY JANE!
STAY BEHIND ME.
WHERE'S PETER?
PARKER WAS HERE? WHERE'D HE GO?
I...I...
S-SPIDER-MAN CAME AND GOT HIM.
YOU SCREAMED LIKE THAT BECAUSE OF SPIDER-MAN? WHY?
I WAS... STARTLED.
THAT'S IT. YOU KNOW MORE THAN YOU'RE TELLING. YOU'RE COMING DOWN TO THE STATION-- NOW.
WAIT! WHAT ABOUT PETER? WHAT'S HAPPENING?
HAS THE WHOLE WORLD GONE INSANE?

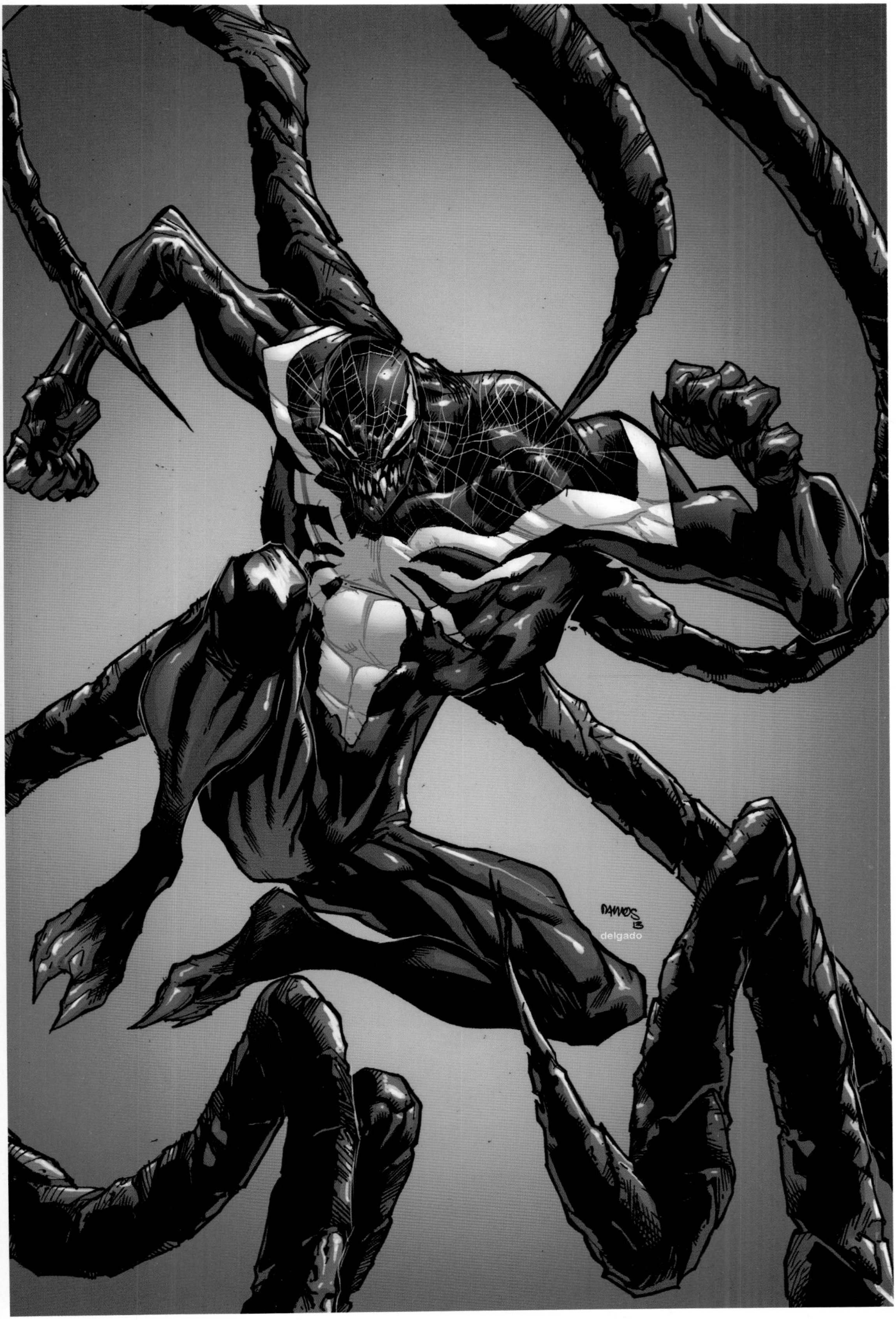
delgado

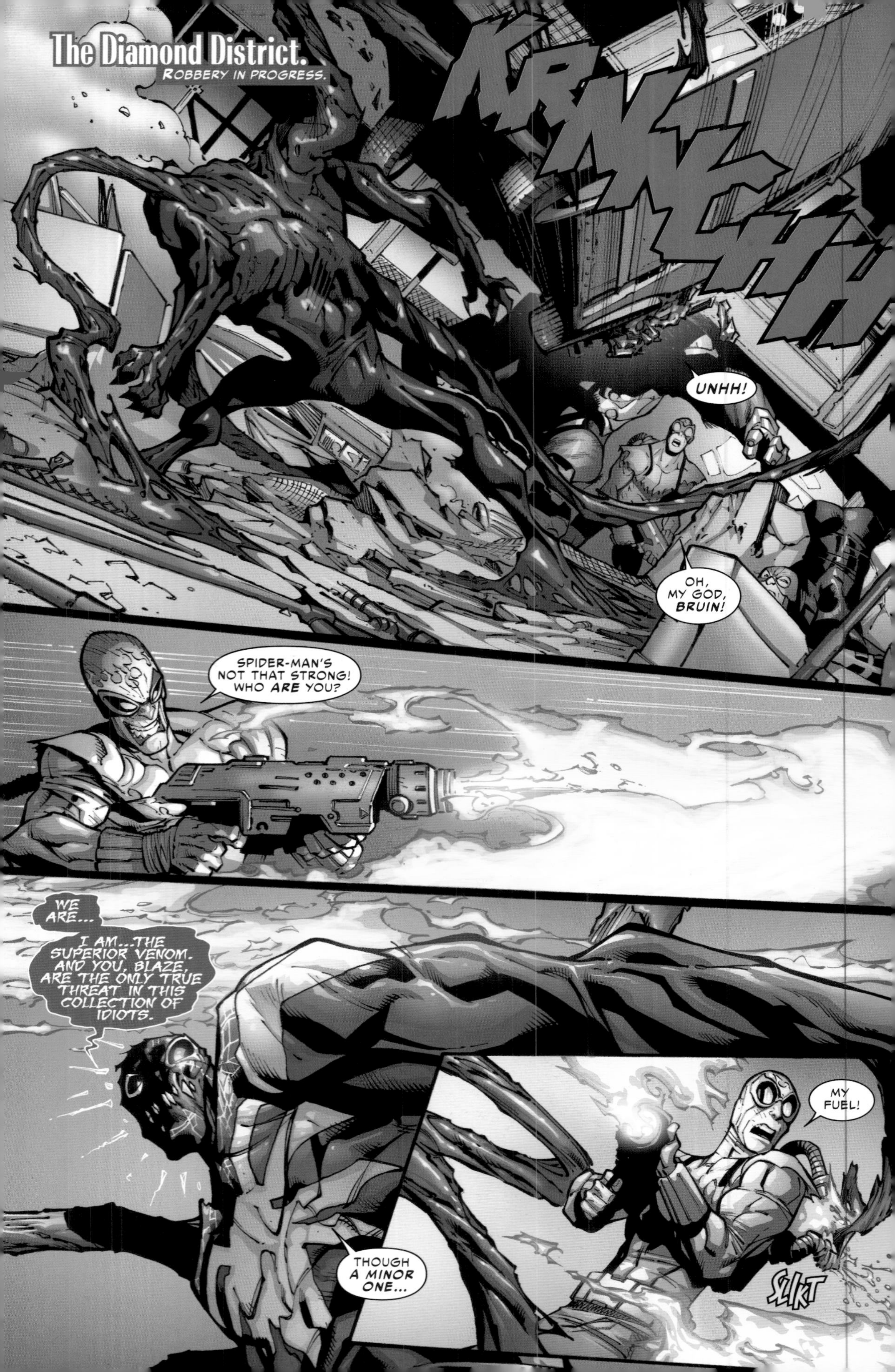
The Diamond District.
ROBBERY IN PROGRESS.
KRAKKCHH
UNHH!
OH, MY GOD, BRUIN!
SPIDER-MAN'S NOT THAT STRONG! WHO ARE YOU?
WE ARE...
I AM...THE SUPERIOR VENOM. AND YOU, BLAZE, ARE THE ONLY TRUE THREAT IN THIS COLLECTION OF IDIOTS.
THOUGH A MINOR ONE...
MY FUEL!
SLIKT

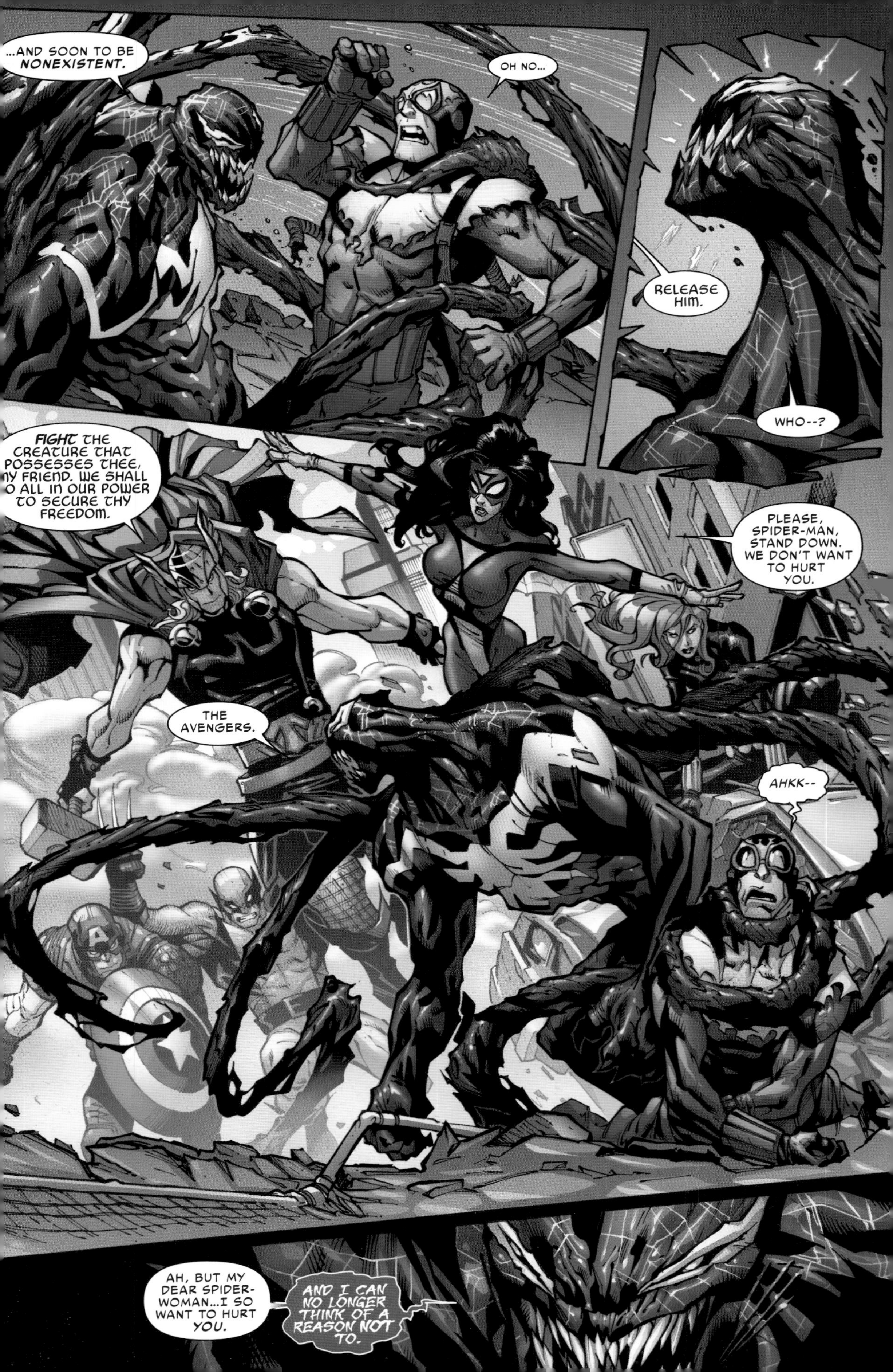
...AND SOON TO BE *NONEXISTENT.*
OH NO...
RELEASE HIM.
WHO--?
FIGHT THE CREATURE THAT POSSESSES THEE, MY FRIEND. WE SHALL DO ALL IN OUR POWER TO SECURE THY FREEDOM.
PLEASE, SPIDER-MAN, STAND DOWN. WE DON'T WANT TO HURT YOU.
THE AVENGERS.
AHKK--
AH, BUT MY DEAR SPIDER-WOMAN...I SO WANT TO HURT *YOU.*
AND I CAN NO LONGER THINK OF A REASON *NOT* TO.

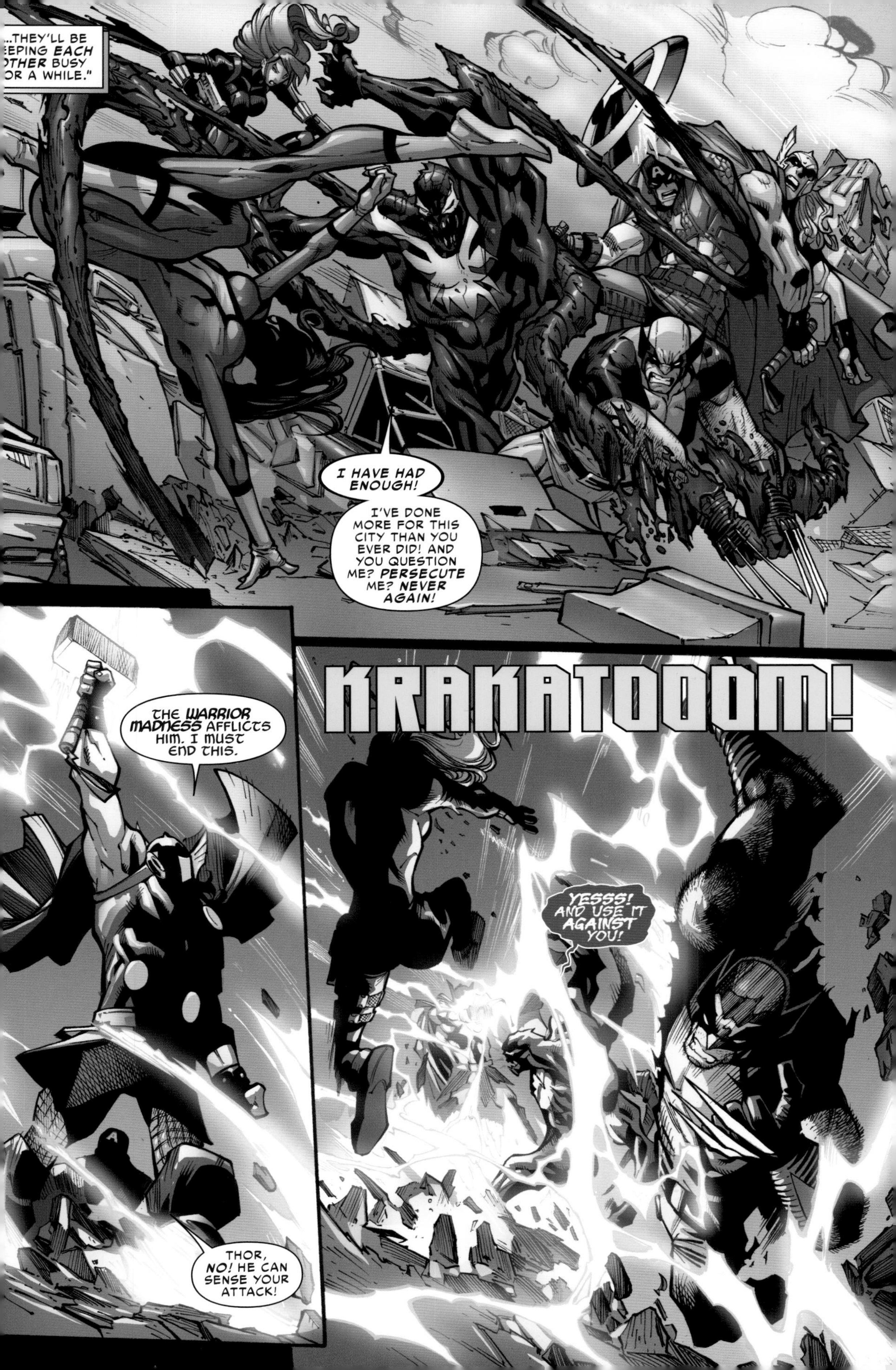
...THEY'LL BE KEEPING EACH OTHER BUSY FOR A WHILE."
I HAVE HAD ENOUGH!
I'VE DONE MORE FOR THIS CITY THAN YOU EVER DID! AND YOU QUESTION ME? PERSECUTE ME? NEVER AGAIN!
THE WARRIOR MADNESS AFFLICTS HIM. I MUST END THIS.
THOR, NO! HE CAN SENSE YOUR ATTACK!
KRAKATOOOM!
YESSS! AND USE IT AGAINST YOU!

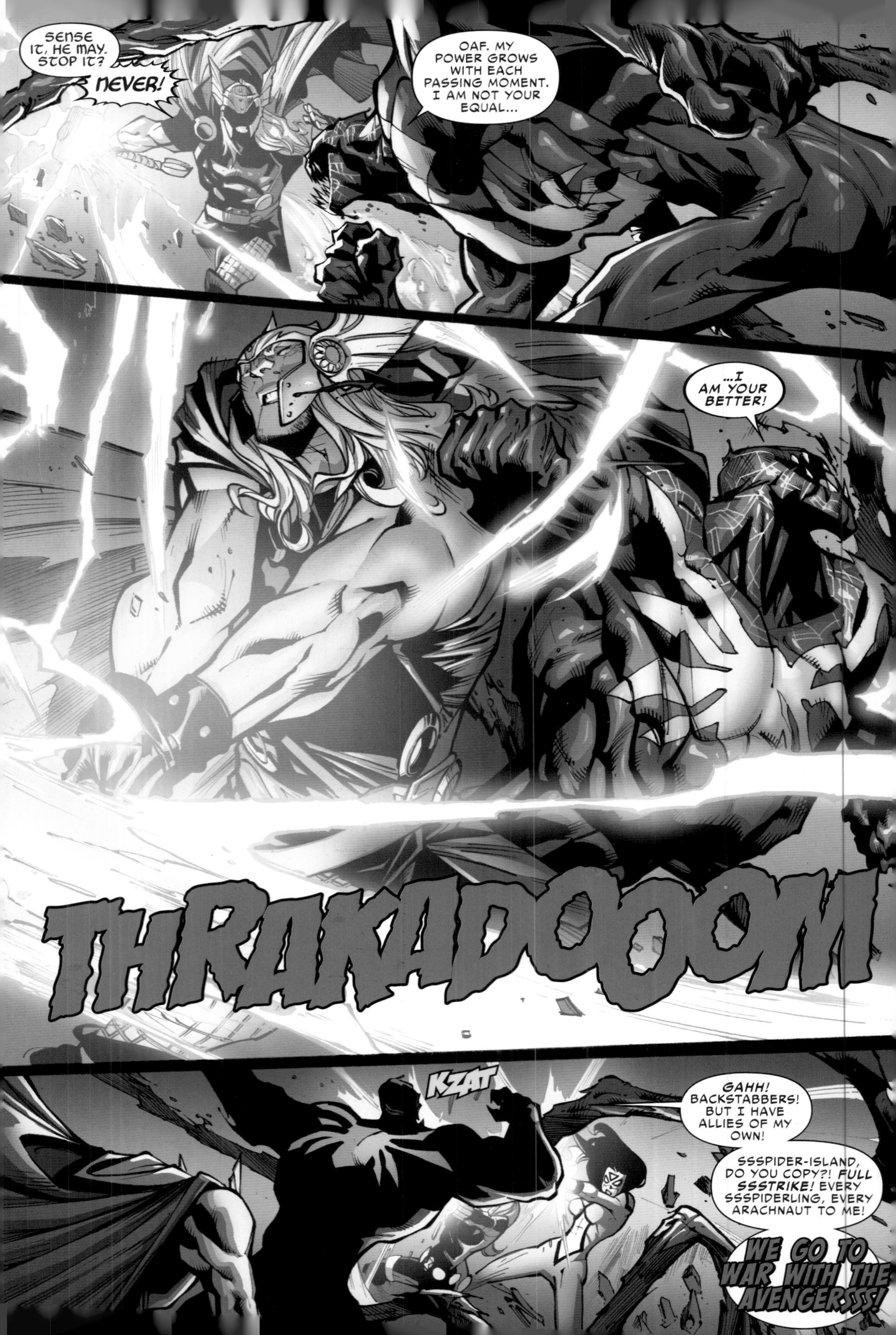
SENSE IT, HE MAY. STOP IT? NEVER!
OAF. MY POWER GROWS WITH EACH PASSING MOMENT. I AM NOT YOUR EQUAL...
...I AM YOUR BETTER!
THRAKADOOOM
KZAT
GAHH! BACKSTABBERS! BUT I HAVE ALLIES OF MY OWN!
SSSPIDER-ISLAND, DO YOU COPY?! FULL SSSTRIKE! EVERY SSSPIDERLING, EVERY ARACHNAUT TO ME!
WE GO TO WAR WITH THE AVENGERSSS!

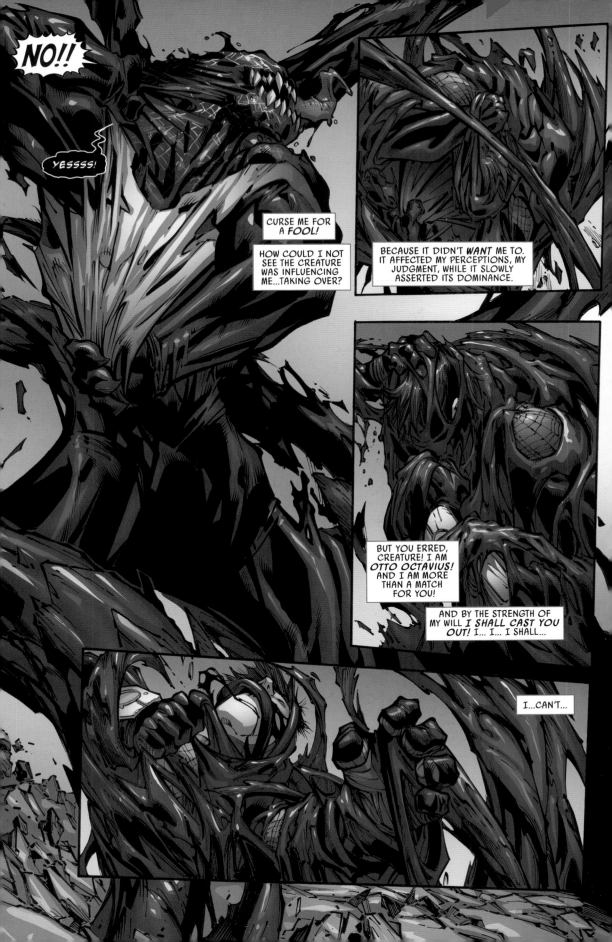

NOW YOU LISTEN TO ME, CAPTAIN. YOU HAVE *NO RIGHT* TO HOLD MARY JANE WATSON. ARREST HER, OR RELEASE HER...

...AND IF YOU CHARGE HER, MY NEXT CALL IS TO MY SON, JONAH...THE *MAYOR OF NEW YORK.*

CALM DOWN, MR. JAMESON. SHE'S FREE TO GO.

BUT I'LL BE KEEPING AN EYE ON MS. WATSON. *AND* PETER PARKER. BECAUSE IF THEY WON'T HELP ME FIND OUT WHY CARLIE COOPER DISAPPEARED...

...I CAN ONLY ASSUME IT'S BECAUSE THEY HAVE SOMETHING TO *HIDE.*

THANK YOU, MAY...JAY. I'M SO SORRY.

ABOUT *WHAT?* WHAT'S GOING ON? AND WHAT HAPPENED TO PETER?

HE WAS ACTING LIKE--MARY JANE, IS HE USING *DRUGS?*

NO. I'LL TELL YOU EVERYTHING, I PROMISE. BUT I--I JUST CAN'T RIGHT NOW.

I'M EXHAUSTED. I NEED TO GO HOME... GET SOME SLEEP. I'LL CALL YOU SOON.

BUT PETER'S OKAY, ISN'T HE?

MARY JANE?

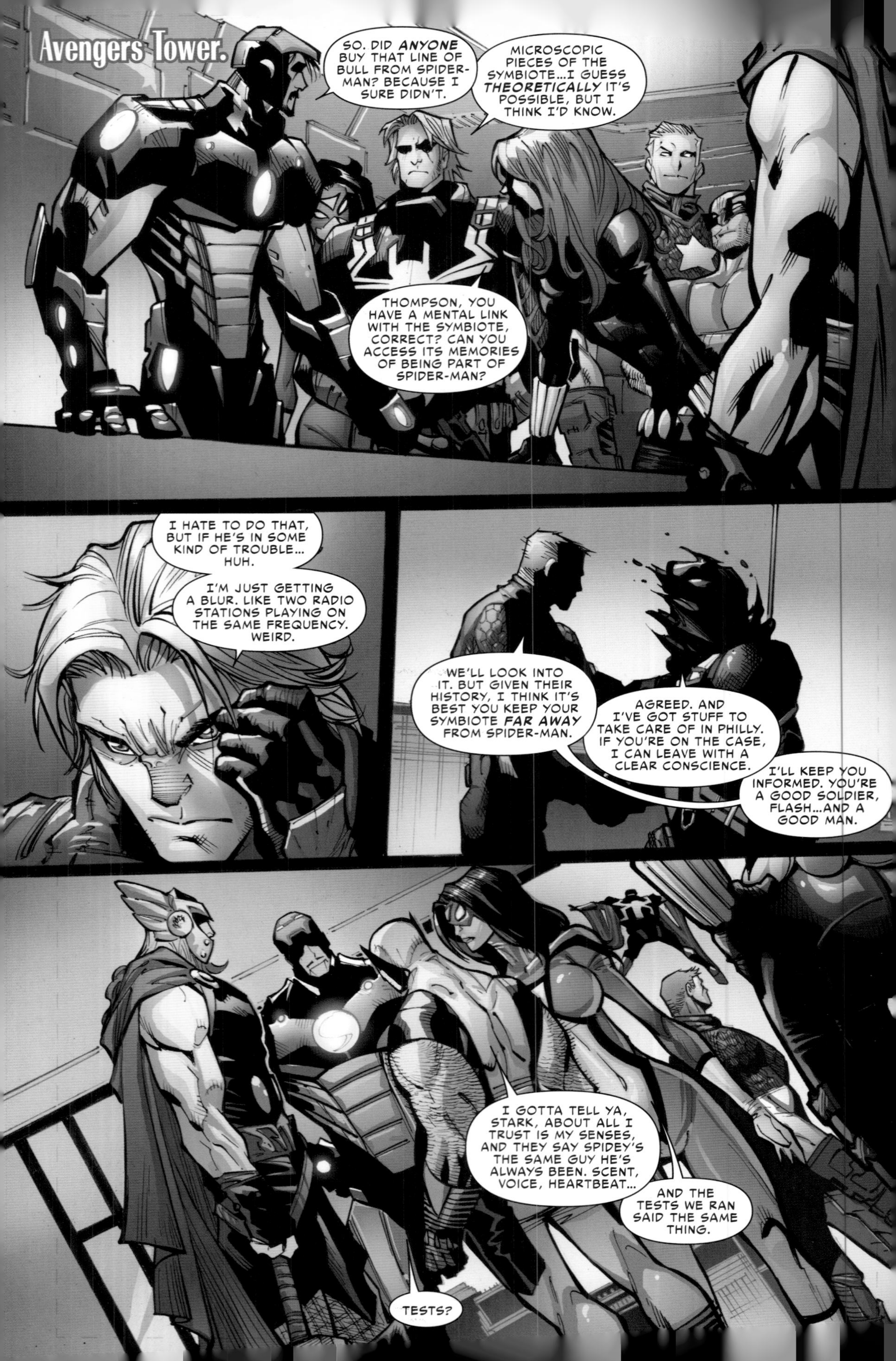
Avengers Tower.
SO. DID ANYONE BUY THAT LINE OF BULL FROM SPIDER-MAN? BECAUSE I SURE DIDN'T.
MICROSCOPIC PIECES OF THE SYMBIOTE...I GUESS THEORETICALLY IT'S POSSIBLE, BUT I THINK I'D KNOW.
THOMPSON, YOU HAVE A MENTAL LINK WITH THE SYMBIOTE, CORRECT? CAN YOU ACCESS ITS MEMORIES OF BEING PART OF SPIDER-MAN?
I HATE TO DO THAT, BUT IF HE'S IN SOME KIND OF TROUBLE... HUH.
I'M JUST GETTING A BLUR. LIKE TWO RADIO STATIONS PLAYING ON THE SAME FREQUENCY. WEIRD.
WE'LL LOOK INTO IT. BUT GIVEN THEIR HISTORY, I THINK IT'S BEST YOU KEEP YOUR SYMBIOTE FAR AWAY FROM SPIDER-MAN.
AGREED. AND I'VE GOT STUFF TO TAKE CARE OF IN PHILLY. IF YOU'RE ON THE CASE, I CAN LEAVE WITH A CLEAR CONSCIENCE.
I'LL KEEP YOU INFORMED. YOU'RE A GOOD SOLDIER, FLASH...AND A GOOD MAN.
I GOTTA TELL YA, STARK, ABOUT ALL I TRUST IS MY SENSES, AND THEY SAY SPIDEY'S THE SAME GUY HE'S ALWAYS BEEN. SCENT, VOICE, HEARTBEAT...
AND THE TESTS WE RAN SAID THE SAME THING.
TESTS?

NEXT: The Goblin War!

VARIANT COVER GALLERY

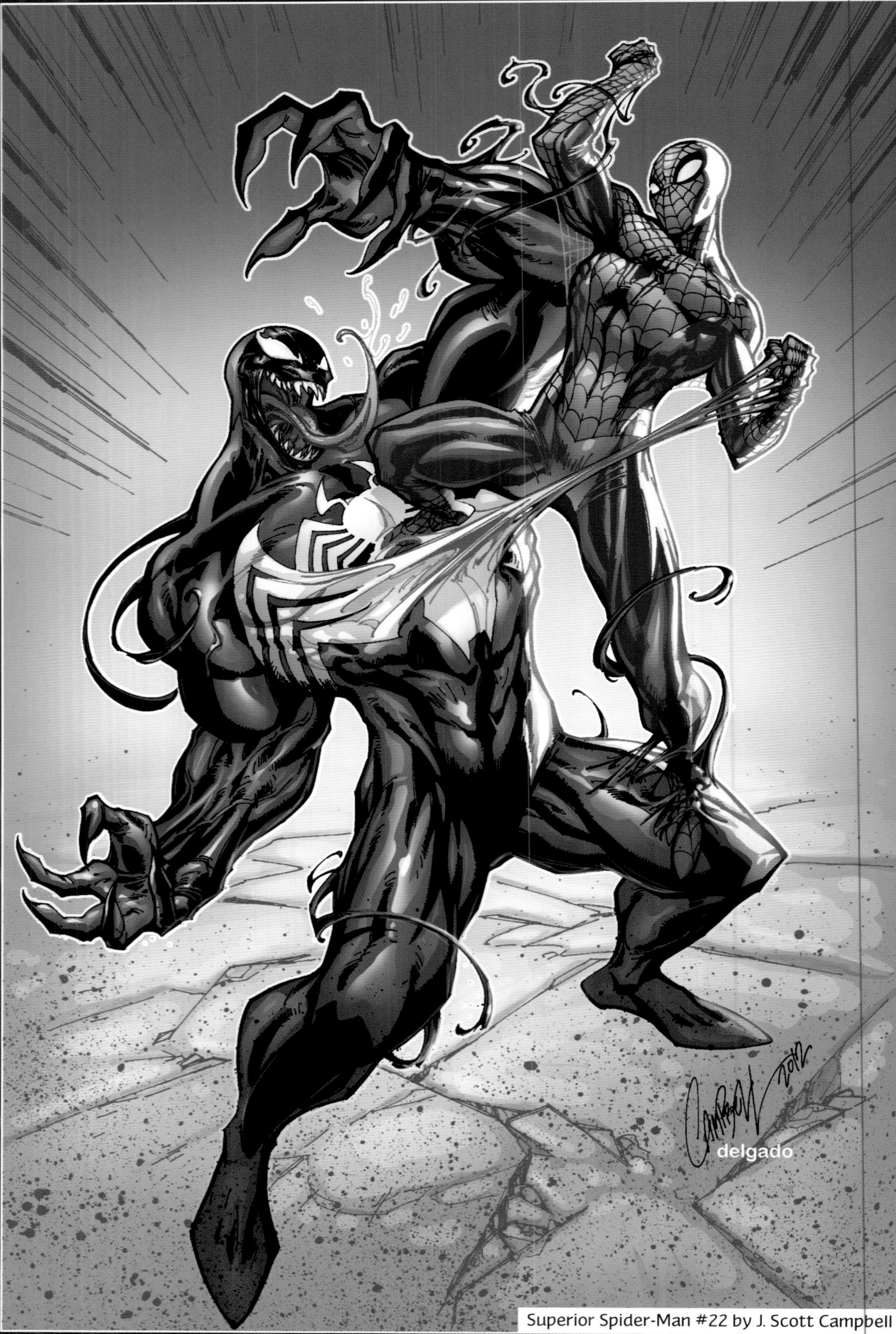
Campbell 2012
delgado

Superior Spider-Man #22 by J. Scott Campbell

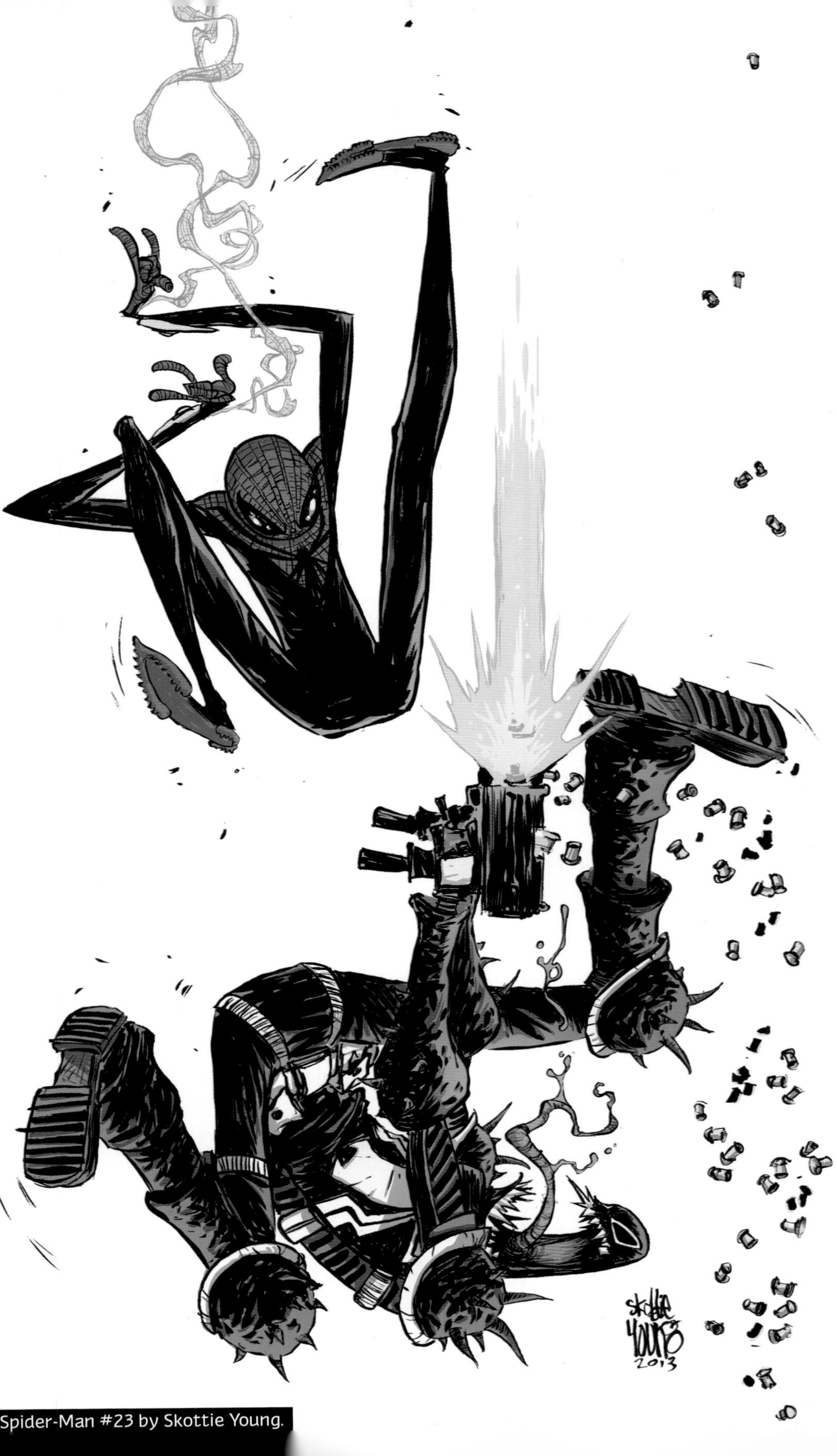
skottie young 2013

Superior Spider-Man #23 by Skottie Young.

Superior Spider-Man #24 by Stefano Casell

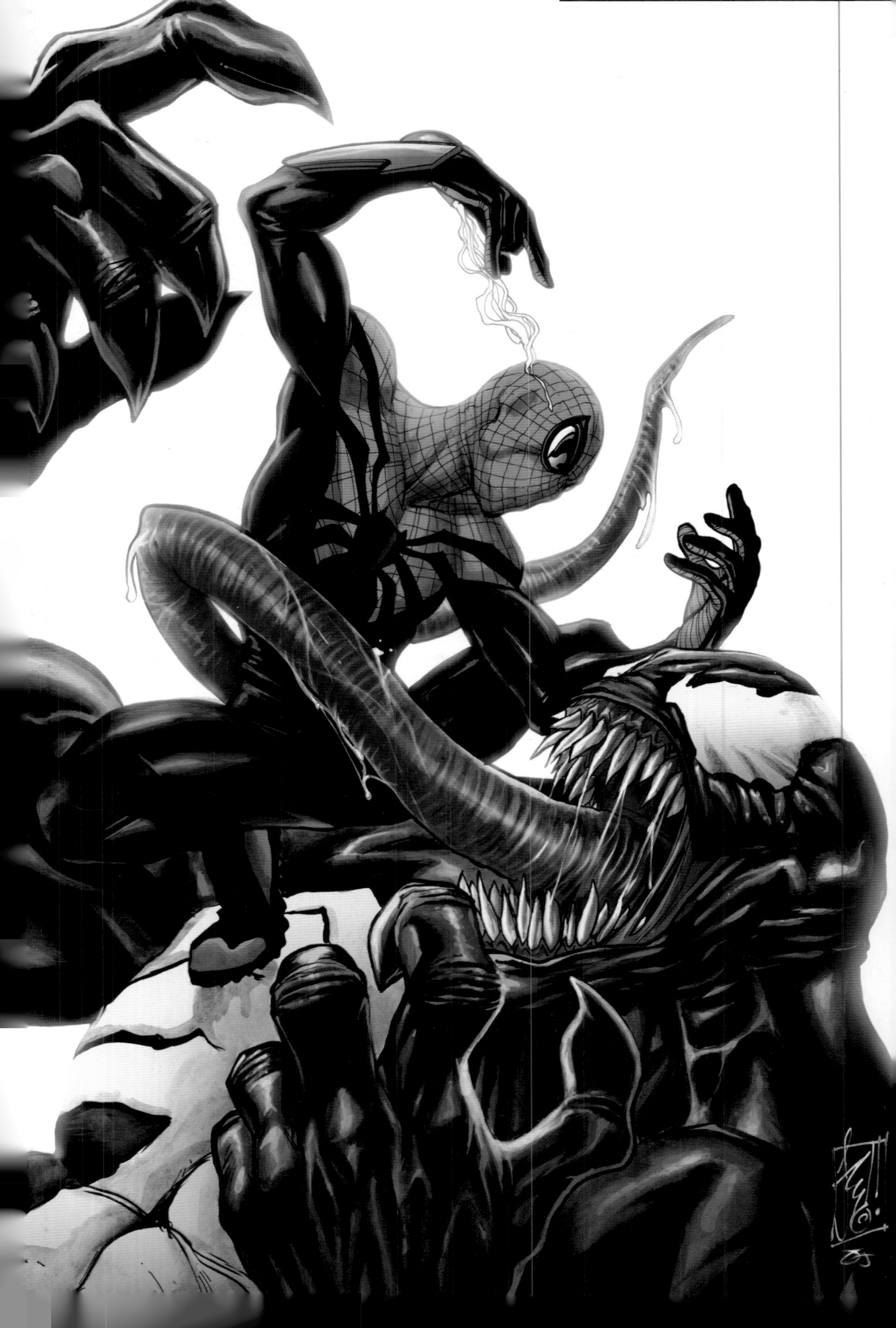

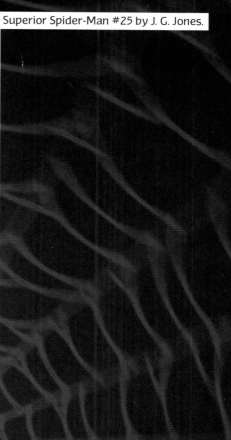

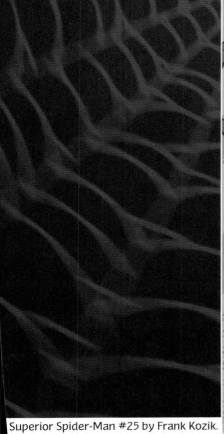

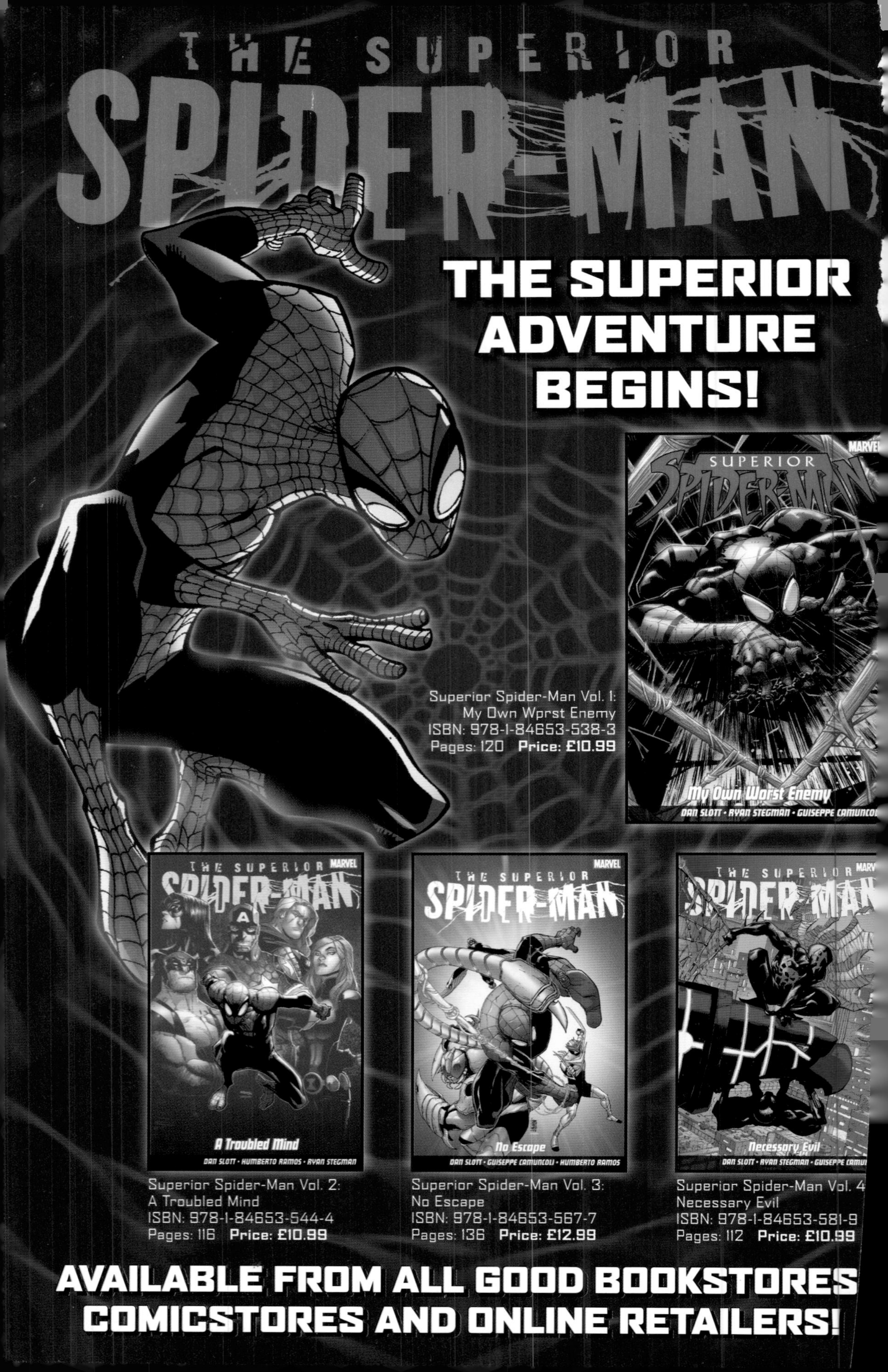
THE SUPERIOR
SPIDER-MAN
THE SUPERIOR ADVENTURE BEGINS!
SUPERIOR SPIDER-MAN
MARVEL
My Own Worst Enemy
DAN SLOTT · RYAN STEGMAN · GUISEPPE CAMUNCOLI
Superior Spider-Man Vol. 1:
My Own Wprst Enemy
ISBN: 978-1-84653-538-3
Pages: 120 Price: £10.99
THE SUPERIOR SPIDER-MAN
MARVEL
A Troubled Mind
DAN SLOTT · HUMBERTO RAMOS · RYAN STEGMAN
Superior Spider-Man Vol. 2:
A Troubled Mind
ISBN: 978-1-84653-544-4
Pages: 116 Price: £10.99
THE SUPERIOR SPIDER-MAN
MARVEL
No Escape
DAN SLOTT · GUISEPPE CAMUNCOLI · HUMBERTO RAMOS
Superior Spider-Man Vol. 3:
No Escape
ISBN: 978-1-84653-567-7
Pages: 136 Price: £12.99
THE SUPERIOR SPIDER-MAN
Necessary Evil
DAN SLOTT · RYAN STEGMAN · GUISEPPE CAMUN
Superior Spider-Man Vol. 4
Necessary Evil
ISBN: 978-1-84653-581-9
Pages: 112 Price: £10.99
AVAILABLE FROM ALL GOOD BOOKSTORES
COMICSTORES AND ONLINE RETAILERS!